LANGUAGE AND PERCEPTION:

Essays in the Philosophy of Language

Frank B. Ebersole
University of Oregon

University Press of America
of America™

Copyright © 1979 by

University Press of America, Inc.™

4710 Auth Place, S.E., Washington D.C. 20023

Printed in the United States of America

ISBN: 0-8191-0776-X

Library of Congress Catalog Card Number: 79-88305

TABLE OF CONTENTS

This is the second of two books of essays in the philosophy of language. The first book, entitled **Saying and Meaning**, is concerned with the philosophy of speech acts. The present volume contains essays on a variety of subjects whose connections are not so easy to briefly indicate. They are concerned with questions about the "relations of language to reality", and perhaps they ought to be called essays in the "metaphysics of language." They deal with questions such as these: Does physical reality predetermine the form of our language? Does it determine the kinds of words in our simple, basic vocabulary? Does our language in basic ways determine the way we perceive reality? Does our language embody the outlines of a certain theory of perception? And does it incorporate a certain view of human actions and of the future? Of course these are not very clear questions, and one of the reasons they are philosophical questions is that they are not very clear.

These questions are expressions of the problems in the philosophy of language which a person inevitably gets himself into while dealing with other problems in philosophy. And these are problems in the philosophy of language which have direct consequences for the way in which one deals with problems in other branches of philosophy. That means, I hope, that in dealing with these problems I am concerned with matters which are fundamental in the sense that a person must run into them over and over again while he is working on any of a large number of different philosophical problems. I do not see them as fundamental in the sense that they are the proper first things to consider, and must, therefore, be got out of the way before one can get on to more advanced things. I do not regard them as stepping-stones, or try to deal with them in a systematic way which might provide a theoretical framework for something more advanced. In short, I do not consider them as problems or topics which can and ought to be considered in their own rights. I am concerned with language in so far as it bears on problems of perception, action, fate, free-will, truth. At times, therefore, these are no more essays in the philosophy of language than they are in metaphysics or theory of knowledge or ethical theory.

Here (in semi-outline) is what the several essays in this volume contain:

Essay 1, "The Family-Resemblance Metaphor." How is one to understand Wittgenstein's dictum to the effect that things are called by the same name because they have family resemblances to each other? Against what is it directed? Is it an improvement over its alternative?

Wittgenstein's remarks seem to presuppose and enforce certain confusing pictures of meaning, "things" and "characteristics." Wittgenstein's view requires that some characteristics be language-dependent and some be possessed by things in themselves. It requires a picture of language as based on "simple words" like "red," which directly refer to observable characteristics of things. But how can one think of "red" as a characteristic which things have independently of language? Concrete and abstract color words.

What is it for things to be "related" or "have relationships" or "family relationships"? Games and names of games.

What do we talk about when we talk about the meaning of a word? Is a survey of the characteristics of things to which a word applies a study of the meaning of the word? Do color names have meanings? What is the meaning of a general, concrete noun? Of a "natural-kind word"? Wittgenstein on pictures. "Applying" words to things.

Essay 2, "Does Language Shape Perception?" is an examination of a view opposed to the idea that simple words are directly connected to visible features of the world. It is the view that our language is always a determiner of what we perceive: what we see is shaped by our language. Our color vocabulary determines whether we see or do not see certain color facts. I examine the thesis (held, among others, by J. L. Austin) that similarities are "natural" but sameness is "conventional": we literally see the likeness and differences among things, but language plays a part in our perception when we see that two things are the "same." Also, the Whorf-Sapir thesis that perception is determined by grammar.

Essay 3, "The Causal Theory of Perception" is an effort to isolate and examine the linguistic facts and the "philosophy of language" upon which the causal theory of perception (vision) depends. By "causal theory" I mean the philosophical view that part of what we perceive is caused in us by the object we perceive. The main part of this essay is an investigation of these questions. Is "It is red" (as a judgment of vision) related to "It looks red" in the way causal theory leads one to suppose? That is, does a thing's being red cause it to look red? And, is the fact that something looks red the sort of fact which can conceivably be given a causal explanation? Is it looks red "weaker than" it is red, as it is red or black is "weaker than" it is red? In order to isolate the relevant linguistic facts, I consider the words "It looks red" only in circumstances which might provoke--or allow for--a causal explanation.

Essay 4, "Does It look the Color It Is?" is an examination of this thesis: A thing always looks red whenever I see (visually) that it is red. Here I consider the words "It looks red" quite generally and without regard to whether they are used to report a fact which might be given a causal explanation. Consider a thing which I see to be red. Now here is the real question: does it look red even though, in the circumstances, it would be puzzling of me to say that it looks red? Does the fact that I cannot say "It looks red" have anything to do with the matter?

In addition to "It looks..." I also examine a somewhat simpler idiom, "It seems to me that I see...."

Essay 5, "The Analysis of Human Actions" explores the question, "What is an action--in addition to being a bodily movement?" The question rests on a mistake. Its abandonment leaves in its stead a program for the "analysis" of actions into component parts. The analysis of speech acts or illocutionary acts into rhetic, phatic, and phonetic acts, is an example. When we speak do we make sounds? Is this program of analysis sensible?

Essay 6, "Truth and Fate: Future Occurrences" examines an argument for fatalism based on what "one might say"--or on "supposals" or "assumptions." What is it for "what one might say" or for an "assumption" to imply something? Can assumptions be correct? "Correct" as opposed to "turns out to be correct." Correctness and truth. Propositions. Three-valued logics.

Essay 7, "Truth and Fate: Future Actions" deals with another argument for fatalism which starts from the fact that certain things we say about a person's future actions imply that the person has no control over his actions. Is "he cannot help himself" implied by what is said? By the truth of what is said? By the fact that someone is in a position to say it? By a proposition to the effect that someone will do something? How to isolate a proposition. Propositions and sentences.

* * * * * * * * * *

Some words about the style. I do not deal with a problem unless it is a real problem for me: I must be entangled in it and it must be more than an intellectual poser. I approach each problem in a way that promises to resolve it as I face it, and this approach predetermines a style for the essay. Hence all but one are philosophical monologues. Essay 6 is the exception. It is a dialogue, and so I am not so immediately and directly in it. I regard it as a preliminary skirmish with the problems that it raises. The monologues differ from one another a bit--because they are experimental and each took a form which seemed most suitable for the problem at the time I was working on it.

Essay 1 is a greatly expanded and, I hope, greatly improved version of a paper which appeared in The Canadian Journal of Philosophy (Vol II, No. 1, Sept., 1972), under the title "Reconsidering Some Passages in Wittgenstein." I want to thank the Canadian Association for Publishing in Philosophy for permission to use. the parts of it which survived my rewriting.

* * *

I include a few pages from the preface to the first volume. They are as pertinent here as they were there, and they will be of as much, or as little, use to the reader.

In trying to follow the advice of students and colleag]es who are familiar with my work, I have tried to write a long explanatory introduction to these volumes. But I have not been able to do so. I made several beginnings, but I could tell that the tone was wrong as soon as they started to come out.

If I understand my advisers, then I know some of the topics which they think I should discuss. I can at least outline the ingredients of the introduction I cannot write.

(1) These several essays are what I think of as "philosophical investigations" or "inquiries." As quickly as I can I try to get a problem for philosophical investigation or inquiry isolated from history and from the doctrines of philosophers and get it "personalized," "internalized." Then I get to work on it--putting to use, where they seem to apply, certain procedures and methods which I have found helpful in dealing with other problems. Among these: (a) I try always to keep the discussion in my own terms and to avoid use of the terminology of the philosophers who have dealt with the problem. I do not want to take on more of its usual philosophical baggage than is absolutely necessary to give it form as a problem. I do my best to tackle the problem as though it were the first time the problem had ever been considered; I try

to think everything clean through as though none of it had been thought about before. (b) Thus, I try to avoid polemic; I try to put down the philosophical urge to array all the many philosophers before me, and to refute them one by one and declare myself the winner. I avoid constructing theories or developing doctrines. I try to stay away from the theoretical, the general and explanatory and stick to particulars, details, to cases. I want to proceed as much as possible by inventing and thinking of examples. The examples I mean, of course, are bits of stories, involving scenes or situations in which a person will properly and sensibly say something or think something. The desire to theorize, though, is often overwhelming, and when it is, there is nothing to do except to face it for what it is. I know of no effective way to do this except to confront it with more and more examples, to present it with the details—the facts. For I know from many past experiences that these philosophical theories which rush in on me not only make me distort the facts, they make me blind to the very facts they have led me to distort. I must not let my desire to theorize turn me away from a close consideration of examples. For once my mind is full of theory, I can no longer see the determining details of an example. There is nothing to do but to be more persistent in forcing the details of examples before myself.

The upshot: I believe that going over the details—I mean the examples—and exposing unwanted theories and explanations as they emerge—I believe that pursuing such things in the right order, in the right way, can lead one to see exactly what he needs to see.

I do not want to give the impression that I have a list of rules which I follow or try to follow. But I'm afraid I have given that impression. I want to say only that when I reflect on things I have done and thought which seem to produce useful insight, then these more-or-less-rules or something-like-guides seem to have been partly responsible for the desired results.

(2) It seems to me that this approach to philosophical problems is almost without precedent. I cannot think of the work of any well-known philosopher with which I can make useful comparisons and contrasts. Well then, these essays are queer. Therefore, I wish the reader could suspend some of his usual expectations. If he is open-minded and persistently reads on I think that his first reactions may change. I believe that many readers will feel that examples are quite unnecessary, and hence they may become impatient with

my sometimes prolonged parading of examples.

(3) I might try to lean on an interpretation of some cryptic, methodological passages in Wittgenstein's Philosophical Investigations, but my interpretation of these passages might very well be mistaken. At any rate, if I say that my philosophical attitudes in these essays were inspired by Wittgenstein's advice, I must add that he does not--in truth--ever follow his own advice.

(4) Still, if I had to indicate what I am up to in terms of some preliminary simile, I should use Wittgenstein's simile of "therapy." What I am trying to do about philosophical problems is what one hopes to do in individual psychotherapy with "personal" or "emotional" problems. But I do not long want this comparison. It is dangerous, and I think it could only be useful in the beginning--in an introduction--and only to put out of mind some of the wrong kinds of things. The disanalogies are too numerous even to begin listing, but one is this. Psychotherapy proceeds on talk, and more talk, and it requires a respondent. Philosophical talk--discussion--does not produce useful results. Philosophy, I think, is strictly a solitary business with pencil and paper, pencil-sharpener and eraser. Philosophical discussion at its best is too quick and slapdash, too meandering; and it is rarely infused with the necessary spirit of mutual inquiry. In particular it is too fast-moving to allow for the construction of and consideration of the proper examples. One must experiment with examples in leisure. When a person first tries to think of an example, he does not know what exact details are needed. One must supply an example with speakers and then one must "hear" their words: their words must be exactly right. "Listening" to the words of imaginary speakers often produces great nervous tension, for many times one has to pause and wonder whether his attitude toward the example is produced by a proper adoption of the life of the example itself, or by the intrusion of his trouble-making philosophical longings. How to resolve this? Go for a long walk. Drive philosophy from one's mind and think again later. Abandon the example and invent another one. Such thinking calls for the kind of time and absorption one finds only in solitude. Nothing but writing (and of course, rewriting and rewriting) has any real promise of bringing the required results; reading can only rarely give a person what he wants, and only on that most rare occasion when he reads just the right thing at just the right time.

(5) "Well, all right," I can hear some impatient critic say, as he prepares to pounce on these essays of

mine. "Why all the elusive side-stepping? So these essays have a therapeutic aim. That does not tell me much: only that they are located on the philosophical map somewhere between Protagoras and Spinoza. Why don't you come right out and say what kind of philosophy you have produced? You owe it to any critical reader to tell him where among the recognized philosophico-historical categories to place these writings of yours."

I imagine that this critic really wants me to use one of his own prepared pigeonholes, and the pejorative title which goes with it. So I shall. These pieces, then, belong in the niche of "ordinary-language philosophy," and if my critic thinks of ordinary-language philosophy as a sickness, then I shall concede that these essays of mine are extreme--perhaps terminal-- cases of it. I really do believe that philosphical problems arise because we have incorrect ideas about the nature of such things as knowledge, truth, value, meaning, explanation..., and I believe that the only way in which we can clear up these problems is to look carefully at examples in which such words as "know," "true," "means," "explains," and others are used. This is "ordinary-language philosophy," I take it, because the examples needed are of an "ordinary" kind-- involving familiar surroundings, people, occurrences, actions, and issues. But if an example should involve technical, scientific or specialist matters, and I understand the example perfectly, then such an example will do just as well as an "ordinary" one. If my problem has to do with a word like "explanation," I may well need some such technical examples. But most philosophical problems do not turn on technical ex- amples; they require instead that one turn to examples in which familiar words and phrases are used in quite ordinary situations.

Many people are going around saying that ordinary- language philosophy has had its day. They say that it was a good thing for awhile: it had something useful to teach us, but we have all learned everything there is to be learned from it; and we had now better get on with more important philosophical business--the busi- ness of theory-construction and system-building. I do not for a moment believe that this is true: I think that ordinary-language philosophy was never given more than a most cursory consideration. And, far from learning a lesson from it, most philosophers merely used it to mildly reshape some of their preconceived misconceptions.

Now I can hear my critic saying, "Aha! I have hit a sore point. Here at last I have drawn you into the polemic you have been trying to side-step." So you have, and I really do not want to engage in such polemic. "Don't you want to convert people to your way of thinking?" I don't know what to say to that. It's certainly not high on my list of desires--but I suppose that I do. "Then why not give it a try?" That's what the whole collection of essays in its way is intended to do. "Can't you give it a short preliminary try?" No, I don't think so. "But suppose you had to: how would you proceed?"

A strange idle prospect: to plan a forensic campaign I do not intend to engage in. How? "We are told that people in the Pentagon do something analogous to that: they plan military strategy for battles they hope they will never fight. How would you begin?" I should first try to get my opponent to agree, in J. L. Austin's rather unhappy phraseology, that ordinary language is the "first word." That much is easy. Where else could one begin? If you are going to examine knowledge, say, or meaning, where can you begin except with things you say, things in which the words "know" and "mean" will figure? Most people seem ready to agree that ordinary language is the first word. If I can get that far, I think I can then show them--contrary to Austin--that ordinary language is the last word. I am convinced that if a person gets hard to work on examples, inventing them, reflecting on them, arranging and rearranging them, then it will never occur to him to go on to the construction of a technical terminology or to turn to another method. No, that is not strong enough. I think he will come to see that a system and its technical terminology is exactly what he does not need.

(6) One last thing: a note on my talk of "pictures." I think that the only proper starting point for a philosophical investigation is with the recognition that we have and hold philosophical theories which puzzle us and disturb us. And I think that we can discover that what puzzles and disturbs us is this: the theories lead us to think that we say things which we do not say, and to think that we would say things that we would not say. What to do? "Remind" yourself over and over and in the greatest detail of what you do say and what you would say. Why do we hold such philosophical theories? I attribute this to our tendency to think in terms of simple, diagrammatic pictures. I for one do actually try to represent things philosophically to myself in terms of visual imagery. I often think, for example, of the mind as a chamber, an arena, a theater--behind my eyes--and I picture myself as a spectator in this arena. I become aware of

things only in so far as they are shown to my inner eye in this inner theater. This picture leads me to think that when I see (visually) an "object," a house, a tree, that I must be aware of something else, a sense-datum. And this in turn leads me to think that when I see an "object," it "appears" to me, or it "looks" in some way to me. In short I think that what I mean by saying that something "looks" so and so to me is that I am aware of some sense-datum. This is wrong--and disturbing.

I try to represent to myself what is involved in the fact that a word "means" what it means. I picture the word on the left of my visual drawing board, and on the right are the "things" of the world: boxes, houses, trees. And from the word I picture a bundle of diverging arrows going forth, aiming at and striking the things which the word "denotes." If I imagine the word to be "grackle," then its arrows would strike all the birds which are grackles. And this now leads me to believe that when I know the meaning of a word I am able to point out the "things" to which it refers. But this is wrong. Many people know what the word "grackle" means, and cannot identify every grackle that comes before them. Being interested in birds, I think I can do better than most, but I do not know exactly how many kinds of grackles are found in the world, and some may be quite different from any I am familiar with. I do know that the females of such species as the bronzed grackle are very different in size and color from the males, and are much more difficult to identify. But neither my general knowledge about birds nor my specific knowledge about grackles is knowledge of the word "grackle" or of the meaning of the word. I know the word "diamond," but I cannot pick a diamond out of a group of diamonds mixed with imitation diamonds. Knowing the meaning of the word is one thing and being able to recognize specimens or examples is something else entirely.

I do believe that "pictures" are responsible for making us produce philosophical theories, and are responsible in turn for leading us astray, puzzling and distressing us. I do not mean, of course, that everyone is keenly aware while philosophizing that he has images in his mind or diagrams clearly before his mind's eye. I mean that he can catch himself thinking in such graphic ways, that he can come to realize that he is thinking in conformity with a simple diagrammatic model. Perhaps even this is too much. Maybe such "pictures" are a personal peculiarity; maybe most people do not think in that way at all. If that is so, most readers will think that I have overemphasized this matter of "pictures." I hope they can see, though, that even if I have exaggerated it wildly, that is of no importance. At most it is an effort on my part to explain to myself how we come to worry and trouble ourselves with misfit philosophical theories. And the important question is not why do we have such theories but what are we going to do about it, since we quite evidently do have them.

1.   THE FAMILY-RESEMBLANCE METAPHOR

I

I want to consider some difficulties which I have on rereading the passages on "common properties" or "common features" and "family resemblances" in The Blue Book[1] and in Philosophical Investigations.[2] These passages are not as easy to read as they once were.

Wittgenstein tells us that we think, or have a tendency to think, that all the things to which we apply a general word have some property or feature in common, and he tells us that we believe it is because of this common property or feature that we apply the same word to them.   In The Blue Book the phrase is "common property"; in Philosophical Investigations it is "common feature." Wittgenstein may have changed from the word "property" to the word "feature" because the word "property" is obviously too limited in its application. We speak of the properties of mercury or neoprene but not of the properties of sandpipers or slatterns. The word "feature" also seems to limited in a way, but he may have chosen this word mainly because it fits his metaphor of family resemblances. I do not think that Wittgenstein wants to impose any special restriction at this point, so I shall use the word "feature" only where it is appropriate, and I shall use the less limiting word "characteristic" where it seems more appropriate than the word "feature."   Thus I assume that Wittgenstein means to examine our tendency to think that a general word is applied to things because those things have some feature or features, characteristic or characteristics in common.

I think it is easy to see that it is only as philosophers, or only when philosophizing, that we think or have a tendency to think as Wittgenstein says we do. Right away this raises many questions, for Wittgenstein urges us to "look and see": he says that when we look and see we shall discover that what we think or have a tendency to think is mistaken. When we "look and see" we shall discover that the things for which we use the same word do not have features in common: we shall find instead that they have overlapping similarities or

---

[1]Ludwig Wittgenstein, The Blue and Brown Books (N.Y., Harper & Row, 1958), p. 17.

[2]Ludwig Wittgenstein, Philosophical Investigations (N.Y., MacMillan, 1953), Sec. 65-71.

1

"family resemblances" to each other. Now this is a surprising turn and a surprising outcome, for rarely indeed can a philosophical "belief" be dispatched so quickly and easily. What is more surprising is this: not only are we expected to dispatch the philosophical belief, we are expected, apparently, to replace it with another. We were wrong in thinking "common features"; we shall be right in thinking "family resemblances." All of this jars because it is contrary to everything we have learned elsewhere from Wittgenstein.

What exactly is the philosophical "belief" about words and common features supposed to be, the one which Wittgenstein says we have? Where can I look for it except in myself? Yet if I find a belief in myself, it may be only my own belief that I find, and not one which is shared by others. This procedure raises the risk that the belief I find may be a peculiarity of my own, and so it will make inappropriate any remarks I want to make on Wittgenstein. Even so the risk is worth taking, for there seems to be only one alternative to it; I may find instead that the relevant "belief" is not mine at all, but is part of some special philosophical system. Then any commentary I might make on that belief would be at best a piece of historical exegesis and criticism.

What philosophical belief about general words do I have to which Wittgenstein's remarks might be addressed? It seems to be something like this. I have the idea that there is a certain large, important class of words, each of which is applied to many items in the world. These words are like labels which we affix to specimens in a museum, zoo, or laboratory. Quite naturally, when I acquire these words, when I make them part of my language, I learn to apply them to the proper things (although, of course, I sometimes—but not often—make mistakes). How could I learn to apply these words except by learning to identify the items to which they apply? And how could I learn to identify the items except by learning to recognize them, and how could I recognize them except by noticing the features or characteristics by which they are marked and distinguished? Hence I come to apply one of these words to certain things because those certain things have characteristics which are common to them and peculiar to them. Those things are distinguished from all other things by just those characteristics. I have this philosophical picture of general words as labels (1A).[3]

_____

[3]In this essay I discuss two such philosophical

2

Now if this were all of my philosophical belief, I could indeed easily show it wrong. I need only to find a word which I might think belongs to the proper class of words but which--contrary to my expectations--is applied to things which do not seem in the required way to possess common and peculiar characteristics. I think I have found many such words. In fact, philosophers long ago noted many such words: for example, the word "healthy" as it occurs in "healthy exercise," "healthy complexion," "healthy body." Do some exercises, certain complexions, and some bodies have common and peculiar characteristics by virtue of which they are called "healthy"? Even examples which the philosophical belief seems tailored to fit do not on examination seem to fit at all. An entomologist will affix the same label to a caterpillar, a chrysalis, and a butterfly. If these share any features or characteristics, I think they are not known to the entomologist. If there are any characteristics they have in common, these characteristics have nothing to do with the fact that the entomologist attaches the same name to them. An entomologist may have a larval specimen and an adult specimen and not know whether they are the same species or not. He may examine each very carefully to see whether there are any characteristics which may suggest that they are the same species, and find none. He may find nothing at all, and then he may later discover that they are larva and adult of the same species.

What I have said so far gives only a partial and misleading expression of my philosophical belief about general words. There is more to it than I have so far indicated, and it is the rest of it that enables me readily to accommodate these exceptions to the belief as a whole. It is the rest of it, too, which is philosophically important. So far, my philosophical story about general words suggests that they are labels or names; it suggests that my only question about these words concerns the way I sort the items of the world for labelling. Do I attach the same label only to specimens which have common characteristics, or do I

---

pictures, each of which I discuss in two parts. For no very good reason I have numbered them IA, IB, IIA and IIB. IA is part of the more inclusive IB; IIA and IIB are correlative parts of the same picture. I shall call IA "the picture of words as labels," IB "the picture of meaning," IIA "the picture of the world of things," and IIB "the picture of the features of things."

3

attach the same label to several different groups of things which are connected to each other in various ways? My belief, or my tendency to believe, that words refer to things because of the characteristics of those things surely comes to mind in order to answer a different question. It is meant to explain not just how I apply the names, it is meant to explain what makes these words names. And more, it is meant to explain what makes these various marks or sounds words rather than mere marks or sounds; that is, it is meant to explain what gives them their meaning. It is meant to tell me in what their meaning consists. When I think philosophically about language, I often think like this. If it were not for language I should be cut off from other people and they from me: I could never know their thoughts and feelings and they could never know mine. There is a physical gap between us and I can bridge the gap only by making signals in the physical world: I can make sounds for the ears of others. And of course they can make sounds for my ears to hear. But if all we had were sounds to go between us we should be no better off than birds or animals. We should have calls and cries, but still no way to communicate our thoughts. Before we can truly communicate, the sounds we make must be words, and the words must have meaning. We could make sounds as crows make sounds, but these sounds do not have meaning as words do. What then must be added to a sound to give it meaning--to make it a word? That is my philosophical question. And the answer I am inclined to give is this: the sound must be made to "stand for" or "designate" things. I must be able to use the words to refer to things, to talk about things, to request things, to tell what I think about things. Reference to things is what makes sounds (and marks, too) into meaningful elements of language. And these elements of language--words--refer to things by virtue of the fact that certain things share certain characteristics. Perhaps not all words refer to things in this direct way, but the basic words of language do--and it is through these basic words that other words acquire their meanings. In understanding the meaning of one of these basic words, I understand that the word reaches out--it is applied to those things of which it is the name, those things which have certain characteristics in common. It is this reaching out, "designating," "denoting" things by virtue of the characteristics of those things which is the meaning of the word in question (IB).[4] My account of the meaning

---

[4]B. Russell: "When we ask what constitutes mean-

of such words will be of this form: "What does the word 'rat' mean?" "It refers to a medium-size rodent with a pointed nose and long tail." "What does the word 'fid' mean?" "It is the name of a pointed tool used in splicing ropes." My philosophical account in terms of common features is meant to give the principle by which words are related to the world and in terms of which their meanings are to be understood. My picture of words as labels (1A) is only part of a picture of words and their connection to things which represents the nature of meaning (IB).

Suppose now that I do as Wittgenstein directs; I examine the things referred to by some word and discover that all do not share common and peculiar characteristics. If I make this discovery while the picture of meaning is before my mind, what shall I say? Something like this: not all the things have the same characteristics, but at least some of them do. So the principle shown by the picture is at work here. What this discovery shows is that other principles must be at work also. Originally, perhaps, the word referred to a more limited group of things than it now does, and then because of various similarities or relations of the members of this original sub-group to other things it was extended step by step to other groups of things. These extensions may have been of practical importance at certain historical periods. We must recognize at least one other principle at work in determining the meanings of our words, the principle of "the economy of language": it is doubtless better to extend the application of old words than to proliferate hosts of new ones.

I can see now that the risk of my philosophical beliefs being idiosyncratic is not the risk I might have thought. For the "theory" I have found myself tending to believe seems to be one widely held by philosophers: perhaps it is even the orthodox philosophical theory. The theory consists of two parts. The first is that in order to understand meaning one must consider primarily the general, concrete words through whose meaning language becomes connected to reality. And the meaning of any of these words is to be understood in terms of characteristics which things must have in order for the words to be correctly applied to them. In well-known philosophical jargon, the meaning of a word consists in

---

ing... we are asking not who is the individual meant, but what is the relation of the word to the individual which makes the one mean the other." Analysis of Mind (London, Geo. Allen & Unwin, 1921), p. 191.

its "connotation." The second part of the theory is this: when we examine the things to which we commonly apply a general, concrete word, we shall often discover that they do not all share common and peculiar characteristics. This is due to the fact that the users of language bring about changes in the meaning of words, and these changes are brought about primarily by their practical and not their theorectical interests. Thus in J. S. Mill's terminology most words come to have "unsettled connotations." They are applied to many different kinds of things which have no one set of features in common, but which resemble each other in various ways. Philosophers, whose interests are presumably theoretical, often regret this aspect of the meaning of words as they are employed in "everyday language," and they feel that in order to engage in clear and accurate thinking they must do something to straighten out the meaning of these words. This is often part of what they hope to accomplish by "analysis" of a word. "Analysis" is intended to substitute something clear and definite for the original vague and indefinite meaning. Yet an analysis is not given capriciously: the intent behind an analysis is not to change the meaning of the word entirely, but to find, to fix, and to preserve the central or most important part of this connotation. Philosophers doing analysis often talk as though they were restoring words to their original, pristine meanings; or if not that, they talk as though they were exposing the hidden but true and proper meanings of the words.

If this is what I believe about the way words refer to groups of things because these groups of things have common features, then my beliefs go untouched by Wittgensteins's observations about "family resemblances." At one time I may have been a bit surprised to have discovered that many words behave as Wittgenstein says they do, but my philosophical picture and the theory it sponsors would not have been seriously disturbed by the discovery. In my philosophical thinking about language I have a place ready for the discovery, and I quickly accommodate my thinking to it.

6

In reading Wittgenstein's discussion in Philosophical Investigations I am in even more serious trouble than this. I might at one time have had a tendency to think that all the things referred to by a general word shared common features or characteristics. I now wonder about this: I wonder whether I could have carried out the exercise which Wittgenstein says I should. I wonder whether I could ever have followed Wittgenstein's dictate to "look and see," because I wonder whether I have a clear understanding of what I am to do. Of course I am to turn to examples, and learn from them whether all things referred to by a general word have some feature or features in common--in virtue of which they are referred to by the word in question.

How am I to find or construct the necessary examples? It is hard to imagine examples in which someone is concerned with the relevant issue. Suppose I imagine an African native named Abu who has learned English at some missionary school. He has just come to America, and finds that his vocabulary is not adequate for life in our society. He comes across many new words, and he asks me about them. One day he says, "I hear that many people ride in Fords. What are Fords?" I say, "A Ford is a kind of automobile." Can I imagine his asking this question: "What features do Fords have?" And if he does ask, what shall I say? "Their features are not much different from those of other cars. Some have four-barrel carburetors, some have lots of chrome decoration, some have bucket seats, some have automatic transmissions...." Now how does the conversation go? "Aren't there any features which all Fords have in common?" "No. I don't suppose so. I think that every feature has been changed from the earliest model, the Model-T, to that of the present time." Am I right about that? Is there no feature which all Fords have always had? Well, even if there is some feature which absolutely every Ford has had, it is not a feature by virtue of which these cars are called "Fords." Am I to reach the conclusion, then, that this example shows that there are no features which Fords have in common in virtue of which they are called "Fords"? But Abu did not ask why certain cars are called "Fords." Suppose, instead, that Abu goes to a Ford museum with me, and after looking at many of the cars on exhibit, he asks, "Why are all these cars called 'Fords'?" (Can I really imagine that?) I say, "Because they were manufactured by the Ford automobile company." Of course that is not the reason that all Fords are called "Fords" and no other cars are

called "Fords." The Ford motor company has manufactured lots of cars not called "Fords"; Mercuries,
Edsels, Lincolns, and others. Then they were
manufactured by the Ford Division of the Ford Motor
Company: the Ford Division, as far as I know, has
turned out only Fords. Even so, it is thinkable that
Fords should have occasionaly been manufactured by one
of the other divisions of the Ford Motor Company, and
it is thinkable that the Ford Division should turn out
some other kind of car. There must be someone at the
Ford Motor Company who has the power to assign names to
lines or groups of cars. Then these cars are called
"Fords" because that person so designated them. Even
so, I do not want to say that all Fords are called
"Fords" because they have one feature in common, namely
that they have been properly designated by someone with
that authority at the Ford Motor Company. The word
"feature" surely does not belong here. I simply tell
Abu that these cars are designated by some authority at
the Ford Motor Company. What will he say now? "Then
it is not because of any feature they have that they
are called 'Fords'." To this, I think I should have to
say "That's right. It's not because of any feature
they have." I may reply in this way without knowing
exactly what Abu's misunderstanding is. Perhaps he
thinks that being a Ford is like being a sports model,
which I take it is a matter of having certain features.
Have I now shown by an example that Fords are not
called "Fords" because they share some common and
peculiar feature? In spite of what the example seems
to show, I want to say that I have mentioned a
candidate worth considering as a common and peculiar
feature, namely this: Fords are designated by some
authority at the Ford Motor Company.
    Abu comes to me and says, "I hear people saying
that they look forward to May. What is May?" I say,
"May is the fifth month of our year." (Of course I may
also have to explain the calendar to him.) Can I now
imagine his asking, "What are the features of May?"
(Or perhaps, in this case, "What are the characteristics of May?") Suppose he does ask--what do I say?
"The trees become green again; the flowers are in bloom
in May; most of the birds have returned; May is a beautiful month--not cold, not hot." I must now try to
suppose that he asks, "Are those characteristics of all
Mays?" And how should I be expected to reply? "Well,
no. The climate here is not dependable. But May is
usually like that: it is usually a wonderful month."
Shall I conclude from this that not all Mays have any
features or characteristics in common? Even if all
Mays were exactly alike--even though all were warm and

8

sunny and freshly green--it would not be because of
that fact that they are called "May." And now I cannot
imagine how Abu's question could be about why these are
called "May." Why what is called "May"? "Why is this
month called 'May'?" "Why is the fifth month called
'May'?" If that is his question I should have to tell
him about the Julian calendar and how "May" comes from
the Latin Deus Maius, meaning "the great god--Jupiter."
I want a question something like this: "By virtue of
what features or characteristics is a certain stretch
of time called 'May'?" and I cannot think of an example
where the question I want would arise. Even so, I feel
that I understand the question, and I am inclined to
answer, "Mays have this feature: they are the fifth
months in the years determined by our calendar, the
Gregorian calendar."

As Wittgenstein seems to dictate, I turn to examples to see whether general words refer to things because those things have common and peculiar features or
characteristics. And I cannot make my examples show
what I want them to. When I imagine someone reviewing
the features or characteristics of Fords or Mays, he
seems to come to the quick and easy conclusion that not
all Fords or Mays have features or characteristics in
common. But the review of features was not addressed
to the question "Why are all these called Fords or
Mays?" When I try to change the examples in order to
make a place for that question, I cannot make them work
out right. I cannot imagine the right question, "Why
are all these called 'May'?" I can find a place for
the question "Why are all of these called 'Fords'?" but
then the answer is not given in terms of features or
characteristics which Fords have in common.

Yet in spite of my difficulty with the examples I
feel that I understand the question "By virture of what
features or characteristics are these called 'Fords' or
'Mays'?" And I am ready with what I consider to be
likely answers. "These are called 'Fords' because they
have this characteristic: namely they were so designated by someone with that authority at the Ford Motor
Company." "These are called 'Mays' because they have
this characteristic: namely they are the fifth months
in the Gregorian calendar." I am surprised that Wittgenstein does nothing to discourage this kind of thinking. If fact, his dictate to "look and see" invites
it. Why am I inclined to think in this way? I can
think of no reason except that my picture of the meanings of general words inclines me in that way; general
words refer to things because those things have common
and peculiar features or characteristics. That is the
way the "original" general words must have referred to

9

things. It is the way the simplest of general words must refer to things. Of course I have no reason for thinking that "Ford" and "May" should exhibit the original or simplest pattern, and so I take my answers as proposals only--as likely candidates. In case they should turn out not to be quite right, I feel that they will give me the main or central instances. In the case of "the fifth month in the Gregorian calendar," I cannot but think that it is exactly right.

In spite of the fact that my examples do not show "designated by some authority at the Ford Motor Company" or "fifth month in the Gregorian calendar" to be features or characteristics of things, all the same I want to say that these are the essential or defining features or characteristics. What makes me want to say this? Again I think I have no way to answer except to look within myself. I believe my thinking is dictated by a very simple picture I have of the things that words refer to, and of the characteristics of these things. I picture the world of things to which words refer (IIA). I picture myself surrounded by "things" --right before my eyes--all of these many, many things which make up the real world. They are there before me, and even if I had no words with which to refer to them, they would still be these, just what they are, with all the many likenesses and differences among them. Then, too, there are the characteristics or features of these things which are marked by the distinctions among my concrete general words (IIB). The "things" are spherical or flat, red or green, bird or beast, crest or trough, sick or well, fruit or vegetable, beef or lamb, earth or air or fire or water.

The things before me exhibit their characteristics: they show them forth. The trouble with this picture of characteristics (and the associated picture of things) is due to the fact that when it dominates my thinking I have no other pictures with which to complement them. Everything in the world must be either a "thing" or a "characteristic." Now there are all kinds of things, and they are different from each other in many ways, and they are alike in many ways. I think of this in terms of "things" and their "characteristics." Hence I must say that any way in which things are alike or different, any way in which they can be contrasted or compared, is a feature or characteristic of the things. Any description of a thing is a description in terms of its characteristics or features. And still I picture this in my mind's eye with squares and spheres which have such characteristics as "red" and "flat." Other features must be like those: there is no other way for features to be. Some features are so simple and obvious I cannot miss them. Others are more complex, but as I develop from infant to adult I learn to distinguish among things in terms of them. Regardless, though, of how complex or subtle, I come to recognize, identify, or characterize things in terms of these features, and thus my vocabulary comes to register more and more distinctions among things: one word for things with this characteristic, another word for things with that.

I believe my thinking is guided by the beautiful, quasi-pictorial simplicity of this.[5] My picture of the world of things (IIA) does not suggest any difficulty in picking out or isolating an individual thing, or in determining what features any thing has. Things with their features are all on exhibit right before me. My picture of features or characteristics (IIB) does not suggest any problems about, or complications in determining what is and what is not a feature or characteristic of things. The features of things do not depend upon my specific inquiries, questions, or reasons for distinguishing among things. By observing the things, I make the determination from my unique place, for once and for all. I mention a few features: size, shape, color; and I add "and so on." "Anything by which things can be distinguished or compared—anything that I can truly say of anything which will properly characterize it." Anything that one can say in describing a thing, distinguishing a thing, identifying a thing—anything at all that one can say of a thing—will ascribe a feature or characteristic to it.

This picture is not a superficial thing: it determines a great deal of my philosophical thinking about language. I find it very hard to be sufficiently alert to its presence and to be aware of the many ways in which it directs my thinking. Now that I mention this, I can see that my very characterization of the influence of this picture has been determined by the picture itself. I said that the picture of things (IIA) does not suggest any difficulty in picking out or isolating things, and I said that the associated picture of features or characteristics (IIB) does not suggest any difficulty in determining what is and what is not a feature or characteristic of things. In short, I thought all the time of a world of units with their intrinsic likenesses and differences. I thought that one of the difficulties I might not take account of was involved in picking out the units or bringing them into focus.

---

[5]In a postscript at the end (pp. 69 ff.) I try to explain this business of "pictures."

11

I thought that the units were there waiting to be picked out. And I thought that they had intrinsic differentiating markers of some kind, and that the difficulty which the picture obscured was that of determining which of these marks is to be counted as a feature or characteristic. In short, I was thinking that the world is full of individual units which have all kinds of distinguishing markers, and that the question was which of these markers we were to call "features" or "characteristics." If I am to examine the picture of things and characteristics and its influence, I must be more perspicacious. I represented the complication which the picture did not present as though it had to do with our use of the words "feature" and "characteristic," as though it were a mere matter of language and did not have anything to do with the underlying reality. I thought that there were markers and distinguishers in reality which we do not call "characteristics" but which have the same status as those we do call "characteristics," and hence they really are characteristics, even though we do not call them such. This way of thinking, I am afraid, results entirely from the picture.[6]

Again, if my picture here is in any way idiosyncratic, the manner of talking which I derive from it is not. When we speak of an item in the world, anything we say of it ascribes a feature or characteristic to it. This seems to be the way I think when I think in logic: I say that in formulae or schemata such as Pa or Qb, any specification for P or Q will designate a feature or characteristic of the things named by a and b.

Wittgenstein urges me to consider the question whether such things as Fords and Mays have common and peculiar features, and he urges me to do so by looking at examples. I know he wants me to see that I am led astray by my picture of meaning and its associated picture of things and their features. And of course I see that the pictures do lead me astray. I am led to think of things and characteristics in a way that does not fit my examples. But having come to the realization that that way of thinking does not fit the examples, I cannot then find a way to test my picture of meaning-in-terms-of-characteristics against the examples at

---

[6]Note in anticipation. By working through some examples it is seen that the "application" of many words depends on factors other than features or characteristics: it depends on such things as ancestry, historical origin, intent, consequences, function.

all. I suspect that Wittgenstein is urging me to do
the impossible. I think that he must want me to keep
and to operate on the picture of things and
characteristics, and then to turn to examples to test
the idea that things are called by the same name
because they have common characteristics. Of course I
cannot do that. When I turn to an example, I have no
way of considering or talking about the characteristics
of things other than that supplied by the example. I
do not think there is a way to carry out Wittgenstein's
dictate to "look and see" which will give the result I
believe that Wittgenstein wants. I think I am supposed
to hold onto the picture of things and characteristics,
and then bring the picture of meaning against examples.
How can I ever do anything like that?

Perhaps I should take another tack entirely. I
cannot bring my picture of meaning, alone, up against
examples, but I ought to be able to see what the outcome would be if I could. So, in the general terms
which I derive from the pictures, I shall try to think
through an example where things turn out as Wittgenstein assures me that they will: the things referred
to by a general word will turn out not to share common
and peculiar features or characteristics.

From my picture of features and characteristics I
get the idea that anything one can say of a thing, anything which applies to this thing as one of a group of
things, will ascribe a feature or characteristic to the
thing. Do games, then, have some feature in common?
Are they all played on boards or with balls? Do they
all involve competition or winning and losing? One can
truly say these things only of some games. Do they all
have any feature or features in common? The trouble in
turning up the right candidate is that it is right before our noses. There is one thing we correctly say of
all of them, namely that they are games. And so, of
course they have that feature in common: all of them
have the feature of being games. That feature is common to them and also peculiar to them, for we do not
correctly say of any other things that they are games--
except in metaphor. Even so, this does not answer the
question I want to ask about games. I am interested
not just in whether they have certain common features
but in whether they are called by the same name because
they have those common features. All games could have
the feature of being games for no reason other than
that we call them all "games." My question is this:
do we call them all "games" because they have some
feature or features in common? Well, it may be that we
call them all "games" because they have in common the
features of being games. How can I tell? How can

13

I distinguish between these two: (1) They have in common the feature of being games because we call them all "games," and (2) we call them all "games" because they have in common the feature of being games? If (2) is right, then of course Wittgenstein is wrong. Since I am now trying to think through Wittgenstein's example, I shall have to assume that (1) is right: they have the feature of being games because we call them "games." Is it then because of some other feature that we call them "games"? Suppose I consider some other likely feature, no matter what, call it P. Then, in turn, (1') P may be a feature which things have because we call them P's. Or, on the other hand (2') we may call things P's because they have the feature of being P's. Again, in the spirit of Wittgenstein's reasoning, I shall assume (1'): Wittgenstein seems to suggest that that is the usual thing. The outcome is this: we call things "games" because we call them P's. But I have not found out why we call them P's. Well, perhaps we call them P's because we call them Q's, and we call them Q's becuase we call them R's, and so on.

What has gone wrong? One part of my picture of things and features (IIB) obviously clashes with the other (IIA). Whenever we use the same word of several things we thereby assure (by IIB) that the things in question have a feature in common--the feature which we attribute to those things in applying the same word to all of them. And these things may have no feature in common other than the feature they have in virtue of the fact that we do apply the same word to them. But my picture of things (IIA) leads me to believe that the things of the world are there before me bearing and exhibiting their features quite apart from my intrusion among those things.[7] I shall have to make peace between the two conflicting pictures. When I consider the words of language and in what their meaning consists, IIA is obviously the more important of the two pictures of things and their characteristics. How could words have meaning unless they were connected to the things of the world through the characteristics

---

[7]Cf. J. L. Austin: "...words are not (except in their own little corner) facts or things: we need therefore to prise them off the world, to hold them apart from and against it, so that we can realize their inadequacies and arbitrarinesses, and can re-look at the world without blinkers." "A Plea for Excuses" in J. L. Austin, Philosophical Papers, ed. J. O. Urmson and G. J. Warnock (Clarendon Press, Oxford, 1961), p. 130.

of those things? But if Wittgenstein is right, not all words are so connected to things. Therefore I shall have to say that only some words are connected to things through the features or characteristics of those things, and that other words are connected to things only indirectly: the things to which they apply have no feature or characteristic in common other than that which comes from the fact that the same word applies to all of them. If Wittgenstein is to be believed, the word "game" is evidently of this kind.

This adjustment may bring peace between the two conflicting pictures, but it brings a very uneasy peace. Being a game is not a characteristic which anything has in and by itself: it is a characteristic which many different things acquire only because they are called by the same name. This suggests that if we look out upon some place in the world where a game is being played, we shall not see a game being played. We shall not see a game because games are not things to be found in the real world. Games are not games but other things which are collected together and thought together under the label "games" because of crisscrossing similarities and relationships among many different things that have become incorporated in the meaning of the word "game." Here, the adjusted pictures obviously lead me astray. When I go to a baseball game the very thing I go to see is the game. "Did you see yesterday's game?" "I certainly did: I'm glad I didn't miss that one." I am asked what the children are doing: why are they making so much noise? I look out the window and I can see that they are playing some game. I may be unfamiliar with the game; I may not know what game it is; but I can see that they are playing a game. Perhaps I should say that I cannot see a game, but even if I cannot see a game I can see that the children are playing a game. There is no one set of characteristics which make a game a game. Therefore there is no one thing which a game is: therefore it is not one thing (or a thing) which one could see. But I could see something going on and know that something was a game—even though a game is not one thing. So I could see that something was a game. This would be a mistake. I am inclined to say this only because I am inclined to misapply a logic lesson. In saying of the children that they are playing a game I think that I am simply saying that this goings-on belongs to a certain class. And I think that I might say this even though I have no way of characterizing the class other than in pointing out its members one by one, remembering no more than that just these particular things belong to this class. Of course this is silly. In saying of

15

the children that I see them playing a game, I am
saying what they are doing. They are playing a game.
I could not say that--correctly and unquestionably as I
do--unless I could recognize a goings-on as a game,
unless I understood what it is to be a game.   If
Wittgenstein is right I could not understand what it is
to be a game unless I knew the word "game."   Being a
game is a characteristic which goings-on have only
because the word "game" is applied to them. Of course,
Wittgenstein does not think that the word "game" is
applied to things as a result only of caprice. He does
not think that one of my language-making ancestors
decided one day to call this and this and that games--
where this and this and that are no more than certain
things that happened to pop into his mind one morning--
perhaps this bone, this prayer, and that means of
making fires are to be called "games."   No. The word
"game" is a part of the order of language: its application is teachable and systematic, and anyone who
knows the word "game" can apply it to things he has
never seen nor heard of.   It is part of an organized
way of life.
     When thinking in terms of the pictures I shall
think that, although we speak of seeing games, we do
not see games directly.   Games are things we see only
because our language has collected together the real
things we see under the label "games."   But this will
not do. "Things which I do not see directly" seem to
be things I see in a mirror, or things I see reflected
in some similar surface.   "How can you claim to see
what is going on in his apartment? You cannot see into
his window from your window."   "No, I can't see into
his window directly. But I can see everything that
goes on in his apartment reflected in the mirror near
the end of the hall."   Of course when I go to a ball
game I do not see the game reflected in a mirror. Even
"reflected in the mirror of language" does not seem an
appropriate metaphor here: it does not seem an apt way
to be colorful or poetic. Perhaps I do not really see
games.   What could I have in mind by that?   "I never
really saw a ghost, although I used to think I did. I
thought the man who worked at night in white coveralls
was a ghost." If I had been nearer the man or if I had
seen him in better light, I should have known then that
I did not see a ghost.   When I think that I do not
really see games, I am thinking that I do not really
see them because of the word "game" and the nature of
games, not because the light is bad, or because I never
have a good seat at the stadium.   Perhaps this is the
way I should put it: although we see these various
goings-on in the world which are called "games," we

16

merely see them as games. When would one see something as a game? "I see international politics as a game." I see much of the behavior of a man and his wife as a game they play with each other." One might say such things in introducing a metaphor or model which he believes throws some light on international politics or on marriage. The acts of nations or of husbands and wives are much more like the moves and countermoves in tic-tac-toe than we are usually inclined to think. The same moves and countermoves are made over and over again. They are stupid games, too; one wonders why people continue at them. Seeing something as a game is not a visual matter at all: it is in no way incompatible with, or an alternative to, anything we say we see with our eyes.

But sometimes seeing as is a visual matter. I see this drawing now as a staircase leading up to the right and now as a staircase leading down to the left; I see it now as the top of the staircase, now as the bottom. In such cases we speak of seeing the drawing as one thing or as another only when we are familiar with the two possibilities. With games we are not familiar with a second possibility. When watching a game of hockey we do not see it now as a game, and then suddenly--see it as the other thing.

Well then we do see games--and other things which have no characteristic in common other than that which they have because they are called by the same name. The things we see must he be of two different kinds: some are the products, in part at least, of our language; some are not. Some things have their distinctive characteristics because we call them by the same names. Other things have certan characteristics in themselves; because they have in themselves these characteristics we call them by the names we do. The two pictures of things (IIA) and their characteristics (IIB) actually complement each other. Because we apply the same word to certain things, these things have a certain characteristic in common: indeed, they have no other characteristic in common. Games are presumably like that--and many, many other things as well: pencils, shoes, chairs, boxes. But not all things could be like that, and not all of the features which things have could depend on the fact that we call the things by the same names. If all things and all features of things were in that way products of our language, then before human beings appeared on the world and evolved a language, there could not have existed any of the familiar things which we recognize by their familiar features. Before there were language speaking human beings, there could not have been rocks and rivers,

17

lizards and trees. And of course there were rocks and trees long before human beings began to walk to and fro upon the face of the earth and up and down on it. But does that absurdity really follow so simply from the view that most of the familiar things of the world are partly the products of our language? When humans speak of rocks and rivers, lizards and trees they know well enough what things they are talking about--and no matter whether these "things" are partially formed by their language. Or rather, the "things" are there, severally, in the world; it's just that without human language they are not grouped and classified. But again, that is not right, because when we identify or characterize a thing by name we are doing more than reciting the fact that this thing before us is numbered among the member of this class--for no particular reason at all. Things, then, are severally in the world, but not lizards, or crabs or brooks or ponds. But of each thing, it is a lizard--if it is; or it is a pond--if it is. Yes, of course. Then that pond may have existed before there were humans on the earth, and also that river and that mountain; of course not that lizard, because lizards never live that long. I can refer to things singly, individually, which might have existed before mankind came upon the world. But "things" referred to by common nouns could not have existed before mankind because without the words there are no such "things." Before there were humans, there could not have been lizards and fish or mountains or prairies. In the beginning, God could not have created mountains or oceans or snakes or grasses, nor could these things have come by earthquake or evolution from previous states or earlier living things.

More importantly--for purposes of the present inquiry--if all things and their features were dependent on language, there would be no way in which any words at all could acquire a meaning. We should not then be able to use language to talk about the world. If all things were what they are because of the words we apply to them, there would be no way to explain why we apply the words we do to them. Language would float in the air with no connection to the world beneath. In fact this whole idea is quite unthinkable and unsayable. Some words must be applied to things because of the characteristics those things have in themselves.

Some things, then, must have some characteristics in themselves. How can I find such a characteristic, one which things have in themselves? How can I find a word which applies to things because of some characteristic which these things have in themselves? When I think of a word like "game" and ask what characteristic

18

a thing must have in order to be a game, I think of many characteristics: involving competition, winning and losing, being a form of amusement, and so on. Although not all games have these characteristics, they are relevant to the application of the word "game": each of them counts in some way toward making a thing a game.[8] By contrast consider the word "red" and ask what characteristics a thing must have in order to be red. Surely there is only one characteristic which makes a thing red, the very characteristic of being red. No other characteristic is relevant; no other characteristic counts in any way toward making a thing red. All red things have the characteristic of being red, and it is precisely because they have that characteristic that we call them "red." And, just as I should expect, I can look out upon the world and see that characteristic of one thing and of another. Through that characteristic, surely, the word "red" becomes connected to various things in the world. One does not need to know the word "red," one does not need to be a language-using animal, in order to see that characteristic. It is plainly there in the world to be seen--waiting, if you like, to have a word bestowed upon it. Undoubtedly, what the originators of language did was to invent a word and assign it to that easily observable characteristic of being red.

What am I thinking here? I think that some words are connected to the world only indirectly through other words, but that some words are connected directly to the world. "Red" is one of those words which is connected directly to the world. It is the name of a certain color found here and there throughout the world. But is "red" the name of a certain color? Most of us know quite a few color names, such as chartreuse, puce, magenta, vermilion. "Do you know the name of this color?" I might ask, and the answer might be "Yes. It's called 'puce'." Would I ever ask, "What's the name of this color?" where the answer is "red"? (Of course, the answer might be "vermilion" or "scarlet.") The answer "red" does not sound in place. Is this because I already know the name of that color?

_____

[8]"Instead of producing something common to all that we call language, I am saying that these phenomena have no one thing in common which makes us use the same word for all...." L. Wittgenstein, **Philosophical Investigations** Sec. 65. In saying there is no one thing in all which makes us use the same word, surely Wittgenstein implies that there are things in some which make us use the same word.

19

What color? The color might be scarlet or cardinal or
vermilion. What am I thinking of as the color red? If
I were a painter I might say "I reserve this part of my
palette for mixing the reds. I use lots of reds,"
where I should count any number of different colors as
reds, including such as burnt sienna, dark maroon, old
rose and pink. I was certainly not thinking of these
as "red." I did not think that, without langauge, a
person would see that all of these many different colors had the same characteristic and thus had to be
called by the same name.

I must have been thinking of one of the several
colors I often refer to as a "bright red." That was
the color of some of the blocks or cards with the help
of which I first learned the color words. When I was
very young I was asked to point out or to pick up
blocks or cards which were green, yellow, blue, and
red. And soon I could carry out these requests without
mistakes. At this point in my life I must have learned
how the word "red" was connected to something which was
directly before my eyes. But when this lesson was
complete I had only barely begun to understand where
the word "red" fit in my growing vocabulary. I went
on, of course, to learn all the bright colors: violet
and orange as well as blue and green and red. And I
learned that these colors shade into each other and
that some of them may be described as orange-red or
reddish-orange, purplish-red or blue-green. The same,
too, with brown, as reddish-brown, or brownish-red.
Even black may be bluish-black and white may be "off-
white" or yellowish. I learned that red can be very
light, shading into pink, or very dark, shading into
maroon.

Now what did I think the word "red" referred to?
Any one of any number of hues and shades and tints between red-orange and reddish-violet and pink and maroon. Any color which is not too light, not too dark,
not too orange, not too violet: colors like crimson,
scarlet, vermilion, cardinal. And why did I think that
that color stood out by itself in the world and struck
my eyes as one thing to be given one name? Of course,
it does not have to stand out in the world; it only has
to be there. But why did I think that with my animal
eyes, untrained by language, I should be able to find
it there?

It is clear, now, that I have been making a mistake. I have been trying to trace what I imagine to be
a direct connection between the word "red" and something presented to my eyes in nature. I have taken
this "thing" as the color red. When the noun "red" is
used in the way I have been talking about--that is,

20

when it is used as an abstract noun--I suppose that grammarians would say that it was used as a "mass noun." If I understand correctly, a "mass noun" is one which does not take the indefinite article; it cannot be quantified by such words as "one," "two," "many," "few"; and it has no plural (if it is singular in form as "red" is). Although the abstract noun "red" might appear not to satisfy these requirements, I think that the appearance is superficial, and that it really does satisfy them. It takes the indefinite article only in a few expressions. An artist, pointing to a part of a painting, might say "What you need is a red here." In this, and in other similar uses, "a red" is clearly an abbreviated way of saying "a shade of red." Also, when it is quantified by "some," "few," "many," it seems to be an abbreviation for "shades of red." "The fall landscape has many reds" amounts to "The fall landscape has many shades of red." Only in these, and in similar expressions, does "red" take the plural--and then "reds" comes to "shades of red." This is typical of mass nouns: their "reference is divided" by making them prepositional objects of a preceding noun which takes the plural, quantifying adjectives, and the indefinite article. In its most common uses, "water" acts as a typical mass noun, and its reference is divided through the use of such phrases as "puddle of water," "many cups of water," "a drop of water."

Although in the uses in question "water" and "red" are alike in being mass nouns, they are unlike in that "water" is concrete and "red" abstract. "Water" is the name of a "material substance," and hence, when its "reference is divided" it is divided into spatio-temporal units: ponds, drops, puddles, glassfulls, and pints. When "red" is divided it is divided into shades, which are not spatio-temporal units.[9] Again

_____

[9]Quine seems to think that, as a mass noun, "red" is concrete. He says that the mass word "water" when used in subject-position is a singular term, referring to a "single though scattered object, the aqueous part of the world." And about "red" he says: "...similarly the mass substantive 'red' in subject position may be conceived as a singular term naming the scattered totality of red substance. 'Color' becomes a general term true of each of various such scattered totalities." Willard VanOrman Quine, Word and Object (N.Y., John Wiley & Sons, Inc., 1960), p. 98.

Part of the difficulty here is that Quine is obviously thinking of someone saying, "Red is a color." I cannot think when one would say that--except possibly it is easy to be confused here because of such expressions as "patch of red" or "spot of red," which make it look as though "red" were a concrete mass noun, and hence that red is a substance like water. As water exists in pools and drops, so red exists in spots and patches. But this is obviously silly. Where "red" in "patch of red" or "spot of red" is concrete, surely it is functioning as an abbreviation for "patch of red paint" or "spot of red pigment" or something like that. ("Put a spot of red here." "Put a spot of red paint here.") And where "red" is abstract in "patch of red" it is short for "patch of red color." (I inspect a set of color patches designed to help children learn color words, and comment, "This set is lacking a patch of red.") That the noun "red" is abstract is perhaps best brought out by comparing it with other nouns which are unquestionably abstract. Consider this sentence: "His most obvious character trait, frankness, is a very rare trait in our day." And compare it with this: "The most conspicuous color in the works of Ion painters, namely red, reveals much of their attitude toward painting." The first sentence could easily be rewritten with "honesty," "sensitivity," "loyalty," or the name of some other trait in place of "frankness." And all these, I take it, are unquestionably abstract nouns. The second sentence could be rewritten with any color name in place of red: "blue," "lavender," "chartreuse." Color names, then, must be abstract nouns. Indeed, it is obvious that they are. ("His trait"; "The name of his trait"; "Its color"; "The name of its color.") The name of his trait and the name of its color are abstract nouns.

It is sometimes assumed that abstract nouns will have some ending which marks them as such: "-ity," "-hood," "-ness," "-ship" (longevity, motherhood, hardness, leadership). This is obviously a most complex matter, and no list of suffixes will serve to mark off every abstract noun. In fact, it appears that in a concrete-abstract pair, it is the concrete which sometimes gets the suffix: horror--horrible; fear--fearful; wit--witty. It makes a difference whether the concrete word is noun or adjective: "-hood" and

---

in answer to a foreigner's question about the word "red," and then it would be, at least partly, a remark about the word "red" and not about red. But that sentence must not be important. Suppose that in giving some advice to students an artist says, "Red is a difficult color to handle." Is he talking about the "scattered totality of red substance"?

"-ship" will make an abstract noun out of a concrete
noun: mother--motherhood, professor--professorship.
If one begins with adjectives, "motherly," "profes-
sorial," then the corresponding abstract nouns are
created with "-ness,": "motherliness," and "professo-
rialness." And, of course, the two sets of abstract
nouns are very different: motherhood is quite different from motherliness. Often a concrete adjective
permits of two abstract nouns which are not equivalent:
pious--piety, piousness; tedious--tedium, tediousness;
sad--sadness, sorrow.

Benjamin Whorf thinks that the structure of our
language leads us to construe abstract mass nouns on
the pattern of concrete mass nouns. Specifically, he
believes that we are led to think of "time" as we think
of "water."[10] According to Whorf, we individuate
mass-nouns by using the "names of body-types" as in
"stick of wood" or "pane of glass" or by using the
"names of containers" as in "glass of water" or "cup of
coffee." Thus, "our language patterns often require us
to name a physical thing by a binomial that splits the
reference into a formless item plus a form" (p. 141).
Whorf thinks that we treat the abstract mass noun
"time" by analogy, and so "...with our binomial formula
we can say and think, 'a moment of time, a second of
time, a year of time'... the pattern is simply that of
'a bottle of milk,' or 'a piece of cheese'." (p.
142-3) Thus, apparently, we are led to think of time as
a substance which can be divided into segments or con-
tainer-sized units, and this Whorf thinks is a re-
grettable effect of our language; it is a distortion because time as directly experienced is no such thing.

I do not recognize in myself any tendency to think
of or picture time in the way Whorf says that I do.
But quite aside from that, there is a question about
whether Whorf has correctly characterized the "grammar"
of mass nouns in English. Whorf thinks that our picture of time has a grammatical origin. He must think,
therefore, that we tend to treat abstract mass nouns on
the pattern of concrete mass nouns. By analogy with
"puddle of water" or "glass of water" we get "one minute of time" or a "year of time."

For one thing, the principle he finds at work
cannot be very general, for surely he does not think
that we have any tendency to containerize jealousy, or

---

[10]"The Relation of Habitual Thought and Behavior
to Language" in B. Whorf, Language, Thought, and Reality, ed. J. B. Carroll (Cambridge, Mass., M.I.T. Press,
1956), pp. 134-159.

fear, or beauty, or disease. (A piece of jealousy, a length of fear, a unit of beauty, a chunk of disease.) For another, we do not often use the expressions he cites, "a moment of time" and the others, and it is not easy to see when we should use them. Perhaps, poetically, "A century is but a moment of time." "Time is a most valuable commodity: do not waste a minute of it." Of course we speak of a moment of "my time" or of "your time" ("Give me a moment of your time"), but that is an altogether different matter. We do commonly use less definite quantifying words and phrases with "of" and "time": "a lot," "a bit," and others. "Be patient: it will take a lot of time." "Give it a bit of time." "But there is a bit of rancor in his words." "I have confronted a lot of hate in my career."

It is sometimes assumed that abstract nouns always come with a grammatical indicator, a suffix which marks them as abstract nouns. And specifically, it is assumed that the abstract noun corresponding to the concrete "red" will be marked by the suffix "-ness." Hence it is assumed that only "redness" is the abstract noun form corresponding to "red." But the word "redness" is too limited: it is used only in very special circumstances. In reporting on my injured arm, I might say, "The soreness is gone, but the redness is still there." Indeed "redness" is another abstract noun, but it is not the abstract noun corresponding to the uses of the concrete adjective "red" as simple color attributors (i.e., not to "red" as in "The package is tied in red ribbon"). One can see to what concrete adjective use an abstract noun corresponds by engaging in the artificial exercise of "translating" an abstract expression into its concrete "equivalent." Thus "The color red is rare in wild flowers" becomes "Few wild flowers are red" or "Red wild flowers are rare." And, I suppose "The redness is still there" becomes "My arm is still red." But this is surely a special idiomatic use of "red," as "red" is also used in "red hair," "red eyes," or "red skin" (the skin of the American Indian). And "redness" seems to be the appropriate abstract noun for all of these. "I have tried bleach and dye but cannot get all the redness out of my hair." "The eyedrops have improved my vision, but they do not get the redness out." "The redness of the American Indian's skin is due to two pigments." "Redness is common in eye infections of that kind." Now try "redness" as the corresponding abstract noun for "red" in its simple color-attributive use. Compare the last example with "Redness is common among wild flowers." This certainly will not do. "Redness of petals is common among wild flowers" might suggest itself as the better expression, but clearly it isn't any better.

However it is with the names of colors, I should be concerned with "red" as it directly "applies" to concrete things. I should be concerned with "red" as an adjective--and hence as it occurs in sentences where red is "attributed" to things. I should be thinking of what is involved in talk of red things. "The male red-shafted flicker has red whisker-marks." "Canadian mailboxes are red." "The tool with the red handle is a mattock." The word "red" in these sentences is the concrete general word I want.

What is involved in saying of something that it is red? I say that the clay near the fence is red. I say that my new neighbor has red hair and eyebrows. If I checked the samples in a standard array of color chips which are nearest to the color of red clay and red hair I might well find that I had checked "sienna" and "ochre," which are not near to the ones marked "cadmium red," "crimson" or any of those which are clearly "bright red" or even "red." These are not examples of what I have in mind. Perhaps we say of some things, such as hair or clay, that they are red, meaning that they are as red as things of that kind usually are. If a flag or a sweater were the color of my neighbor's hair I should not so readily say that the flag or the sweater was red. Looking out my window at dawn, I say to Emile, "The whole sky is red this morning." If I ask Emile to pick the nearest color from the standard color chips, he would pick "orange." I say to Jeanne, "I love those red flowers that have just blossomed in your garden." If Jeanne were asked to pick the color which comes closest to that of the lupines in her garden, the flowers to which I refer, she would pick "magenta." This color, too, is a long way from those marked "red"--or those which we usually think of as red when we review the colors in the color chart. In many cases when I talk to someone of something being red the person knows what color I have in mind, and often it is not the color of the red blocks I played with as a child, the ones which my grandmother used in giving me my first lessons in colors. If I tell someone that I just bought a red sweater--and I want to be explicit-- I shall perhaps add, "It is slightly greyed and rusty red, a salmon color." If someone comes to me and says that he cannot find a mail box, I might say, "Do you know what you are looking for? The Canadian mail boxes are red, you know." Again, I might feel that I should say "bright red" or even "scarlet."

I see no easy way to summarize all of this. Perhaps sometimes when we say that something is red, without elaboration or qualification, we mean that it is

25

"bright red" or something near the color of a child's red blocks. Whether my remark that something is red calls for elaboration or qualification seems to depend on the thing I am describing, the person I am talking to, and the reason for my description. I can think of no way of summarizing without losing important details. Perhaps this: to say of something that it is red, simpliciter, is to say that its color is some shade of "bright red," not too grey or pink, not too orange or violet--and how much variation of color is permissible will depend on circumstances.[11]

If this is about right, then how am I to imagine that the red things in the world somehow stand out for me to recognize, independently of the fact that I know the word "red" and other color words? What reason have I for thinking that my animal eyes--unaided by language--would survey the things in the world and somehow note as belonging together all of the many things which are red? The color adjective "red" ("bright red"), I am inclined to think, must be one of the simple words of my language. It must somehow mark out, and register, something given to me by nature.

I ought to be able to imagine how it was with me before I acquired language--when I was a small child. I want to ask whether, before I knew a single word, I was aware that all red things belonged together in the

---

[11]Philosophers often write as though the application of the word "red"--taken as a "simple" word--was a very simple matter. They seem to think that any question about it can be answered in a few sentences, although they do not give the same, or even compatible, answers. Of the question, "Why are we able to name [red] things as we do?" D. F. Pears says "...ultimately there must be some exit from the maze of words, and, wherever this exit is made, it will be impossible to give an informative reason except by pointing.... Still at the place where the exit is made it is always possible to give a detailed reason like 'We are able to call red things red because they are red,' which is too obviously circular even to look informative." ("Universals," Philosophical Quarterly, Vol. 1, 1951)

A. J. Ayer says, "...very often we have no way of saying what is common to the things to which the same word applies except by using the word itself. How else could we describe the distinctively common feature of red things except by saying that they are all red?" in Problems of Knowledge (Baltimore, Penguin Books, 1956), p. 11.

proper way. I mean "belong together" in the sense that they could properly be said to be red--although I do not speak and do not know anything about speech. Are the red things "there," waiting to be picked out and described by one simple adjective? Do all the bright red things somehow earn the same adjective: a ripe tomato, a drop of blood, a sunset cloud, a bottle of cranberry juice? "Same adjective?" I know nothing of adjectives; I know nothing of words; I cannot describe or characterize anything. I crawl and cry and peer and chuckle. But I must be aware that things have colors. Don't the red things all deserve what is coming to them--when finally I learn the adjective "red," and apply it to them all? When I learn it, doesn't it fit just right: isn't it perfectly natural? These seem silly things to ask. What am I trying to think? "The word 'red' fits the red things in nature." "The red things deserve the word which will come to them." "The red things, as they are in themselves, earn the same adjective." I must get all these metaphors from the picture I have of simple words. The simple words must apply to things because the things are alike in some significant respect. When I look upon the world as an infant I do not know what likenesses might be significant and what they might be significant for. I have no words. I do not know what a word is--so I do not know what a concrete general word is or a simple word or a color word. If words are connected to things in the world, I do not know how they are connected. I do not know what to look for in things that might make them "earn" or "get" the same word. I have no comprehension of what it is to "get" the same word. The ideas of "likeness" and "same" and "significant" I get at the same time I get my language and in connection with it. As a small child, I have no language. I cannot imagine that, as a pre-linguistic child, I might make such observations as "these deserve the same word, those do not."

Perhaps I am thinking like this. There are many times when I see something, but I do not know how to identify it, and I do not know its name or how to talk about it by using its name and perhaps other parts of the most suitable vocabulary. So perhaps I say in that way that there was something about all red things that deserved a common label, even though I didn't know what the label was. Suppose that I have been reading a book on American trees. After finishing it, I say to my Uncle Fred, "I've never seen a chinquapin tree. I wonder where I can find one." He says, "But you have seen a chinquapin tree. There was one growing just out-side your grandfather's house. I know you saw it when you were ten years old, when you were spending the summer there, because I remember that you sat on the back step and watched your grandfather trim that tree." So, of course, I did see a chinquapin tree, long before I knew anything about trees, their features, their classification or their names.

And in that way, I undoubtedly saw many red things, before I learned my color vocabulary. Suppose that I had been born with vision, but that I became blind at an early age, say four. Later, when I am twelve, I ask my father, "Did I ever see a red thing?" He would surely say, "Yes, you had a red wagon when you were three years old." I might say, "I don't rememeber it at all. I certainly don't remember seeing it." And he might reply, "Oh, you saw it all right. You had perfect vision then." So in that way I might have seen a red wagon. But that is not enough to show me that red things stand together in the world somehow, and that my eyes can pick them out. I cannot remember seeing the colors of things.

Sometimes I can see something and not realize what I have seen, and someone may tell me what I have seen, but unlike the former cases, I can remember all the details necessary to recognize it or identify it and to talk in appropriate ways about it. As we are leaving the zoo, I say "I wish I had seen a mandrill." My companion says, "You did see a mandrill. I saw you standing for a long time looking at it. It was the large baboon with the striped face and purple rump." "Oh, so that was a mandrill." Although at the time I saw it I did not know it was a mandrill, I remember it very clearly. I remember every feature of the animal: I watched it carefully and for a long time. So now I could recognize a mandrill anywhere; I could easily pick one out of a whole zoo full of animals. That is the way I think I might have seen red things when I was a small child. I did not know the word "red." I did not know any words. Yet I was prepared to pick all the red things out and separate them from things of other colors, before I had begun to acquire my language.

In what way could this be the same as being able to recognize a mandrill? When I watched the madrill at the zoo—not realizing what I was watching—I already knew a great deal about animals. I knew roughly how they were classified, and in what characteristics one kind differed from another. I knew how they reproduced. I knew that the sexes differ, and that the young are quite small and differ from the parents in many ways. When I said that I could recognize a mandrill anywhere, of course I exaggerated. But the exaggeration was understandable. I could probably

28

recognize a living, healthy normal adult male mandrill, at least during the spring breeding season, when his rump is purple. I do not know all the ins and outs which make the word "mandrill" a complex word.

I had no analogous knowledge about colors. But isn't that irrelevant? There is to be no analogous knowledge about colors. Colors do not differ in sex or by age. Nothing needs to be known about colors to see everything that is relevant in classifying and naming them: it is all open to the untutored eye. That is what makes "red" a simple word. Can't I just remember how it was, before I could speak or understand the words of my parents? Didn't I see that these things are red, those things blue, and so on? NO. That is not right: I didn't see that these are red, or that those are blue. I didn't see that that tree was a chinquapin and I didn't see that the baboon in the cage was a mandrill. I do not say, about such things, retrospectively, "I saw that..." unless at the time I was able to recognize the thing as one of a certain kind or class. I did see this red wagon, that red block, and that red pitcher. But the fact that I say these things is not enough to show that I saw them as somehow belonging together. Then I must have seen that they were, in the proper way alike: that is, I must have seen that they were shades of bright red. "That" has crept in again. I did not see that they were all shades of red. Then what did I see?

I am to remember being impressed by a certain visual quality of some things: their being red. I am to remember that I was aware of it, before I had a color vocabulary, before I had any language at all. But what is that visual quality of being red? It is what I attribute to a thing by an adjective, and moreover a color adjective, but not a color adjective like "puce." And what do I attribute to a thing? How can I think of it without thinking that it incorporates the fact that the thing is not too orange (or yellow), or too purplish, or too light, or too dark, or too brown? It is impossible to think of this without illegitimately smuggling in all of the many ideas which derive from or are tied up with my language. I cannot think of these things without the word "red" in the background, and my grasp of the word is partly reflected in my knowing when I should say "This is red...," "Being red...," "I want red," "Make it red," and similar things, and my knowing when to qualify and why and in what way. I cannot really think the idea that I was aware of red things in the world before I knew my language.

I cannot think of "being red" as independent of language any more than I can think of "being a game" in that way. They are both language dependent. But isn't that a confused thing to say, because "being red" is not language dependent in the same way as "being a game"? Being a game is language dependent because the many things which are games have nothing in common other than the fact that the word "game" applies to them. Can I say the same of things that are red? Or isn't it rather that I cannot understand what being red is without understanding other color words, the idea of shade--the whole color vocabulary and the ways in which we talk of colors? I cannot know what bright red is without knowing how it stands among the other colors. There is all that, of course. Yet isn't it also true that the bright red things do not have anything in common--anything visual that is? I cannot find any one way that they all stand out and impress my animal vision. I cannot see that there is anything among all the bright red things that makes them earn the adjective "red." But now I think I do not understand what question I am asking myself. Don't they have, in themselves, a sameness, or only similarities? It does not help to rephrase the question.

I am inclined to think that "red"--"bright red"--is language dependent only because of the color differences among bright red things: there are many, many shades of bright red. A truly simple word would correspond to the name of just one of these shades. I mean, the truly simple color adjective would correspond to the name of a specific color. A word for a specific color is the word I want. What do I have in mind as a specific color? I mean a color with a certain definite hue, a definite brilliance and saturation, a definite surface, a definite sheen. I mean a color which cannot be distinguished from a particular sample I now have before me. I mean the color which I shall ascribe to all the different patches which I obtain by painting in the same way bits of the same surface from the same can of thoroughly mixed paint. A specific color is what I am looking for when I am trying to match the color of a wall--in order to paint a new, but well sized, plaster patch.

We do not have words for such colors, of course, but I can make up such words when the situation calls for them. I shall say that anything is "bory" which has a color indistinguishable from this color sample I have before me. It is not surprising that our language does not have such words as these, so of course I cannot be thinking of "simple words" of our language. If I add such words, can I possibly think that they are the simple words I want? Characterizing things with such words will not be a simple matter. I must realize that when I match colors in one light they may not be indistinguishable when the light changes. So in describing the color of a thing the best I shall be able to do is characterize it as "bory," say, under certain light conditions. But how shall I know when I am seeing things under these particular light conditions? The human eye is notoriously bad at judging when the light is the same as it was before, and no simple description will do, such as "noon sunlight in early June at latitude 41 degrees." In order to ascribe specific colors to things, I shall have to carry with me not only a color sample, but also a color-temperature meter. Also, of course, I must be careful never to characterize something as "bory" because it is indistinguishable from something else I have correctly characterized as "bory." Two surfaces which may be indistinguishable from my "bory" sample may not be indistinguishable from each other, even in the same light and at the same time. There is no way I can be released from my color-samples and I shall be able to make duplicate sets of the required color samples only with the greatest of difficulty. So, it appears that words which are used to ascribe specific colors could come to be used only in connection with phrases like "same light for purposes of color-determination (color-temperature)," "indistinguishable in every color factor." Such specific colors as "bory" undoubtedly occur very rarely in the world of nature: I may go about with my color-sample and meter for years without finding a single bory object. If the simple common nouns of my language are the nominal forms of such adjectives, then the common nouns will name very uncommon things. The idea that such words could be the simple words of language now seems fantastic.

How can I think that it is through such words as these that language acquires its connection to the world of things? How can I believe that nature supplied me--independently of language--with this idea of and sensitivity to exact indistinguishable shades of color? In saying this, I feel somehow as though my question had slipped away from me. For even though I could not understand the name of a specific color without knowing the meaning of many other words, and even though I could not master the application of a specific color word without learning techniques that require a knowledge of optical theory, still these color-characteristics which I succeed in ascribing to things may be characteristics of things in themselves. After all, "bory" is not connected to other color words in the way that "red" is connected to "orange" or "greyed." But how could language rest on such words as "bory"? They

31

could not be the "original" words of our language as I was thinking that simple words would be. They are not the first words I learn as a child because such colors strike my untutored eye and can easily be pointed out to me. The distinction between language-dependent and language-independent seems to have slipped away from me. The distinction slips even further away when I remember that the characteristics of being a box or being a ball are, in all likelihood, like the characteristic of being a game. So if I say that a box is bory or a ball is bory I am stating a language-dependent fact, even though "bory" may be an absolutely simple word. I do not imagine that my animal eyes just see bory before them: they see bory things. They see bory twigs or bory stones. But these things, in all likelihood, are partially products of my language. My animal eyes would see only the real things, things in themselves. What, I wonder, are the things in themselves which I am supposed to be thinking of if they are not such things as balls and boxes and blocks? The further I think about this the more impoverished the real world of things in themselves becomes.

The whole idea of words being connected with things (IB) seems to lose its foundation. I cannot think of words on the one hand and things on the other, and then think of connecting the words to the things because of the features one finds the things to have. I cannot think of things except as they are formed by words. At this point I am tempted to dispose of my picture of words and things and to replace it with an entirely different one. Language is a device for converting "things-in-themselves," "the undifferentiated continuum," "pure experience"--we do not know what it is or where it comes from--into the things we see. This is the picture, I take it, which leads to remarks like these of Ernst Cassirer:

> Language does not enter a world of completed objective perceptions only to add to individually given and clearly delimited objects... names which will be purely external and arbitrary signs: rather, it is itself a mediator in the formation of objects. It is, in a sense, the mediator par **excellence**, the most important and most precise instrument for the conquest and construction of a true world of objects.[12]

12E. Cassirer, "Le Langage et La Construction du

I am tempted to replace my original picture with this one, but only until I think of some of the sad and ridiculous consequences to be drawn from this one. For now dogs and bluejays do not see any of the things we do. A dog cannot see a bone; a bluejay cannot see an acorn. Bones and acorns are things formed out of the flux by our language acting through our eyes; since dogs and bluejays do not have our language, then of course they do not form bones and acorns for their eyes to see. But does this estimate of the perceptual powers of dogs and bluejays really follow from the view? Without language there are no "completed object-ive perceptions." Language is "the most important... instrument for the conquest and construction of a true world of objects." And dogs and bluejays have no lan-guage. Thus they cannot be aware of a true world of objects. Bones and acorns? But they see! No one wants to deny that. And I do not want to say that we are wrong when we say that they see such things. We are extending our language--which applies primarily to humans--to cover the abilities, behavior, and actions of animals. Then they do not really see. What does it mean to say that bluejays do not really see acorns? "The bluejay just looks as though he sees the acorn. He really finds it by smell." "No, bluejays have practically no sense of smell. He really sees it, but he appears to be looking in the other direction." He really does see it then. No: that is what we say he does. Well, dogs see bones: that is, we say that they do, and that is good enough. I do not want to deny that they do. It's just that they do not see them as bones. But do we see bones as bones? I mean that dogs do not recognize them as bones. I train my dog to pick the bone out from a group of objects, and to fetch it when I say "bone." One day I disguise the bone: I smear it with moist clay. I say "bone" and off my dog goes. He looks over the group of objects. He doesn't recognize the bone. And then he does. He picks it up and brings it to me.

What am I trying to say? The world is not at all the way I see it or think it to be. Then I am mad. My picture of things and characteristics makes me think strange things. There are the things before me with their characteristics open to my eyes. And now I want

Monde des Objets," Journal de la Psychologie Normale et Pathologique, XXX, (1932), p. 23. John Cook provided me with this quotation, after persuading me that I would be wrong in using a quotation from Benjamin Whorf.

to deny that. Then there are no such things and their characteristics--only incomplete, unconstructed objects which I cannot talk about until my language has formed them. Of course my language has formed them: these objects, the only ones I know. But no language has formed them for dogs or bluejays.

What am I to think of Wittgenstein's point about "family resemblances"? Is it meant to replace the principle given by my picture? Is it meant to replace it with another principle, namely that words refer to things because of "family resemblances" among these things? The principle of my picture is: "same feature, same word." This being the principle, this gives the key to the way language is acquired; it shows its "original" workings. In connection with this, I have another picture: the things one sees with his animal eyes and hears with his animal ears give the markers for assigning general words. Does Wittgenstein mean to suggest that our animal senses show us the sets of overlapping relationships, "family resemblances," which we need for assigning words to things? Does he mean that these are somehow found in the world and presented to us, independently of language? Does he mean that we see the overlapping "family resemblances" among a group of things-in-themselves, and because of that we assign the same word to them?

It is hard to understand what could be meant in saying that one who knows no color words, one who had no language, could see a characteristic common to all red things, namely their being red. Is it any easier to understand what could be meant by saying that he could see overlapping similarities or relationships among red things? When are two things similar in color? Is orange-red similar to violet-red in some way that orange-red is not similar to orange or violet-red to violet? Is a red liquid in a bottle similar to a ripe persimmon? They are different kinds of color, but they may be exactly the same. After comparing them carefully, a painter might mix the same color to use for each of them in a still life he is painting. He might say that each is a slightly tinted vermilion. If they are in this way "exactly the same," surely they are not "similar." I might say something like this of some painting: "The colors of the sea and the colors of the beach are similar--I mean that they are all subtly tinted and transparent." Two colors can thus be similar and not be of the same hue: the colors of the sea are blues and the colors of the beach tans. Two colors can be similar by both being brilliant and saturated to the breaking point. They may, against a background of other colors, jump off the canvas and smite the eye. Except when doing philosophy we do not lose track of the fact that things are always similar in this way or in that, the similarity depending always on the context, the question at hand, the subject matter, the point of the comparison. Things are not just similar in and by themselves. Do red things have some relationship to each other? I do not know what "relationship" here could be, unless it is one of those relationships which are represented in the familiar color-charts found in dictionaries. But it is not by virtue of having such a relationship that certain things are said to be red.

So, in trying to think in a perfectly general way of the consequences of Wittgenstein's remarks, I come to an impasse. I can only resolve it if I can sensibly maintain that some features are language-dependent and some are not, and only then if I have a way to determine for any given feature whether it is one or the other. But even for a simple quality like "red" I do not know what it means to say it is a feature of things in themselves, in complete independence of language. Nor, on the other hand, do I have any grasp of what it means to say that it, being red, is dependent upon language. As soon as I relax from my philosophical tensions a little I am inclined to say, "Well, the word 'red' is the name of a color." But when should I say such a thing? Perhaps a foreigner has managed to learn a great deal of English without mastering the color words. One day someone asks him the riddle, "What's black and white and read all over?" He gets the answer "newspaper" and he laughs politely. Later he asks me to explain the joke. "I know what black and white mean, and I know that printing is black on white--but why is it funny for a newspaper to be read all over?" I explain, "It's a pun on 'read' and 'red'." "But what does 'red' mean?" "Oh, it's the name of a color. You mean you don't know the English color names." This is too far-fetched.

What alternative remains? There does not seem to be any way to think of features or characteristics of things in a perfectly general way. I had better forget the logician's jargon and turn away from the picture which dictates it or something like it (IIB). Instead I can try to let the way we talk of features or characteristics determine how I talk of features or characteristics. I had best turn to examples where we talk of features or characteristics. An entomologist attaches the same name to a caterpillar, a chrysalis, and an adult butterfly: he calls these three very different "things" by the same name. I ask him why he calls them by the same name and he says, "Because they

35

are three stages in the life-history of one insect." I
now ask, "Do the three have some feature or characteristic in common in virtue of which you call them by
the same name?" "No." "Are there any relationships
among their features in virtue of which you call them
by the same name?" What is his answer? He says, "The
features develop and change and disappear as successive
stages in the life-history of one species of insect."

Did I ask him the right questions? Could he have
understood my last question, "Are there any relationships among their features...?" I am trying to ask him
about the matters which, according to Wittgenstein, determine our use of the same name for many different
things. I must turn to the text of Wittgenstein. When
writing of games he says that we shall find overlapping
similarities. When writing of language he says that
the "phenomena...are related to one another in many
different ways. And it is because of this relationship, or these relationships, that we call them all
'language'." He summarizes solely in terms of
similarities: "...we see a complicated network of similarities, sometimes overall similarities, sometimes
similarities of detail." Then he adds the metaphor of
"family resemblances." (Philosophical Investigations,
65-67).

My main question about the text is this: Wittgenstein writes both of similarities and of relationships,
of things being similar and of things being related;
am I to think that being related is something different
from being similar? In many cases it certainly is.
The "family resemblance" metaphor suggests a case where
the two are quite different. Suppose we look at photographs of three faces, A, B, and C, and we are struck
by the similarity. "The three people look very much
alike." We study the photographs and analyze the similarity with results much like those which Wittgenstein
suggests. A and B have the "same" chin or a "very similar" chin, B and C have the "same" brows or "very similar" brows, A and C have the "same" cheeks or "very
similar" cheeks and so on. Thus we explain the fact
that they look alike. There is an entirely different
question to which we may now address ourselves. "They
certainly look alike. I wonder whether they are related?" Here the question of whether they are related is
not decided by examining and comparing their features.
They may be cousins, or two may be brothers and the
other an uncle. The same difference is present in
other cases. Hawks and owls have certain obvious similarities but they are not very closely related. Owls
are more closely related to cuckoos than they are to
hawks. "Relationship" is still another matter.

Whether the three people in the photographs have a close relationship or not may well be a question about whether they live in the same house or whether they are good friends or something like that. I'm not sure what a "close relationship" among hawks and owls would be. Possibly tick-birds and water buffalos have a "close relationship." At any rate this is a matter of having a close relationship, not a matter of "having relationships to each other." Besides "close relationships" what other kinds of relationships are there? There are relationships that are strained, long and enduring, peculiar, shameless, infamous.... But of course none of these has anything to do with the application of general words.

Wittgenstein writes as though "being related to one another" and "having relationships" were pretty much the same thing. This leads me to believe that he was not thinking of uncle or cousin or having a common ancestor or common origin or anything of that kind as relevant to "being related." I can only say that I must read Wittgenstein as implying no more by "related" and "relationship" than is implied by saying that things are "similar." Consider the college curriculum. Tell me what functions two courses are designed to fill, and I can tell you whether these functions are related. I may say, "They have related functions." I think this is a question of the contributions they are expected to make to the whole college education and to later life. I may say, "Their functions are similar." These are not the same, of course, but both are understandable remarks. I think that Wittgenstein must be thinking of something more like similarity and relatedness as they apply to functions, where at any rate being related is not a matter of having a common ancestor or common origin. But in this case the language "having relationships" does not seem to fit. "A bank and a loan company have similar, though not identical, functions." "Their functions are related." Not, I think, "Their functions have many relationships." Also, "features" or "characteristics" seem to have no place in these examples. What are the features or characteristics of the purposes of a course in elementary logic? What are the features or characteristics of the functions of a bank?

I think that Wittgenstein intends his "similarities," "relations," and "relationships" to be a matter of the features or characteristics of things. In spite of the difficulties in reading Wittgenstein in this way, I think that he means no more by "relations" and "relationships" than "similarity," and he is thinking of similarity as a matter of sharing certain, but not all, features or characteristics. As this stands, it is apparent that it will not do. This implies that whenever we compare or contrast two things to which the same general word applies--that is, whenever we discuss the similarities between the two--we are prepared to specify "features" or "characteristics" of the things upon which the similarity depends. When we consider Wittgenstein's own examples, this does not seem always to be the case. It is not true for "languages." English and German are similar in a way that neither is similar to Hopi. That similarity in part consists in the fact that both English and German have the same grammatical parts of speech. But surely it is not a "characteristic" of the English language that it has this and that part of speech. And it is not a "characteristic" of the German language that it has the same parts of speech as English.

But what of games? Baseball and cricket are similar games. That is, they are similar in a way that neither is similar to polo. Among other things, they are similar in that both involve batting a ball and running bases. Are those "characteristics" of baseball? Is it a "characteristic" of baseball that the players bat a ball? Or a "characteristic" of baseball that the players run bases? The language of "characteristics" sounds out of place here. But when someone says of two things that they are similar, the nature of his comparison may be vague or misunderstood. Then one can ask him, "In what way do you find them similar?" or "In what respect do you mean they are similar?" And he can be expected to say in what way or in what respect they are similar. Although Wittgenstein does not say so, let us be generous and say that he means by "similarity" a sharing of features, characteristics, ways or respects.

It still seems obvious that we do not use the same word of a multiplicity of things because they have similarities to each other. A larval woolly bear and an adult woolly bear are not similar in sharing certain features or characteristics. Nor is there any way or respect in which they are similar. They are simply not similar at all. And yet they get the same name.

In trying to be fair with Wittgenstein, one might say, "Of course he was thinking here primarily of games. And of various kinds of games it is the similarities based on features which determine our use of the same word for all of them." But is it so obvious that that is so? Must it be so?

When I turn again to Wittgenstein's discussion of "games" I am puzzled again about what exactly I am expected to do when I "look and see," and what exactly I

am expected to find when I do "look and see." I have
been thinking all along that I am concerned with any of
some large class of words--"general concrete words" or
general nouns--words, that is, which apply to many
things, as opposed to proper names, which apply to individual things. I have been thinking of the "things"
to which these words apply as the concrete, particular
"things," the individual stones and bushes, the single
events or occurrences, which go to make up the world I
perceive. These are the entities I try to represent in
my picture of things and their characteristics. And
so, I am concerned with the question of how I understand the "generality" in these general words. What do
I learn when I learn that one of these words applies to
this and this but not to that? Do the things to which
I apply the same word have common and peculiar characteristics by which I recognize that the same word applies to them, or do they have overlapping similarities
to each other? When I "look and see" for the word
"game" I naturally think that I shall look at the particular activities and goings-on which make up the
playing of a game: the playing now of this game of
croquet on the lawn, that game of chess in progress in
room twelve at the chess club, this afternoon's game
between Oakland and Cleveland at the Oakland Coliseum--
which started at 2 o'clock and will probably be finished before four-thirty, and which is now at the bottom
of the 4th inning with the score tied 2 all. Wittgenstein does not ask me to survey particulars in this
way. Instead he asks me to look at "board-games,"
"card-games," "ball-games": "look, for example, at
board-games, with their multifarious relationships.
Now pass to card-games; here you find many correspond-
ences with the first group, but many features drop out
and others appear. When we pass next to ball-games,
much that is common is retained, but much lost" (Sec.
66). When I think of board-games in order to determine whether they have "multifarious relationships"
with each other I naturally think of backgammon, monopoly and Uncle Wiggley: I do not think of two or more
people sitting across some table at some particular
time playing out a game of monopoly. The particulars
have already been swallowed up in a general classification. Again when I think of characteristics which
all games seem to involve, such as skill and luck,
Wittgenstein directs me to look at the parts played by
skill and luck, and at the difference, for instance,
between "skill in chess and skill in tennis." So I
think of the game of chess and the game of tennis, not
of this particular game of chess between Abel and Mabel
or of the third game in the first set in yesterday's

tennis match between Adolph and Gerald.

Why should I think of the scheduled or unscheduled activities which make up a particular match or contest or early afternoon's amusement? After all, these are particular games, but they are particular games of tennis, or baseball, or horseshoes. Of course not all of the particulars are games that I can recognize by name: people can play a game and make it up as they go along--so that the progressing game is not duck-on-the-rock, not tipcat, nor any other recognized game. But most games will belong under one of the known headings or another. So surely I can carry out Wittgenstein's directions by thinking of recognized games such as ice hockey, or pinochle, or musical chairs. When I think of those I am thinking of classes of particular games. But am I? When I think of the word "game" I think of the word which applies to all particular individual stretches of activities which make up games and no matter whether they are games of ice-hockey, golf or tictactoe. "What are they doing?" someone asks, and I say "They are playing a game." "Can't you be more specific?" "Yes. They are playing tictactoe." That is all very well--if that is what I think when I think of chess or baseball or solitaire and ask whether they have common and peculiar characteristics. But I could think of "the game of baseball" or "the game of chess," and I should not then be thinking of a label, more specific than "game," to apply to what people sometimes are doing. What are we talking of when we talk of "the game of baseball"? "After the Black Sox scandal, a commissioner was appointed to maintain the integrity of the game of baseball." In this case I should be thinking of an established social entity which stands to the particular games much as the American judicial system stands to a given court-room trial. I may say that those two teams are playing the game of baseball as it should be played. I might say that this is a poor exhibition of the game of baseball. Or I might say of a certain team that its style of play does credit to (or discredit to) the game of baseball.

In each of these cases it is clear that by the phrase "the game of baseball" I am not referring to a class of particular games which fall under the same heading because of their characteristics or similarities. Nor am I talking, in the abstract, of the characteristics or overlapping similarities in question. I should not be surprised by this. The phrase "the game of baseball" does not have the proper form for a high-level general noun-phrase. Suppose I ask Wittgenstein's question about pens or about the word "pen." Do all pens have anything in common? Do they all have metal nibs or liquid writing material? And so on. The phrase "the pen" will not come into my talk. When I talk of "the pen" I am on another subject. "The pen was invented in ancient Egypt," "The pen is mightier than the sword."

"The game of baseball" is an abstract noun-phrase. When I think of the game of baseball, I am not thinking of games of baseball--not all of them, or most of them, or some of them. "The game of baseball is a gentle-manly game" is not equivalent to "All games of baseball are gentlemanly" or "Most are gentlemanly." To speak of the game of baseball, I need not use the phrase "the game of baseball"; the noun "baseball" itself is often an abstract noun. "Baseball is a gentlemanly sport," "Baseball is a slow-paced but dramatic sport," "It is a characteristic of baseball that it generates heated arguments about the application of the rules, but there is practically no pressure to change the rules." In this respect "baseball" does not differ from other general nouns. It seems that a great many nouns can be used both as general and as abstract nouns. "There are five birds on the feeder" as opposed to "Birds are the chief warm-blooded flyers." (Compare this with "The bird is the chief warm-blooded flyer." Here, the plural is the abstract form of the noun alone. "The albatross is the greatest natural flying machine." "Albatrosses are the greatest natural flying machines.") It seems there is some potential for the abstract hidden in almost every noun. I must be careful, then, that I do not compare baseball--in the abstract--with golf or chess--in the abstract. I want to compare one game of baseball with another, and one game of baseball with one game of tennis and so on, in order to determine how all these many different goings-on have come to be reckoned under the one name "game."

The general concrete phrase I want, then, will be "game of baseball" (and its plural "games of base-ball"). "What is that?" "It's a pen". "What is that?" "It's a game of baseball." That's the way the phrase should work. But something is wrong. The ques-tion "What is that?" cannot be asked, out of the blue, for a game of baseball. Instead the blunt question will surely be, "What are those people doing?" And the answer will be, "Playing a game of baseball." "Games of baseball" are played. But of course "a game of baseball" is not a thing that is played as a trombone is a thing that is played. The question might be, "What is that goings-on over there?" And then the an-swer will be, "That is a game of baseball." That is what I should expect. A game of baseball is an

41

organized human activity and hence a goings-on. "That is a game of baseball," "That is a game of baseball being played," "They are playing a game of baseball" are all roughly the same. And I might be able to determine that the goings-on was a game before I could determine that it was a game of baseball--just as I might be able to determine that something in the grass was a frog before I could determine that it was a cricket frog.

I am to be concerned with the question, "What is it about all these different goings-on which makes me call them all games?" I must compare this and that goings-on which are games of baseball with this and that goings-on which are games of Old Maid, and so on. The considerations for "game" will be of the same kind as for "game of baseball," it's just that there will be more of them for "baseball" than for "game." (As the extension is decreased, the intension will increase.)

There is something which comes to the front immediately when I consider, say, "games of baseball" which does not come out so immediately with "games," and that is the fact that the players, managers, and coaches regard themselves as playing the game of baseball. In the case of organized American major and minor league baseball, the players, managers and others agree to be bound by the rule-making and the rule-enforcing bodies. They accept its methods for training and appointing umpires and score keepers. And so on. Is that a characteristic of this game of baseball, today's game between the Dodgers and Giants? Is it a characteristic or feature of this game that the players and managers and others regard themselves as playing the game of baseball? What, after all, is a **characteristic** or feature of this game or of any game? I do not know what I should do if I were asked to list the features or characteristics of this game between Atlanta and the Mets. Even if this is not a feature or characteristic, it is a respect in which this game can be compared with others. "These games are alike in that the players in both think of themselves as playing major-league baseball." But not all games of baseball are alike in this respect. Consider a sand-lot game. Here the players are not bound to any organization. Nor are they bound by any rule-making or rule-enforcing bodies. Quite the contrary. It is a characteristic of sand-lot ball that many of the rules are made up to suit the circumstances and changed at will. Agreements on the rules are precarious, there is much controversy; the rules are frequently bent and changed. Suppose that I see a game being played on a sand lot by nine boys: I mean a total of nine boys on both teams together. The nine form two teams, but two boys seem to play on both teams. There is pitching, batting, and base-running; it's not clear how many bases there are, nor how many strikes or balls are pitched. I have reason to wonder what game they are playing: stickball, rounders, baseball, or maybe some form of work-ups. The more I watch the game the more puzzled I become. How shall I find out? Suppose I ask one of the players, "What game are you playing?" and he says, "It's baseball--it's the best we can do with these guys and this equipment." So the players think of themselves as playing baseball. Isn't that definitive? Certainly it is, if the player who answered my question knows what he is talking about. If he is a very young child, and it is apparent that he and his companions know very little about baseball, then I might not accept his answer "We're playing baseball" as an answer to my question. I might say, "These children think of themselves as playing baseball, but they've got it all wrong. I don't know what you might call that game they're playing." In any case, what the players think of themselves as playing is a relevant consideration. Is this a respect in which this game is similar to major-league baseball? This game is not at all like major-league baseball. It is clear that the game is not a game of baseball because of its similarities with major-league baseball or with some other more easily recognizable game of baseball. I noted the similarities and I still had a question about the game. What the players can mean to be playing can help to answer my question.

Cannot the same consideration be relevant to determining whether some activity is a game? Suppose I see a rough and rowdy goings-on in a wide alley. There are two groups of boys and they appear to be fighting--but the procedure is very stylized and is obviously subject to great restrictions--perhaps rules. Some people withdraw and retire; no one seems to be seriously hurt. But the participants engage in this affair with great fury and apprehension. Well, when it is all over, I shall ask some of the participants what they were doing. "It's a gang war. Over the years we've had to agree on the ground rules." "It's a game we made up. It's rough but it's fun. Sometimes it almost gets out of hand." Isn't what they think they are doing relevant? Isn't it definitive? If so, then it is a game because they have agreed that what they do is a game-- with these rules, these restrictions, and so on. It is certainly not a game because there is some respect or respects in which it is similar to some other games.

Consider this example. Suppose that after a

43

shipwreck I am cast up on a small South Pacific Island. The natives help me build a hut and show me how to obtain food. Weeks go by, and although I do not learn much of the language, I observe the people carefully. They have a surprisingly advanced culture. Among other things I find that the young men regularly play a game which I take to be sand-lot baseball. They form two teams, which take alternate turns at bat. They count balls and strikes and run bases, but the number of balls and strikes varies from game to game, as does the number of bases. Sometimes they have a catcher, sometimes a back-stop, sometimes neither. In short, the rules vary a great deal--and the variation seems to depend in part on the number of players. Also, the length of the game varies; sometimes it goes on all day, sometimes for just a few innings. There are often heated arguments among the players.

Suppose, now, that as I learn their language I am able to ask them questions about this game. I learn what I expect--that the rules are much like baseball. But one thing comes as a surprise. They insist that they invented this game. They have never heard about baseball, and they are certain that no sailor or visitor ever brought this game or gave them any instructions or suggestions. They invented it, and it has evolved here on this island in complete independence of any outside influence. At first I disbelieve this, but when I learn about the history of their game and the history of the people I begin to think that they might be right. It is entirely possible that they should have invented this game entirely on their own.

When, at last, I am rescued and return home, what shall I say about their game? I think I shall not want to say "They play sand-lot baseball"--not without explanation. I think that I should, instead, say "They claim to have invented and developed a game which is just like sand-lot baseball." I think I should say "If indeed they invented the game, it is remarkable--because it is a game just like our sand-lot baseball."

Now suppose that I find the published journal of an American sailor-explorer, and in it I learn that he spent nearly three months on this island in the year 1909. He describes the islands and its inhabitants in great detail. There can be no question but that he visited my island and lived with my people. Among other things he explains that he taught them to play baseball. He showed them how to make bats and leather-covered balls, and taught them the rules of baseball. Now, surely, this information will affect what I say about the game. I shall now say "They play sand-lot baseball--which they learned from an explorer in 1909."

What has changed my language from "a game just like sand-lot baseball" to "sand-lot baseball"? Certainly no new characteristic which I discovered. I did not learn that the game is similar to baseball in some respect that I did not know about before. I learned something about its history. Have I kept it quite clear that I am concerned with what I call this game and that game, the particular daily games which the natives play, the goings-on and not "the game" they play? The two are really inseparable. Before I learn of the sailor's diary I do not call that game the natives played on July 12 a game of sand-lot baseball, because "the game" the natives play does not have the right origin or history.

Something besides features, characteristics, respects in which things are similar, seems to determine the application of general words in even the simplest of cases. Suppose that on a plain sheet of white paper there is a little irregular figure; then right beside it there is another which is exactly the same in size and shape and color--and in every other characteristic. One of these may be the figure I penned on the paper and the other an unwanted spot or stain which inexplicably got on while the paper was in my desk drawer. Of course I should be amazed that the two were so much alike: but still one would be the figure I painstakingly penned, and the other an ink spot.

Far from helping me to dispel some confusions, these passages from Wittgenstein seem to encourage them. They lead me to believe that I can raise and answer perfectly general questions about why we do and do not apply general words to things. But when one turns to examples which show us questions about why we apply words to things, the questions are of many different sorts, and the answers are of many different sorts. A dictionary might define the word "caw" thus: Noun. Refers to the sound made by a crow or to any similar sound. Here "similarity" enters the definition given by a dictionary. George makes a harsh sound and Herman says "That is a strange caw." I ask Herman "Why do you call that sound a caw?" Herman says "That's a good question. It certainly doesn't sound like one, does it? But my neighbor, George, made the sound over there behind the barn, and he's trying to imitate a crow. He's been working at it off and on for several hours." The sound is called a "caw" because of the intent of its maker. Is that a feature or characteristic of the sound? If it is, it is not the feature or characteristic which all "caws" have. Is it similar in some important way or respect to other caw-sounds? It is not significantly similar at all. Through the

45

intent of its maker, does it acquire some similarity to other "caws"? It is just not similar to others at all, and that is precisely why the explanation brought in the intent of its maker.

To bring this enquiry to an untimely end I shall mention one more difficulty I have with the passages in Wittgenstein, mainly in order to get a glimpse of topics for futher investigation. I have called IB "the picture of meaning" because I think that it somehow represents the nature of the meaning of words--or at least of certain fundamental words, those concrete general words through which language gains its connection with reality. The meaning of concrete general words consists in the way they are connected to the things they denote. I picture this connection as effected by the properties or characteristics of those things. And I read Wittgenstein as urging me to replace the idea of "common and peculiar characteristics" with the idea of "family resemblances." He says that it is because of the family resemblances among things that the same word is applied to each. And so he invites me to survey the things denoted by general words in order to determine whether they share certain characteristics or whether they have only various similarities to each other. And if they have "overlapping similarities," he urges me to see what those similarities are and to see how they connect the various things referred to by the same word. Now I quite naturally think that a survey of this kind for a certain word will give me a clear grasp of the meaning of that word. I quite naturally think that an understanding of the relevant characteristics or similarities will give me an understanding of the meaning of the word.[14]

And now when I turn away from my picture of meaning and from Wittgenstein's remarks I am quite lost. What are we talking about when we talk about the meaning of a general concrete word?

(1) First, adjectives. Asbury has just read in the paper that there is to be an exhibit of native art at

---

[14]Incidentally, I am not alone in reading Wittgenstein this way. George Pitcher takes Wittgenstein's remarks as a discussion of meaning. He says that Wittgenstein's review of the word "game" shows that "no general word has a unitary meaning." He explains: "As I use the term 'unitary', a word has a unitary meaning when its meaning constitutes an indissoluble whole. That is, the statement or formulation of its meaning refers to certain definite characteristics and something must have all of them for the word to be applicable to it." George Pitcher, The Philosophy of Wittgenstein (Englewood Cliffs, N.J., Prentice-Hall, 1964), p. 219.

the museum. He tells me what he has read, and asks, "What does 'native' mean in this phrase, 'native art'?" I answer, "It means 'produced by the original inhabitants of the area--as opposed to those who came later.' In this case it is the work of Indians and Eskimos." That seems straightforward enough. I explain what "native" means in the context with which Asbury is concerned. But I have not done what my picture of meaning would suggest. I have not discussed the characteristics of native art or addressed myself to the question of whether all native art works have common and peculiar characteristics or family resemblances. Asbury might have had another, and very different question: "What are the characteristics of native art?" If he had, how should I answer that question? What are the characteristics of native art (in this context, of course)? "A certain child-like simplicity, a symbolism which shows preoccupation with hunting and fishing." That answer is right, and good enough, I think; but even so, if I have found a painting with these characteristics, it remains for an expert to tell me whether it is a work of native art. And the reason I must turn to an expert is not that the expert knows the meaning of the word "native" and I do not. He knows the means by which one can identify a native art work--he knows whether all such works have certain characteristics, or some only, or whether different ones have different similarities to each other. But I know the meaning of the word "native" in the phrase "native art" without knowing any of these things.

Another example--perhaps a better one. Imagine a foreign student who has been speaking English for over a year and who is eagerly trying to increase his vocabulary. He says, "I overheard a man say that he had received in change a counterfeit twenty-dollar bill. What does 'counterfeit' mean?" What do I tell him? Something like this: "'Counterfeit' means 'imitation; not genuine.' A counterfeit bill is one that is made in imitation of a real one; it is illegal to make counterfeit bills." Can I imagine his asking, "What are the characteristics of a counterfeit bill?" And what should I say? "The texture of the paper is sometimes a little different. So is the color. The little lines in the pictures and decorations are almost never exactly the same in every detail. But often only an expert can identify a counterfeit. And there is certainly no one characteristic by which they can always be detected." Here it is quite clear that "the meaning of the word 'counterfeit'" is one thing and "the characteristics of counterfeit bills" is another entirely. One

48

can know the meaning of the word "counterfeit" and not be able to recognize a counterfeit when he sees one.

(2) Try an adverb. "He thinks apishly." "There you go again, trying to increase my vocabulary by using words I do not know. What does 'apishly' mean?" "It means "in the manner that apes are thought to do things, that is, in imitation or as mimics. It means 'in an imitative, or unoriginal way'." Does this tell the characteristics which are common and peculiar to all cases of thinking apishly? Or is that another matter? "Everything Donnie does he does enormously." "I do not understand the word 'enormously' used in that connection. What does it mean?" "It means 'exceeding the usual, the rules or norms—in grand style'." Now, what of the question, "Are there any characteristics of all things done enormously?" Who could have such a question? It seems so obvious that there are no characteristics common to every bit of enormous behavior. Whatever the question is, it is not a question about the meaning of the word "enormously."

(3) Verbs. "When he took over the chairmanship he inherited a passel of big problems. He did not have the power to change things much, but he did what he could to ameliorate conditions." "I do not know that word: what does 'ameliorate' mean?" "It means 'make tolerable'." Are there certain characteristics of all acts of amelioration? Again, the answer is so obviously "no" that it is hard to understand the question. And again, it is certainly not a question about the meaning of the word "ameliorate." With adjectives, adverbs, and verbs, the matter seems quite clear. There are understandable questions about the meanings of words and straightforward answers using the language, "The word means...." Of course, one might not ask about the meaning of a word: he might instead ask "What is native art?", "What is counterfeit money?", "What does it mean to do something enormously?" or "What does it mean to ameliorate conditions?" But if the word is new to the questioner and the questioner is especially interested in the word, there is no reason why he cannot ask "What does the word mean?" I can directly answer such a question about the meaning of the word, but in doing so I do not consider whether there are characteristics common and peculiar to all native art works, counterfeit bills, enormous behavior, apish thinking, and ameliorative acts.

(4) Nouns. All is not so simple with common concrete nouns. As my primary and clearest cases of concrete general words I have been taking the names of birds, trees, articles of furniture and such, and it is

for just such names that I am most strongly inclined to invoke my picture of meaning. I am inclined to think that these words refer to things because of the characteristics of the things, and that a grasp of those characteristics (or family resemblances) is an understanding of the meaning of the word.

Yet I do not ordinarily ask for the meaning of such words; and when I do, I am not answered with the formula, "The meaning is ...," or with the words "... means...." Wheaton has received a postcard from a friend who is vacationing on the California coast. The friend writes "Fine place, but the whimbrels make a lot of noise at night." Wheaton has never seen the word "whimbrel" before; consequently he does not understand his friend's postcard message. He comes to me for help. Even though he thinks the word "whimbrel" is an interesting word, and even though he says as much, he will not ask "What does this word 'whimbrel' mean?" He will likely say, "That word 'whimbrel' has a weird sound. What on earth is a whimbrel?" And I, of course, shall say, "A whimbrel is a brown shorebird with a long decurved beak."

He will not ask, "What does 'whimbrel' mean?" He will ask "What is a whimbrel?" And this seems always to be the question about a noun which is the name of an animal, a plant, a tool, an article of clothing--a "thing" or medium-sized piece of dry goods. But this is not the question for all common nouns. "He says I am an ingrate. That's a nasty sounding word: what does it mean?" "It means 'one who is ungrateful; one who is not appreciative or thankful'." One can ask for the meaning of "ingrate," it would seem, and one can answer, "It means...." "My father writes, 'Don't let Carson's occultations disturb you.' What does 'occultation' mean?" "It means 'concealment,' 'hiding from view'." Now it seems quite all right to ask, "What does 'occultation' mean?" and quite all right to say, in this situation, "'Occultation' means 'concealment'." I cannot imagine an analogous situation in which anyone would ask "What does 'whimbrel' mean?" and in which I should say, "'Whimbrel' means 'brown shorebird with decurved beak'."

Why can we explain the meaning of some common nouns with the formula "It means..." and not others? Paul Ziff[15] thinks that the difference is this: one can say "It means..." of a common noun only when the application of the common noun is governed by "necessary and

---

15Paul Ziff, Semantic Analysis (Ithaca, Cornell University Press, 1960), p. 185.

sufficient conditions." I do not know exactly what necessary and sufficient conditions are supposed to be, but I suppose that when one gives the necessary and sufficient conditions for a word's application he gives a formula by which any specimen, sample, individual, case, or instance of the thing to which the word applies can be recognized, identified, or picked out. If that is the force of Ziff's suggestion, then I do not think it is correct. Is every noun of which we can say "It means..." governed by such necessary and sufficient conditions? Are there necessary and sufficient conditions for "ingrate" and "occultation"? Perhaps I need other examples. "The author writes 'A fluster came over me.' What does that word 'fluster' mean?" "Fluster means 'a state of agitation and confusion'." Are there conditions by which one can recognize a fluster--in himself as well as in others?

This noun "fluster" and also the nouns "ingrate" and "occultation" are derived from or closely allied to adjectives: "flustered," "ungrateful," and "occult." It would appear that a very large number of such words are in the same boat; that is, I mean that the words of which we can ask "What does it mean?" and of which we can say, "It means so and so" are in this same boat. "He is a devotee of occultism, you say?" "What does the word 'occultism' mean?" "It means 'belief in mysterious powers that control our lives'." This word, of course, comes from the adjective "occult." There is surely no reason for believing that all the adjectives which I am suggesting here, and then all of the corresponding nouns, are alike in being subject to definition by necessary and sufficient condition.

Ziff suggests not only that if we can say "It means..." the noun is governed by necessary and sufficient conditions, but also, if a noun is governed by necessary and sufficient conditions then we can say "It means...." Consider this: Cargrove does not understand what he hears because he does not know the word "flush." He says "That man said that he was dealt a flush on the first hand." Cargrove needs help. He is about to ask me a question and I think his question will be "What is a flush?" not "What does 'flush' mean?" And I think that that is his question even if he is interested in the word: he may find it a very odd word. But however Cargrove puts his question, the answer is this: "A flush is..." and not this, "'Flush' means...." The answer is: "A flush is a hand in which all cards are of the same suit." I should suppose that if anything is governed by necessary and sufficient conditions, a flush is. The explanation of what a flush is gives those conditions: all cards of the same

51

suit.   With this explanation, Cargrove should be
equipped to recognize a flush whenever he sees one.
Yet this is a case in which the question "What does
'flush' mean?" is odd indeed, and the formula "'Flush'
means 'hand in which all cards are of the same suit'"
doesn't sound right.

What then is the difference between a common noun
of which we can say "It means..." and one of which we
cannot?   The examples I have suggested are all nouns
connected with adjectives or which have an important
adjectival form.   But that is not true of others.   Consider this example.   Suppose I am telling someone about
the dance of the bees.   I say, "If, after watching the
dance of the worker bee, you are going to calculate the
direction of the flowers which she indicates, you must
realize that she makes an allowance for windage."   My
listener says, "'Windage'?   What does that word mean?"
"'Windage' means 'influence of the wind'."   Here, then,
is an example of a noun, "windage," which is not connected in any evident way with an adjective or
adjectival form.

Here is another.   "It says here, 'The bells ring,
but nowadays we cannot speak of their tintinnabulation'."   "What   does   'tintinnabulation'   mean?"
"'Tintinnabulation' means a tinkling or jingling
sound--the kind of sound distinctive of a bell or of
bells."   But is that reply exactly right?   Isn't
"'Tintinnabulation' means..." just a bit careless? and
shouldn't it be "A tintinnabulation is..."?   No, I
think I am being too fussy.   Surely either will do.

The question I am asking is this: what marks a
noun as properly subject to the question "What does it
mean?" and to the reply "It (the noun) means...."?   And
I cannot see what the answer is, if indeed there is any
one answer.   Somehow something about the word, its
sound, its strangeness, must serve to concentrate
attention on the word; but that is not enough.   For a
moment I think that it must be a word in which a phrase
exists which is a near equivalent, which might often be
substituted for the word.   But, of course, the
questioner could not know this--even when it is true.
And anyway it is wrong as an answer to my question, as
the case of "flush" seems to show.   "Flush" is quite
interchangeable with "a hand in which all cards are of
the same suit."   Yet the answerer of the question, who
knows this, will say, "A flush is..." and not "'Flush'
means...."   Also, when looking for likely examples of
nouns about which we would say "It means...," it is
hard to avoid thinking of abstract nouns.

I really do not know what to say about this.   But
whatever the answer, it remains clear that there is a

large group of nouns of which it would be odd or improper to say, "It means...," and for a very large part of this group I think I can see why it is odd or improper to say "It means...." I am thinking, of course, of those words which are the common (not proper) names of "things"; the nouns which are names of species of insects, ferns, trees, fish, birds, bacteria, and also articles of clothing, coins, hands in cards, letters of the alphabet, games, tools, pieces of furniture, styles of furniture, cooking utensils, and also minerals, bodies of water, geological forma-tions, chemical substances, and many more. These are names of species and genera and sorts and kinds of "things" which fall under or within some larger classes. These (the more specific) names "place" things within and among other things which are related and differentiated in all sorts of ways. Any speaker of a language, who is prepared to ask for an explan-ation of one of these words, will be familiar with most of the larger main "kinds" and with the manner in which distinctions are made within that kind. He will know how cooking utensils and articles of furniture and clothing are distinguished one from another, and in a general way how species of birds, animals and plants are distinguished. So, when he needs to have such a word explained, his real question is "Of what kind of thing is this the name?" "What is a maduro?" "A maduro is a dark-colored and strong cigar." "What is a simile?" "It is a figure of speech in which one thing is explicitly compared to another." "What is a hyacinth?" "A plant of the lily family having spikes of bell-shaped flowers."

Some of these words are governed by necessary and sufficient conditions. Such, I imagine, is "zeta." "'Zeta' is the name of the sixth letter of the Greek alphabet." Or "surd" in mathematics: "A surd is an ir-rational number." In the case of these words the ex-planation may equip a person with all or nearly all he needs to know in order to recognize or identify speci-mens when they occur. But the great majority of these words are not governed by necessary and sufficient con-ditions, and those which are not so governed are the more interesting words philosophically. The word "whim-brel" is one such. When I explain the word "whimbrel" to Wheaton, I say, "A whimbrel is a brown shore-bird...." I know how Wheaton's question arose, I un-derstand what he needs to know, and I know pretty much what I can presuppose. He knows that the word "whim-brel" is a name: he does not know what it is the name of. For all he knows, it may be the name of an animal, a piece of machinery, an organization of people, a ceremony--he knows only that, whatever it is, it makes a noise at night. And consequently I can answer his question by telling him which of these many possibilities is the right one. "Migrant shorebird" will do, or medium-sized shorebird," or "shorebird with a decurved beak." And because of the context in which the question arises, perhaps I shall add, "Whimbrels migrate by night and call a great deal." A very sketchy characterization will do. I tell him that "whimbrel" is the name of a species of shorebird. His question arose because he did not know the word "whimbrel": it did not arise out of an interest in ornithology or natural history. I should only bore--and probably confuse--him if I were to carry on about curlews, sandpipers, plovers and such and discuss their various ranges and plumages. I feel certain that "species of shorebird" is enough for Wheaton. He will not misunderstand. I suppose, of course, that he knows a little about the way species and families of birds are distinguished, that he knows how a shorebird differs from a duck, and other general facts which are pretty common knowledge. I do not try to equip him to recognize or identify a whimbrel--even if I could.

The question about such a word is "What is it the name of?" And in this respect such common nouns are like proper names. "I called Millburn to my side." "Who or what is Millburn?" "Oh. Millburn is my cat." Also, for a proper name, we do not say "It means..."; that is, we do not say this in discussing the kind of question I have been examining. We might say of a proper name "It means..." if we are talking about its etymology or translating it from some foreign language from which the name comes ("Godwin" means "friend of God.") In this way we can also say of a common name that it means so and so. ("Titmouse" means "small thing," "penguin" means "white head.") This is "meaning" in a different sense from any with which I am concerned. The nouns of which I imagined we might say, "This word means..." are not of this sort. "Windage," "ingrate," "occultation," are not names; or rather, I mean that when we explain their meanings we do not say, "That is the name of...." Windages and occultatons are not groups or kinds which are parts of groups and kinds; nor do they have groups or kinds as parts of them--which together compose a subject for classification. I do not know what to say about the word "tintinnabulation," but surely it is not the name of a sort of sound.

John Stuart Mill said that proper names have no meaning, but that is wrong--or at least misleading. The question of whether a word has meaning arises only in very special circumstances. "What did you have for lunch?" you ask. And I say, "Some left-over mulligatawny." You know me as a lover of nonsense, and are naturally suspicious. So you say, "Come on now. Is that a real word or did you make it up?" "Of course it's a real word," I say. And immediately you realize that my answer does not put your suspicions to rest. "I mean, does it have a meaning or is it a nonsense word?" "Yes, it has a meaning. Mulligatawny is an East Indian curry soup." In this way I could say that the names of trees and games and tools and such had a meaning, or had meaning; and I could say the same, too, for proper names.

There is a circumstance in which a person will ask for the meaning of a common name. He will ask for the meaning of some word which is a common name when he does not know that the word he is concerned with is a common name. A person named Avery might run across the word "hoopoe" in a word list, perhaps in a list of words which some poet thinks are the funniest words in the English language. Then he might say, "I don't know what this word is at all. How do you pronounce it?" I say, "who poo." "What does it mean?" he may now ask. I cannot say, "It means...," but I shall not go speechless. I shall probably say, "It is the name of a bird found in Europe and the near East. The bird has a thick curved beak and runs on the ground." Of course it would be ridiculous to say, "'Hoopoe' means 'a bird with a thick curved beak which runs on the ground'." I should answer in the same way a person who asked about a proper name. ("'Antarctica' is the name of the body of land around the south pole.")

Avery asks "What does 'hoopoe' mean?" and I answer, "A hoopoe is...." What shall I say of this? Did I reject his question? I told him what he wanted to know, and he could not have asked a different question. He had no way of knowing what form my answer had to take: he did not know whether the word was a name, a verb, an interjection, or what. He is certainly not surprised or upset by the fact that when he asks, "What does 'hoopoe' mean?" I do not reply, "'Hoopoe' means...." Suppose Avery had asked me, "Do you know the meaning of this word 'hoopoe'?" I think I should have said "Yes," and gone on to explain, "A hoopoe is...," and after I told him what a hoopoe is, he would then be in a position to answer "Yes" to anyone who asked him "Do you know the meaning of this word?"

So, what shall I say about the "meaning" of such nouns? In some respects they are like proper names. I cannot say of such a word "It means...", and when I do talk about its meaning I shall usually talk about its

55

etymology--what the word means in its original language or meant some time in the past. I do not want to say that such words have no meaning, because I am not concerned with the question of whether they are nonsense words. But also, and for the same reason, I do not want to say that they have a meaning. A person--like Avery--can ask about such a word, "What does it mean?" and I can answer him, without rejecting his question or feeling that there is anything wrong with it. I can know what such a word means. That is, if someone asks me, "Do you know its meaning?" I shall say "Yes," again without feeling that there is anything wrong with his question and without feeling that my answer is forced out of me or that it is good enough for the circumstances maybe, but not theoretically correct.

Avery asks me, "What does 'hoopoe' mean?" and I answer him, "It is the name of..." or "It is...." How shall I characterize my answer? Haven't I said all there is to be said? But I am asking the question "What do we talk about when we talk about the meaning of a word?" and I am examining cases of such talk. I can tell someone the meaning of adjectives or verbs or certain nouns. But what of a noun like "hoopoe?" Can I tell someone its meaning? Can I explain its meaning? Can I tell someone what it means? Well, not quite in the same way as I can for an adjective or a verb. Suppose that Avery had asked his friend McKay about the word "hoopoe" and McKay could not help him. McKay sends Avery to me, and now, later, McKay comes to me and asks, "Did you explain the meaning of that word to Avery?" Certainly I shall say "Yes." So I can take this as justification for saying that I explained the meaning of "hoopoe" to Avery. And hence when I am thinking philosophically about words and their meanings, I shall say that one can explain the meanings of such words as "hoopoe." And one explains the meaning of such a word by telling what it is the name of. It will surely be all right to say those things, as long as I do not lose track of the details, as long as I remember that I say the things in a certain way and at a certain point while engaging in a philosophical investigation.

So I explained the meaning of the word "hoopoe" to Avery. He now knows what the word means. (If someone asks him, "Do you know the meaning of this word?" he says "Yes.") Even so, he probably could not recognize a hoopoe if he saw one. Only if he became a bird student would he become concerned with such a question as whether all hoopoes have the same characteristics or whether they have "overlapping similarities." But then he would be concerned with how he could identify a

hoopoe of either sex and in any plumage, and not with a
question about what the word "hoopoe" means. When
Avery asked me, I knew the meaning of the word "hoopoe," but I could have known the meaning of the word
without knowing whether all hoopoes have some certain
characteristics or whether they are "connected by
overlapping similarities." Since in fact I know a
little about birds, I should never have supposed that
all hoopoes share some certain peculiar characteristics. But also I should never have thought that the
issue of whether they did or did not have common and
peculiar characteristics had anything to do with the
meaning of the word "hoopoe." Thus, "hoopoe" is like
"native" in "native art" and like "counterfeit" and
"apishly" and "ameliorate" and other words, where the
question of meaning is one thing and questions about
recognition or identification are different things
entirely.
      Still my picture of meaning (IB) can lead me to
think that the meaning of a general word consists in
the features or characteristics common to to those
things to which the word applies. So my picture of
meaning is the source of great confusion. And if I
were to replace "features or characteristics commmon to
things" with "overlapping similarities" the confusion
would be the same. If I were to characterize the male
and the female hoopoe as similar in some way, and the
female and immature as similar in another way, and so
on until I had connected all hoopoes by overlapping
similarities, I should be making no contribution to an
understanding of the meaning of the word "hoopoe."
Such a characterization would be quite irrelevant to
any question about the meaning of the word "hoopoe"--
though it might be relevant to some question about the
biology of a bird plumage, or even to some question
about the identification of the species. My picture of
meaning led me to think that in the original and
simplest case a word must refer to things because those
things had common and peculiar features or characteristics, and those features or characteristics determined
that the word applied to just those things. The meaning of the word is given in terms of those characteristics: the meaning of the word is its "connotation."
Consequently I read Wittgenstein as offering a commentary on the meaning of general words, and I tried, following his suggestion, to think of overlapping similarities in place of common features. Wittgenstein
invites this interpretation by saying that it is "because" of overlapping similarities that a word applies
to them (Sec. 65), and he suggests that it is the
overlapping similarities which "make us use the same

word for all" of the things to which a word applies.

When I explain to Avery the meaning of the word "hoopoe," I gave him a non-specific characterization of the "thing" (bird) which the word refers to. That is, I tell him that it is the name of a species of bird. When I consider this at a time when my picture of meaning is operating strongly on me, I feel that such a general characterization of the things referred to by the word could not give the word the meaning it must have. The meaning given by that explanation is not definite and complete. Such an explanation would not sufficiently determine the application of the word to things in the world, and it is, after all, the things of the world that we expect to talk about when we use the general words of our language. My picture of meaning leads me to think that in learning the meaning of a word I must learn to recognize, pick out, point to, identify the individual things to which the word applies—whether I do this by "common properties" or "overlapping similarities." Otherwise how should I ever be able to talk of the things of the world, for are not the things of the world the particulars which we identify, point to, pick out, call for? The picture of meaning gives me the idea that a clear-cut simple model of someone teaching another the meaning of a general word is presented by someone teaching another to point out or to fetch the items to which the word applies. However, when I turn away from the picture and look at examples, I quickly see that this activity is not so much connected with teaching the meaning of a general word as it is with teaching one how to recognize and identify the various things to which the word applies. It is the kind of activity characteristic of field trips taken by classes in botany, ornithology, or geology, or the kind of thing considered in lectures on recognizing counterfeit money or purchasing native art objects for a museum.

Still it is hard to shake the hold of the picture. I am inclined to think that an undetailed characterization of the things referred to cannot give a complete understanding of the word's meaning. Yet when I explain to Avery the meaning of the word "hoopoe," he does not complain that I have left something out. He does not object that I have given him an incomplete or defective explanation of the meaning of the word. He does not ask to have the rest of the meaning explained. (What could "the rest of the meaning" possibly be?) If, sometime later, Avery becomes a bird watcher, he may learn all sorts of things about hoopoes. He may become adept at identifying any hoopoe in any plumage, of any age, throughout any part of its range. In acquiring this ability, I do not think of him as having learned more of the meaning of the word "hoopce." (Again, what could "more of the meaning" mean?) After I have explained the meaning of the word to Avery, he is equipped to explain the meaning to others, and he can do that whether he becomes a bird expert or not. If someone comes to him with a word-list containing the word "hoopoe," he will tell his questioner the same sort of thing I told him. Even if he were a humble and cautious man, he would not say "I can only tell you part of its meaning; I cannot tell you all of it because I am not a bird expert." He would certainly not think that the questioner should take a course in ornithology in order to learn the full and complete meaning of the word. (What could "full and complete meaning" mean?)

What about a simple word? Again, consider the word "red." It is not clear how one should understand the question, "Do all things to which the word 'red' applies have the common and peculiar characteristic of being red?" Nor is it easier to understand the question, "Do the various things to which the word 'red' applies have overlapping similarities?" But surely when we teach a child the word "red," we teach him to recognize and sort things by characteristics or similarities. Well, however we are to describe what we teach a child when we teach him to sort his blocks into piles of red, green, yellow, blue, we say that we are teaching him colors or that we are teaching him the color words, such as "red," "blue," "yellow".... We do not say that we are teaching him the meaning of the word "red," or the meaning of the word "blue."

In order to find a place for talk about the meaning of the word "red" I suppose I shall have to imagine a foreigner who has acquired much English but who, for some strange reason, does not yet know the word "red." When he first runs across it, he may ask, "What is the meaning of this word 'red'?" How shall I answer? If I know his language, or at least the required part of it, I shall doubtless say something like "'Red' is English for 'rot'." But suppose I cannot offer a translation. Then I shall doubtless say, "Red is a color. It's this color," and I shall find a sample of red. It is hard to imagine any misunderstanding of this. Can I really imagine, for example, that the color words in his language are quite different from those in English? If something like that is the case, then I suppose I shall have to go about teaching him color words much as I teach a child. Then there is no longer any place for talk of the "meaning of 'red'" or "the meaning of 'mauve'." Yet in learning the English color words, this man will be putting himself in a position so that if he ever were asked by a foreigner "What is the meaning of 'mauve'?" he could answer the question. So in this indirect way, the teaching of color words is concerned with their meanings. Perhaps then color words do fit the picture of meaning better than any others. Suppose that a foreigner runs across the word "mauve" and asks what it means. I say, "Mauve is a color--a delicate bluish red." He might well go on, "You mean this color?" "Is this mauve, too?" "But this isn't mauve, right?" That is, he might very well think that he did not have an adequate grasp of the thing until he could pick out the color in question, and distinguish it from other shades of violet. Still, he will not think of himself as learning more and more of the "meaning" of the word "mauve." And we shall not think of him as "knowing the meaning of the word completely" when he can always pick out a mauve patch and have no hesitations. It is hard to know what to say about "the meaning of the word 'red'."

With other words, like "hoopoe," "native" (as in "native art"), and "counterfeit," the question about meaning is quite different from questions about recognition and identification. The two questions are distinct in a way that they may not be for "mauve" or "puce." This is not the way my picture of meaning leads me to think it will be--whether I am thinking of the picture in terms of the characteristics of things or similarities among things.

Well, then, if the meaning of a general word is not given in terms of the characteristics or the overlapping similarities by which things may be identified and recognized, what is the meaning of a general word? Why should I feel impelled to ask this question? In the beginning I asked this question, and then I allowed a picture in my mind to dictate the answer: the meaning of a general word is the characteristics which distinguish the things to which the word applies. And now I have seen that that answer will not fit the examples. When I explain the meaning of a general word, I do not discuss the characteristics (or similarities) of the many things to which the word applies. If that answer, then, is wrong, do I expect there to be a right one? Do I expect "the meaning" of any general word somehow to be always the same thing or perhaps several different things with overlapping similarities?

In **The Blue Book**, Wittgenstein offered a suggestion: he suggested a method for determining what the meaning of a word is.

Asking first "What's an explanation of

meaning?" has two advantages. You in a sense
bring the question "What is meaning?"down to
earth. For, surely, to understand the meaning of "meaning" you ought also to understand
the meaning of "explanation of meaning."
Roughly: "let's ask what the explanation of
meaning is, for whatever that explains will
be the meaning."[16]

Do I read this correctly as saying "Let us ask what an
explanation of meaning explains, and whatever it explains will be the meaning?" If so what do I explain
when I explain what the word "hoopoe" means? I explain
what a hoopoe is. And what do I explain when I explain
what "native," "counterfeit," and "red" mean? I explain what a native art work is, what a counterfeit
bill is, and what color red is. The meaning of a
general word is what the things which it refers to are.
This does not seem to help me get a grasp of "meaning."
It only brings out the fact that "what does 'hoopoe'
mean?" and "what is a hoopoe?" are related questions.
And the same with "What does 'native' in 'native art'
mean?" and "What is native art?" And perhaps even for
"What does 'red' mean?" and "What is a red thing?"
     Wittgenstein does not say, "ask what the explana-
tion explains"? He says, "ask what an explanation of
meaning is." And that surely is different. But what
is an explanation of meaning? What sort of question is
that? Is this an appropriate and proper answer? An explanation of the meaning of a word answers the question of one who asks about the meaning of a word. And
what is his question? Or, better, what is he asking
for? What does he need? Is it always the same? Well,
in my examples it is the same for "native," for "counterfeit," and for "red." It is also the same for
"apishly," "enormous," "ameliorate," "ingrate," "occultation," "tintinnabulation," "windage." The
questioner has read something or heard something which
he does not understand, and he does not understand it
because he is unfamiliar with one of the words in it.
He wants to know whatever he needs to know about that
word in order to understand what he has read or heard.
And, of course, that is what I tell him--enough to
understand what he has read or heard. It is not surprising, then, that even in cases where it might seem
relevant, I do not tell him enough to enable him to

---

[16]Ludwig Wittgenstein, The Blue and Brown Books,
Par. 3.

recognize or identify any specimen he runs across. For, of course, I could not tell him that: in most cases I am myself unable to identify all or even some of the instances to which the word applies. And if his question were about identification he would not ask me; he would enroll in a course in ornithology, in art-dealership, in chemistry or minerology, or in engraving and printing of currency.

This is not the nature of the question or the answer, though, for the word "hoopoe." The question about "hoopoe" arose out of curiosity about a word on a list of words. The questioner does not fail to understand anything said or written; he simply is unfamiliar with an isolated word. Though the question arises in a different way, my answer fits the same pattern. I tell him what he would need to know in order to understand something which was said or written--something which contained the word 'hoopoe." After all, many questions can arise about the meanings of words, questions which do not start from something said or written. Suppose that I am working a cross-word puzzle. Twenty-four across asks for a word which means "greenness, freshness." The word has eight letters; it starts with "v" and ends "ity." The word "viridity" pops into my mind, and I wonder, "Or is it virility?" I ask someone, "What does 'viridity' mean?" He says, "It means 'The quality of being green or fresh'." He confirms my first hunch; I put the word in; and it all works out right.

Maybe the lexicographer begins with idle questions about this word and that. We all have these questions at some time or another. "That word 'ruthful' comes into my mind. I must have heard it or read it--I don't remember where. I wonder what it means?" "'Ruthful' means 'full of pity.' You should have guessed; it's the opposite of 'ruthless'." Such idle questions may start a person on the course of becoming a lexicographer, but if he becomes a lexicographer he soon goes beyond such idle questions. He will undertake to write entries for a systematic dictionary, and he will want the entries for words to be as complete, as carefully drawn and precise as he can make them. We do not always have the same one reason for asking about the meaning of a word. But whatever our reason, and even though our question grows out of idle curiosity or out of the hard-working and systematic concerns of the lexicographer, isn't the answer always the same? When we explain or give the meaning of a word we give what one would need to know in order to understand something said or written. Is this then the key notion running through all explanations of meaning? The meaning is what one needs to know about the word in order to understand something said or written which contains the word.

When a person is engaged in the business of giving a definition of a word does he always try to state what one would need to know in order to understand something said or written--something which contained the word? Is he always addressing himself to a potential lack of understanding or to some positive misunderstanding? No. Dictionary writers are usually engaged in such an enterprise, perhaps, but not always. One cannot construe every dictionary entry as an answer prepared in advance to a practical question about the meaning of the word. Dictionary writers put entries in a dictionary for words about which it is quite impossible to even imagine any relevant misunderstanding or lack of understanding. Some of the words which have been of most concern to philosophers are exactly of this kind: it is really impossible to imagine someone not understanding something because of the presence in it of one of these words. I am thinking, of course, of such words as "good," "true," "beautiful," "ought," 'right," "see," "know," and many, many more.

When, in the proper alphabetical course, a dictionary writer comes to the word "good," for example, he will not stare at it dumfounded. He will write an entry--certainly not with ease or a sense of certainty--but he will write one. How will he manage to do this? I suppose that, having worked on many other words, where thinking of an answer to a question about meaning can be his guide, he has come to understand that certain procedures are appropriate. These may give him some rules of thumb to follow when preparing definitions. Perhaps such as this: wherever possible give synonymous words or phrases--or at least as near synonymous as possible--and then explain the differences. Or this: make sure that the near-synonymous word or phrase will substitute for the word in all of its possible grammatical occurrences. If he is careful in following this rule, he will not give for "good" the definition "a general word of commendation."[17] Or at least he will not suggest that the word "good" cannot be used except when making commendations. Suppose I say of a new novel, "If that is good, I will eat my hat." The word "good" is not used here in

_____

[17]He commits here what John Searle calls the "speech act fallacy." John Searle, Speech Acts (London and New York, Cambridge University Press, 1969), p. 136.

commendation.   The word "good" does not make for
commendation in "That is not good" or in "Try to make
it good." He will instead write, for the definition of
"good," "commendable, admirable." Note now that if
this definition is understood as an effort to give the
"meaning of the word 'good'," it answers a question
which is quite different from questions about what
makes for goodness. Consider the phrase, "good tennis
racket." If considering this sentence provides an
occasion for a dictionary writer to ask the question,
"What does 'good' mean in this phrase?" then he might
well decide that the answer is "commendable, admirable." But there are other altogether different
questions, such as "What makes a tennis racket good?"
or "How can I recognize a good tennis racket?" What I
am trying to suggest is that there are two quite different concerns here analogous to the two very different concerns one might have with common nouns or
general names. "What does 'hoopoe' mean?" is one question; "How can I identify a hoopoe?" is another--quite
distinct.

     If I am on the right track here in what I have said
about the dictionary writer's dealings with words like
"good," "true" "ought," then I think it clear that a
philosopher has reason to proceed with great caution in
his questions about the meaning of "good," the concept
of goodness, the nature of moral obligation, and other
such questions. I should think that the philosopher
would have to look to the practices of the dictionary
writer as the only pattern available for understanding
his own questions and for giving his own answers or
"theories." I cannot think of any other example or ex-
emplar to which he could turn. Then he will take note
of the fact that with such words as "good" the dictionary writer is not on his usual safe ground, and
that his procedures with the word "good" are dictated
entirely by the status of his "rules of thumb." When
he finds these rules difficult or impossible to apply
for other words, it is of no importance because he can
ask, "What should one say to a person who does not know
the word...?" In the case of "know," "good," "ought,"
there is no recourse to this decisive grounding question.

     The words "good," and "ought," "beautiful" and
"right" are exceptions. For most words, a dictionary
writer can be guided by asking himself, "What should I
say to a person who does not know this word and who
wants to understand something which contains the word?"
This is a question which we all meet quite frequently.
Someone asks, "What does this word mean?" and we tell
him whatever he needs to know in order to understand

something he has heard or read. This circumstance provides us our clearest example of an explanation of the meaning of a word. In similar circumstances, though, a person may fail to understand something because he does not know one word, and that word may be a noun. Then he will ask, "What is a _____?" and we will answer by saying "_____ is the name of..." or "_____ is..." without creating confusion. I think that I may talk of this reply as an explanation of the meaning of a word also. "A whimbrel is a brown shorebird with a decurved beak" is thus an explanation of the meaning of the word "whimbrel." "A carbine is a short light rifle--the kind originally used by cavalry or horsemen." This can be an explanation of the meaning of the word "carbine." Through such explanations a person can come to know the words "whimbrel" and "carbine." He can read with perfect understanding all sorts of sentences containing those words, such sentences as these: "Whimbrels nest in fresh water swamps, but they winter near salt water," and "The carbine is the rifle most often carried by guerrilla troops." As likely as not he will not become an expert on birds or an expert on the history and manufacture of firearms; he may never be able to recognize a whimbrel or distinguish carbines with certainty from other similar types.

This is the way it is with many--perhaps most--of the common nouns in my vocabulary. I know many names of trees and shrubs, metals and minerals, styles of architecture, and silverware, but I cannot identify the things to which those names apply, and if for some reason I need to identify a specimen I should consult an expert on the matter. I know the word "diamond," but I cannot distinguish a real diamond from other similar minerals. I know what "pewter" is, but I could not tell it from any number of other similar alloys. Of course this is a commonplace observation about speakers of a language and their knowledge of many common nouns. Yet though it is commonplace, my picture of meaning makes me want to deny it. When I am possessed by the picture I think that the meaning of a noun has to lead me to the individual things it names. I think that my understanding of the meaning must be able to guide me in picking out and recognizing any individual to which the word applies. And this is fantastic; if that were so I could not speak English without being an expert in chemistry, minerology, geology, art history, entomology and so on and on through every field which distinguishes and classifies the objects of its study. The picture leads me to think that each person who knows the meaning of a noun must be able to identify the "things" to which it applies. In truth, most people can--and do--know the meanings of many, many such words, while only a very few are able to identify the things to which the words "apply."

How can a person learn the meaning of a common noun so easily? "'Morel' is the name of a mushroom-like fungus which looks like a sponge." "A fisher is a car- nivorous, arboreal, weasel-like mammal." I can give an effective explanation of the meanings of words like "morel" and "fisher" by simply telling what they are the names of. "A type of fungus." "A weasel-like mam- mal." Then I shall add a most sketchy characterization of the species or genus or type or kind of thing in question. That is quite adequate: it is all that is needed or wanted, although sometimes a little more is called for. When more is called for the circumstances make that requirement quite plain. ("The whimbrel calls at night.") How can this be--how can it be so simple? What kind of question is that? How can it be indeed? It is. It is a plain, obvious fact that we explain the meanings of many words in exactly that way. It can only be my picture of meaning that provokes me to ask this question.

Is there anything useful I can say to such a ques- tion? Sometimes platitudes and commonplaces will help. Of course the person who asks questions like "What is a morel?" or "What does the word 'hoopoe' mean?" is a speaker of the language (English). He does not ask his question in a linguistic vacuum, nor does he expect an answer which will satisfy someone in a linguistic vac- uum. (What is a linguistic vacuum? That must be the stage in the acquisition of language of a new-born child, the zero-state, before the acquisition of lan- guage has begun.) The person who wants a word like "whimbrel" or "morel" explained already knows much. He knows the main different sorts of things which are classified and given names, and he knows how distinc- tions are made within each sort of thing. He knows that many distinctions call for a great deal of spe- cialized knowledge and that they can be made only by one who has become something of an expert. Only a bacteriologist can distinguish among the many kinds of bacteria; only a chemist can distinguish among the many different kinds of acid. We explain the meaning of a word to a person against a background of this knowl- edge. "A kagu is a long-legged crane-like bird found in the South Pacific." Well, the person to whom this is addressed knows what sort of creature a bird is. He knows that birds are classified by their structure, their anatomy, and he knows that their behavior has a lot to do with their structure. A woodpecker could not

66

peck wood unless he had a hard sharp beak and a thick skull. He knows, no doubt, that the sexes of birds often differ in color and size. He knows that the young do not look much like the adults. We count on his knowing what a crane is and how it differs from a sparrow.

Mostly I must make clear how the explanation of meaning fits in his knowledge of language--as opposed to his knowledge of birds and animals and such. Now I must be very careful, though, because it is my picture of meaning that gives me the idea that these two are separable. And I am fighting against just that idea. He needs to know about birds to know the meaning of "kagu," and he could not know the meaning of "kagu" without knowing a good deal about birds and beasts. Still I can represent his knowledge as having to do with language. So he brings a knowledge of language to the explanation of "kagu," and consequently he knows immediately that some phrases will make sense, others will not--and other things of that sort. He is prepared for "abnormal kagu," 'hybrid of kagu with something," "albino kagu," "dead kagu," "embryonic kagu," plucked kagu." Also he knows that "bronze kagu," "wooden kagu," and "mechanical kagu" are entirely different matters. An albino kagu is a memeber of the species "kagu"; a bronze kagu is not. A mechanical kagu is a toy, perhaps. A wooden kagu might be a kagu-decoy.

"'Azurite' is the name of a glassy mineral, blue to black in color." This will be addressed to a person who knows that minerals are classified by such things as hardiness, texture, crystalline structure. He will know, perhaps, that color is not a reliable mark of identification--that many minerals come in several color forms. And so it goes. Has the unrest which provoked my question been dissipated? Different people bring different amounts of relevant knowledge to such explanations and definitions. Every speaker of a language (English) knows a lot about some fields and next to nothing about others. In some areas he might be an expert or he might be able to become an expert with a little more study. An expert in minerals will identify them by chemical test and microscopic examination. If ever a person needed an expert he would know how to go about finding one. The common nouns of our language are simply not ties to the "things" of the world in the way my picture of meaning leads me to think that they are. They could not be.

Of course not all common nouns are like "morel" or "kagu." When some are explained to me, I am immediately able to recognize a sample, a specimen, or an instance when I run across one. "A **parka** is a long shirt or jacket with an attached hood." "A **mesa** is a flat-topped rocky hill with steeply sloping sides." If the words "parka" and "mesa" were unfamiliar to me and I were given these explanations, I think that I should then be able to recognize a parka or mesa when I came upon one or the other. And so I think that there are some common nouns which fit with my picture of meaning. But this is a dangerous thing to think because my picture was not intended to explain some and only some common nouns, and certain adjectives, and some few other words. It was intended to explain the "meaning-dimension" of language in its entirety. And my survey of the meaning of common nouns certainly shows that the picture is most misleading--both in its original form and in its "family resemblance" form.

Suddenly, I am inclined to think that most of the common nouns I use in everyday life must be such that I can readily identify instances--"things"--to which they apply: toothbrush, fork, pencil, automobile, highway, drugstore, man, woman, child, stairway, coffee cup, sandwich, ice-cream, easy chair, sofa, shoes, overcoat, teapot, cookie, mother, father, uncle, radiator, sandwich, wheel, typewriter, friend, student, book, window, door, desk, tree, bush, fireplace.... I must be able to recognize, identify, and deal with samples, specimens, instances--otherwise I should not be able to live as I do in the world of things and of other people. And, thinking this, the picture comes back upon me, and possesses me again. I make a mistake which allows it to come back--I see it now, but I do not always see it. The mistake is this: Whenever I recognize, pick out, refer to, talk about "things," I think that in doing those things I must be exercising linguistic competence. My mastery of the words must lead me directly to the things to which they apply. When I think this and at the same time turn away from details to the task of "constructing a linguistic theory," I am back where I started from. I think of words. They are the units. Speakers must know all sorts of things about words in order to have "linguistic competence." They must know how to put the words together to form sentences. These are the rules of grammar. And then there must be rules which give the words meaning. What are the rules of meaning? They are like the entries in a dictionary: they state the meaning for each word. My mastery of the meaning enables me to bring life out of a senseless string of words.

Now I have made this great mistake--so great a mistake that, like the great lie, I can believe it. I try to think all that is required to enable me to talk about things and people and events and actions and to represent it all together somehow as knowledge of the meaning of words. For meaning is what enables me to bring life to words. But I have just gone through examples which show that by "meaning" I understand what one must know about an unfamiliar word in order to understand something heard or read. When a person knows the meaning of a word, he is not automatically put in a position to recognize an instance to which the word applies. The knowledge required to recognize, pick out, identify, is not always--or even often--knowledge of meanings.

I try to represent "meaning" as some body of knowledge, an internal dictionary, something which gives me an essential part of what is required in order to be a speaker of my language. This is not coherent. It is a semi-pictorial distortion of a simple truth: sometimes I need to learn the meaning of some word in order to understand something I have heard or something I have read.[18]

---

[18]In connection with the topics of these pages I was told that I ought to read Hilary Putnam--particularly an essay called "Is Semantics Possible?" (in Language, Belief, and Metaphysics, ed. by Kiefer and Munitz, N.Y., State University of N.Y. Press, 1970). And that was good advice. Putnam is the one to read all right. He quite clearly sees that a person may know a "natural kind" word without being able to identify specimens to which the word applies. Only a specialist may be able to identify specimens or examples. This is not exactly the way Putnam puts the point, but I do not think that I have distorted it in putting it this way. He is the only philosopher I know who has seen this, and perhaps if I had read this essay at the right time I might have been saved a lot of hard work.

Putnam's interests are so different from mine, I hardly know how to comment on much that he says. He is more interested in the necessary, the analytic, the a priori than he is in meaning. But he gives a general account of what is involved in "conveying the meaning" of a general-kind word. It involves giving a "stereotype." And also giving one the idea that there is a "test" to determine the "extension" of the word-- although the test may be known only by an expert. This account would seem to apply only to one of his word-examples, namely "aluminum." If the word in question were "termite," what would the stereotype be? A damp-wood termite? A subterranean termite? A winged female reproductive? A wingless female? A worker? A soldier?

Are "sterotypes" required for all of these? Then surely there ought to be an explantion of their relation to each other. And what is the "test" for a termite? Putman thinks that a sample will do as well as a stereotype. And then knowing the "test" seems to be knowing how other specimens are "similar to" the sample. It seems clear that he is thinking only of "aluminum" and not of "termite," and that he has overgeneralized from the case of "aluminum."

Postscript: On "Pictures"

What I say here about "pictures" is true to the spirit of Wittgenstein if not true to any letter. Wittgenstein believes that our philosophical thinking often takes the form of a "picture," and that the picture is meant somehow to represent "our grammar" (Philosophical Investigations, 295). The picture seems to give us the solution to a problem, but we feel uneasy about it (325). What we need to do is to examine the "application" of the picture (374): we must explore "what is to be done with the picture, how it is to be used." "But the picture seems to spare us this work: it already points to a particular use. This is how it takes us in" (p. 184).

I find it puzzling that Wittgenstein should talk of the "application" of a philosophical picture. I do not know how to read this. What is involved in our knowledge of how to continue a series? We may be inclined to think that it is having the formula in mind. Wittgenstein reminds us that we must not forget the "application" of the formula--that is, our mastery of algebra. Now if Wittgenstein means that the "application of a picture" is something similar, then there is nothing similar for a philosophical picture--except, of course, being able to elaborate a philosophical theory; and finding that this is so will be of no help to me. One might think that by "application" he is referring to the particular experience or occurrence which suggests the picture, which the picture seems to fit. But Wittgenstein contrasts "application" with that (423). "The picture is there. And I am not disputing its validity in any particular case. Only I also want to understand the application of the picture." Perhaps, after all, we are to understand "application" as he uses it of the algebraic formula for a series. Then the moral is this: philosophical pictures have no application. At any rate, pictures mislead us: they give us an incorrect idea of the way words are used. "This picture...stands in the way of our seeing the use of the word as it is" (305). The picture "held us captive" (115).

With regard to "meaning" Wittgenstein speaks of only one picture--the picture of words as names of objects. "In this picture of language," he says, "we find the roots of the following idea. Every word has a meaning. This meaning is correlated with the word. It is the object for which the word stands" (1). This picture leads Wittgenstein mainly into an examination of "names," "real names," "logical atomism," and into the idea that the mind affects the relation between

71

word and object. He does not track the search for
"common characteristics" directly to the influence of a
picture. Therefore I am on my own in supplying the
pictures I have called "the picture of meaning," "...of
the world of things," and "...of the features of
things." They seem to me to be natural outgrowths of
and elaborations of "the picture of labels"--which, I
take it, is the picture Wittgenstein had in mind.

What does Wittgenstein mean by a "picture"? I have
always taken it that he means an image in the mind's
eye. "When we look into ourselves as we do philosophy,
we often get to see... a picture" (295), "...we have
got a picture of our heads..." (402). I think he means
something that we visualize, and sometimes something
which is graphic or diagrammatic. "'The mind seems
able to give a word meaning' --isn't this as if I were
to say 'the carbon atoms in benzene seem to lie at the
corners of a hexagon'? But this is not something that
seems to be so; it is a picture" (p. 184). But it is
possible that all this talk of pictures is no more than
a bit of metaphysical jargon. Wittgenstein nowhere
explains it. I do not feel very secure in my
interpretation, and I do not want to pretend to offer a
definitive exegesis.

I feel safer on my own. At any rate, I believe
that our thinking is often determined by a picture in
the mind's eye; it is often something like a drawing or
diagram. When we think about words and the meanings of
words--in the ways with which I am concerned in this
essay--I really do believe that we think with just such
pictures. I mean that we have images and that we visualize or imagine diagrams or drawings. When we think
of a word as the name of a thing, I believe that we
visualize the thing and imagine its name written or
printed on it. This may be one of the reasons that we
are so ready to think of words as themselves "things":
they are the labels on things. In themselves they have
no more life or meaning than does a label or a sticker
or a tag. Words are paper and ink, and they are
"physical things" in the same way that paper and ink
are physical things. And when we think of the "things"
which words refer to--"the world"--I believe that we
think first and foremost of things which we can easily
visualize, trees and houses, brooms and hoes; and even
of "things" in a diagrammatic way, circles or squares
or triangles--the kinds of things we might draw on a
blackboard as representatives or stand-ins of the
"things of the world." Thus when we think of the characteristics of things it is quite natural to think
first of shape and size and color; when we think of
words whose meanings are given by characteristics, we

think of "round" and "small" and "red"; we would not likely think of "unconscionable" or "homesick," or "omnivorous," or of the words "game," "counterfeit," "caw" or "whimbrel."

It is not just about words and meanings that we think in terms of pictures--graphic representations. I believe that when we are given to philosophy we think about a great many matters in this way. We think of the mind as an enclosure--perhaps in the head, behind the eyes. Therefore, we have before us the contents of our own minds, but we have no way of knowing the contents of another's mind. Wittgenstein notes, "'I cannot know what is going on in him' is above all a picture" (Phl. Inv., p. 223). When we see something, we really see a picture on the wall of the mind. Seeing is viewing with an inner eye a moving picture on the wall of the mind. It is viewing a show in an inner theater. In dreaming we do the same. Vision and dreams are the same; only the causes are different. Hence it is easy to imagine how dreams might deceive us as Descartes thought they could. The will is an arrow of force sent from the mind out into the muscles which it makes to move. Time is a line along which the present moves--from the past into the future. Blindness is "a darkness in the soul or in the head of the blind man" (424). Memory allows us "to look into the past (as if down a spy-glass)" (604). I do not mean, of course, that we think only of such pictures or diagrams. I mean only that we do think of them and that they suggest to us many of the other things we think: they suggest and determine many parts of our philosophical "theories."

What is the importance of this idea that our philosophical thinking is determined by pictures? Perhaps not much. Some people tell me that they do not have such pictures. And although I believe that really they do even though they say that they do not, perhaps they really do not. They may do their philosophical thinking entirely without imagery, without picturing anything. Teachers of philosophy, I should think, often show that they are thinking in terms of pictures, because they often draw pictures or diagrams of just the kind I am talking about on their blackboards in order to represent various philosophical views to their classes. I suspect that philosophers are not aware of the extent to which their thinking is determined by pictures. I think it takes some effort in self examination to find that pictures in one's mind lie behind one's thinking; and I think there is a resistance to acknowledging it even when it should be quite apparent. The important question, though, is not "Do

73

pictures direct me in constructing philosophical theories?" It is "Now that I have produced these philosophical theories, what shall I do about them?" I start by facing up to the fact that they confuse and puzzle me. And then I think that what I should do next is expose and lay before myself in great detail the many, many ways that they mislead me. I think I should look at the facts and note in great detail how my theories led me to deny them or misrepresent them. The relevant facts, of course, are the facts about how I talk--what I should say when. This is, or at least is part of, what Wittgenstein did about the philosophical theories which first came to him and then worried him. And this is what others have done also. Now, when a person takes this attitude toward his philosophical theories, he is led to take a certain attitude, too, toward the pictures which produce them. He sees the pictures as the sources of misleading and confused thinking. He sees also that it is hard always to be aware of their presence and to be aware of just how much dirty work they do. This leads him to talk of his pictures often with some contempt, and to describe them in overly simple terms, to make a caricature of them and to tell a ludicrously exaggerated story of the way they work on him. All this may be excellent self-therapy, but it makes it difficult for him to help another person realize that pictures lie behind his thinking, too. Many people who read Wittgenstein's many characterizations of philosophical pictures and the way they work will quite understandably say, "I do not think in that simple-minded, silly way. My philosophical theorizing is not directed by anything like those ridiculous pictures."

I do believe that often a simple picture directs our thinking when we philosophize and determines the form of what we think and say. For example, throughout this long essay I have been saying that I "apply" general concrete words to things. I have been thinking of "words" and "things" in such a way that I am willing to characterize my saying something--any something--about a thing--anything--as "applying" a word to it. When I say "That is a nuthatch," I "apply" the word "nuthatch" to a certain "thing" (bird). And even when I say "The hoe is in the tool-shed," I "apply" the word "hoe" to a certain "thing" (tool). And when I say, "He intentionally remained silent," I "apply" the word "intentionally" to some thing which someone did--or did not do. At one time I thought I could distinguish between complex and simple words in terms of their applications. To apply a complex word such as "chair," or "carrot," I must know more about a thing that I can

74

determine by the use of untutored senses. Things in and by themselves are red, blue, green, and whatever else can be said of them using simple words. "Red" is my paradigm simple word. To apply the simple word "red" I need to know nothing. All that is relevant to its application is presented to my eye. My investigation shows me that I cannot really understand this distinction between complex and simple, but it does not, so far, lead me to question the idea of "applying" words.

Why do I use this word "apply"? Where does it come from? When, after all, do I "apply" something? I may have to apply an old rule to a new case. A court may have to apply a law to an unforeseen situation. I could not be thinking "apply" in these ways when I think of applying a word to a thing. Applying laws or rules requires thinking about the purposes of the law or rule; it requires stretching or bending things a bit. It results from or affects a decision. Applying a word does not--except in unusual cases--involve such considerations. If I am a biologist confronted with a new and strange organism, I may decide to class it as a fungus rather than a moss. But when I tell someone that the bird nesting in the mailbox is a bluebird, I do not make any decision or stretch or bend language in any way. I do not concern myself with the purposes of any classification system or the consequences of deciding about the bird one way or another. And this is the way I usually "apply" words--without all these considerations involved in decision-making.

A farmer whose son has just taken a Ph.D. in biology may want the son to come home and apply some of the things he has learned. Of course he wants him to improve the yield of the cornfield or to think of a way to eliminate the tansy ragwort from the hay. Applying what one knows is doing something useful or practical with it. Marconi applied several well-known principles of physics when he invented the wireless. Nothing of this kind is involved in applying a word. I do not have to do anything practical or useful with a word in order to apply it. I do not know quite what it would be to do something useful with a word. I might discover that if I say a certain word to the neighbor's dog, then he will stop barking. That would be a practical consequence of **saying** a word, not of the word itself.

I sometimes apply myself to a task at hand. That means that I work assiduously at it, pay close attention, refuse to be distracted. In order to apply a word I do not usually have to be diligent or carefully attentive. I do not have to avoid distraction or make any special effort.

I apply the second coat of paint over the first. I apply an ointment to a rash, a bandage to a cut. I apply a label to a bottle. This must be the kind of "application" I have been thinking of. I apply words to things as I apply labels to glass jars: "blackberry jam," "quince preserves," "spiced pears." This is the sense of "apply" which is easy to picture. It may be the basic or original sense of the word. Sometimes I do apply words in just this way: I put them on bottles, jars, cans, and boxes. But this is not what I do when I accuse someone of negligence, try to describe my feelings of loneliness, or tell a person how to exterminate his hornets. I do apply words in this way whenever I say something or write something. But now I can think of words in general, and of concrete words in particular, and ask myself, "What gives them meaning?" "What are their meanings?" And I find myself reviewing simple sentences, and thinking of what I might say at one time and another; immediately I think that when I say something about a thing I apply a concrete general word to it. What could lead me to think this way? I believe that I think of "words" as though they were printed or written before me, and I think of "things" as though they were objects a short distance away--in my direct line of sight. And I think that I put the word in front of the thing. I move the word towards it. I see the thing through the word. The word is painted on transparent flexible plastic. I gesture toward the thing with the word. I hold the word before me and thrust it toward the thing. In short, I think that I try to picture something, to visualize it. This, of course, is what I mean by the "picture of words as labels."

Saying something of a simple sort is like putting a label on a bottle. There remains the question "What gives the meaning to words?" Well, that has to do with the bottle and its contents. The bottle is not the meaning; neither are its contents. The meaning of a word is not what it is properly applied to. So the meaning must be given by the characteristics of the thing which the word properly applies to. And now I think I have the most mischievous and confusing picture of them all: the picture of things and characteristics. I visualize a ball, say, and a cube; their characteristics are their shapes and their colors. One is red; one is green. Even more, I think that sometimes I try to visualize the characteristics of things as marks or checks or X's upon the face or the edge of my geometric representation of things. And this, I think, leads me wildly astray. What, after all, is the picture supposed to fit? Whenever I characterize or describe a thing I ascribe one or more characteristics to it. Whenever I compare or contrast two things I do so in terms of their characteristics. The whole of language, or at least the whole heart of language, consists of "individual expressions" and words for characteristics. There are subjects and predicates-- for things and their characteristics. So I think that all of my talk about any thing is a series of comments on its observable markers. Any talk about a thing is like a description of its shape and color. And the possession of these characteristics by a thing determines whether or not I "apply" a word to that thing. Or more accurately, perhaps, the possession of certain characteristics by a thing will determine entirely whether I shall count that thing as one of a kind or type that I have in mind. Is this game to be counted as a game of baseball? Look at its characteristics; they will tell you whether it is baseball or cricket. Of course, I am confused in thinking this way. This picture leads me to overlook all sorts of factors which I use in determining whether a thing is one of a cer- tain kind--such factors as origin, development, his- tory, purpose, intent, function, consequences, social status, ancestry, use.

This picture readily melds with my picture of mean- ing, and the two in combination produce more troubles. They lead me to think that I understand the meaning of a word in terms of such visible characteristics as col- or and shape. Therefore if I am to explain the meaning of a word to someone I must enumerate to him the char- acteristics by which he can identify an instance of the thing in question. But this is not so. When I explain to a person the meaning of a word like "hoopoe," I tell him that "hoopoe" is the name of a species of bird found in the near East, that it runs on the ground and has a long, thin bill. I may not tell him this exact- ly, but it will be something like this. I shall give him a little less information about the bird--or a little more. But I shall not enumerate the character- istics by which the bird can be identified. I shall certainly not discuss the changes in plumage, the difference between the sexes, or the similar character- istics of any of the species with which it might be confused. My purpose is not to train a field ornitholo- gist, but to answer a question about the meaning of the word "hoopoe." And it is a mistake dictated by my picture to think that the meaning of such a word is given in terms of characteristics or resemblances suf- ficient for the identification of the thing named by the word. I know the meaning of many such general

77

concrete words and I cannot identify instances of which they are names. I know the word "gold" but I cannot tell pure gold from alloy or distinguish gold from other similar metals. These things are simple, obvious truths--except that my picture leads me to overlook them, or worse, it leads me to deny them.

2. DOES LANGUAGE SHAPE PERCEPTION?

Consider these passages from "Verifiability" by Fredrich Waismann.[1]

> ...a fact is noticed; and by being noticed it becomes a fact. 'Was it then no fact before you noticed it?' It was, if I could have noticed it. In a language in which there is only the number series 'one, two, three, a few, many,' a fact such as 'There are five birds' is imperceptible.
> Noticing a fact may be likened to seeing a face in a cloud, or a figure in an arrangment of dots, or suddenly becoming aware of the solution of a picture puzzle: one views a complex of elements as one reads a sort of unity into it, etc. Language supplies us with means of comprehending and categorizing; and different languages categorize differently.
> 'But surely noticing a face in a cloud is not inventing it?' Certainly not; only you might not have noticed it unless you had already had the experience of human faces somewhere else. Does this not throw a light on what constitutes the noticing of facts? I would not dream for a moment of saying that I invent them; I might, however, be unable to perceive them if I had not certain moulds of comprehension ready at hand. These forms I borrow from language. Language, then, **contributes to the formation in the constitution** of a fact; which of course, does not mean that it **produces** the fact.

In this paper I want to examine some aspects of these ways of thinking.

When I think long about the matter, I am driven to hold a certain view about language and its relation to the world as it is revealed to me by my senses. I come to the conclusion that the world is partially formed and molded by the language I speak. The things, qualities, relations and facts of which I am apprized by my

---

[1]In **Essays in Logic and Language**, ed. A. Fleur (New York, Philosophy Library, 1951), pp. 140-141.

senses are not the wholly brute and objective things I
might first take them to be. My language enters into
and becomes a part of these things, qualities, relations and facts.

But this is not my original naive view of such matters. When first I philosophize about language and the
world, I am inclined to think just the opposite: language is one matter and the things that I see, hear,
taste and touch are other matters entirely, and I think
that the two are related to each other in a most adventitious way. The world contains rivers and mountains
and trees and robins and pencils and fishhooks. Many
kinds of things are to be found in the world and I can
easily note the distinctive traits and features of each
of these many kinds of things. After my senses have
given me a fair inventory of the world, I learn that my
language has a name for many of the kinds of things to
be found there. When I learn my language it is only
necessary that I observe a few things of which some
word is the name and I can quickly generalize from
those few observations. I can see in what way these
are alike and belong together, and I quickly learn that
the same word applies to all things of that kind because they are alike in an easily observable way: they
share visible characteristics. As far as my perception
or observation of the things is concerned I need no
more perceptual acumen than is possessed by any other
higher animal. All animals can and do make similar
distinctions among things. A towhee distinguishes
easily between a hawk and another towhee. A cow eats
fescue and avoids tansy ragwort. Of course towhees and
cows--and even chimpanzees--have no language. But they
make the sensory discriminations which are required in
order to have a language. The world revealed to them
by their senses is much the same as the world revealed
to me by my senses. The difference between man and the
other animals is not a difference in sensory ability.
The main difference between a language-speaking and
non-language-speaking animal seems to consist in this:
the language-speaking animal has got the idea of a
"word" or sound or mark which "stands for" or
"designates" each of the many things which his senses
show him are of the same kind. (The idea of a word as
a general name is the idea that dawned on Helen Keller
on that exciting day with her nurse at the pump. She
suddenly got the idea that things have names.)

This is my first philosophical view of words and of
things which words denote. But it will not stand up
under close examination. I think of the word "pencil,"
for example, and then I think of all the pencils I can,
and I am unable to find any characteristics common and

peculiar to all these pencils. Rather I soon persuade myself that there are none: pencils of various different kinds, indelible, colored, mechanical, china-marking, can be thought together as having at most "overlapping similarities." And the same, I discover, for many, many concrete general words. Therefore, I am not apprized of "things" in the way I thought I was by my animal senses. In the way I thought of a pencil, there are no pencils to be seen: there are only mechanical pencils to be seen or marking pencils to be seen; and on further thought there are probably not even those. Various mechanical pencils, too, may have only overlapping similarities with each other, and the same with marking pencils. Yet, I do see pencils. I see several of them on my desk now, and I can see a pencil even when it does not stand out clearly. If someone asks me about an object which is partially hidden in the deep grass I may say, "That's a pencil"; then if he asks me how I know, I may say "I can see that it is a pencil. Come over here where you can get a clear view of it." I do most certainly see pencils, and when I make out something of the right kind--not too deeply hidden--I can most certainly see that something in the grass is a pencil. Therefore what I see cannot be one of a certain multitude of things which strike my eyes with their common visible characteristics. I see things and their characteristics; but seeing a pencil is more than that. A contribution is made to what I see by my language: the visible object is partly revealed to my animal eyes, and partly a product of my language. As soon as I specify pencil as what I see, the function of the word "pencil" comes into play. It enters intimately into the thing I see-- more intimately than is suggested by this description of seeing a pencil. It is misleading to suggest that in seeing, I do something called "specifying" a pencil as the object I see. I do not see something and then classify it or specify it "pencil." I simply see a pencil. But I would not--could not--see a pencil if I were not a language-speaking animal whose language contained the word "pencil." Seeing a pencil is not a matter of opening the eyes and having some perception come already marked or branded "pencil" anymore than it is a matter of having some perception which I, upon reflection, mark or classify "pencil." There is one thing, seeing a pencil, and only upon philosophical reflection can I see that my language enters in the most intimate way into the thing, the pencil which I see. If the society which speaks my language had not grouped things in the way they do--into pencils, pens, erasers, paper clips, and so on--and had not thought of

81

things in the way they do--if all this had not become incorporated into the language which I speak and concentrated into the word "pencil," then I should not be able to see a pencil.

I can see the workings of language here in my perception because in thought at least I can separate the elements which enter into it. On the one hand there are things of various lengths, diameters, shapes, colors, materials--and on the other hand the fact that they are all pencils. And they are seen to be pencils, not in the sense that they are seen and then recognized as pencils, but just seen as pencils. Still the ease with which I can separate the elements in thought must come from the fact that the elements are sometimes genuinely separate. After all, I can and sometimes do see something which I do not recognize right off as a pencil. "What is that bronze-colored metallic thing?" "I don't know." "Oh, I see now. It's an old mechanical pencil."

And just as the elements are sometimes quite separate, and sometimes separable only in thought, so sometimes they must not be separable at all. There must be some perceived things in which language plays such an intimate part that without language they simply do not exist as things to be perceived at all.

Pointing to a sky nearly full of cirrus clouds one day, my friend Kleinmetz says to me, "Look at those clouds. There is an arch fingerprint. Do you see it?" I look curiously and politely, but I must ask, "What on earth is an arch fingerprint, and what does it look like?" Kleinmetz tries to describe the pattern of an arch print. I continue looking, but with no success. I cannot see it. Kleinmetz is so excited about the phenomenon that he takes a Polaroid photograph of the cloud, and after its three-minute development he shows me the photograph. "There it is--clearly--in the photograph," he says. I can no more see the arch fingerprint in the photograph than I could see it in the sky. Later Kleinmetz takes me to his home and shows me a book with drawings of fingerprints. He shows me the drawing of an arch fingerprint. I stare a long time, running over the configuration of its lines in my mind. Then he shows me the photograph he has taken of the cloud. And instantly I see the arch fingerprint in the clouds. First I could not see it, and now I can. One who has never seen an arch fingerprint cannot see one in the clouds or in a photograph of the clouds. Language changes my vision in that way, I am inclined to think. After all, doesn't Kleinmetz's explanation of the phrase "arch fingerprint" make my perception of the arch fingerprint possible? No, not exactly that.

Language does not enter into my perception in quite that obvious and direct way. I did not ask Kleinmetz a question about the phrase "arch fingerprint." I asked him "What is an arch fingerprint?" But the fact is I had never heard the phrase "arch fingerprint" before: it was entirely new to me. If someone had asked me about the meaning of the phrase, I could not have explained it to him. I did not ask Kleinmetz about the meaning of the phrase, but after he showed me the drawing of an arch fingerprint I came to know the meaning of the phrase, and I could then have explained to someone what the phrase "arch fingerprint" means. So, in that way, my coming to know what an arch fingerprint is involves my coming to know what the phrase "arch fingerprint" means. Also, after Kleinmetz shows me what an arch fingerprint is, I can use the phrase "arch fingerprint," where before I could not. I can now talk about arch fingerprints: I can ask questions about them, describe them, direct someone's attention to them, comment on their variety. Still, it is not the language part of Kleinmetz's explanation that turned the trick in my perception of the arch fingerprint in the sky. It is the fact that he showed me a drawing; so by direct acquaintance I learned what an arch fingerprint is. Even so, I am inclined to think that language is involved in my perception, and specifically that the phrase "arch fingerprint" plays a decisive part in it. An animal eye could never, by itself, pick out and fasten on the particular intricate pattern. That complex could never register itself on animal consciousness. Somehow--I do not know how--the ability to see that pattern and knowledge of the phrase which refers to it in language are inextricably connected to each other. If it were not previewed, as it were, in the vocabulary of our language, it would not be viewed at all. It is too complex, too intricate, too artificial--too difficult to fasten attention on. If there were not some way in which it was marked out and made permanent, the eyes alone could never fasten upon it and pick it out. So even though I do not actually have to learn the phrase "arch fingerprint," it is inconceivable that I should see an arch fingerprint, particularly that arch fingerprint in the clouds, if that pattern were not somehow registered on the permanent record of things in the language of my society. And that is the same as to say that its name has become part of my language. So, in this more indirect way, the phrase "arch fingerprint" is essential to my seeing the arch fingerprint in the clouds. If I did not learn the phrase "arch fingerprint," I should at least have to keep in mind some other phrase which came to the same thing or very much the same thing: perhaps "any pattern like that," where "that" could be a drawing in a book.

First I could not see an arch fingerprint in the clouds, and now I do. The fact that I see it now is made possible by my having learned the phrase "arch fingerprint" or at least by the fact that I have become conscious of the place which that phrase has in my language. I look at the clouds, and I see that pattern there. Surely my eye, by itself, could never have picked out that pattern. The pattern would never have emerged from the blurred tangle of clouds. Those wisps of cloud might be seen in the form of an endless number of different patterns—or in none at all. Surely I see the arch fingerprint only because my language makes it possible. And more than that: there is an arch fingerprint there to be seen only because it is one of the categories of my language. A crow cocking his eye to the sky will not see an arch fingerprint in the clouds. Nor will a deer grazing in the meadow, though the sky be unobscured and in his field of view.

Suddenly I feel all at sea. These metaphors give me no satisfying grasp of language or vision. I began with a philosophical picture of words and the well-marked things to which they refer. And in a reaction against that picture I have drawn another. The things we see do not stand in external relations to one another. The things we see are in part the product of the words and phrases which refer to them. I turned to the examples in an effort to find this "theory" shown in them: seeing pencils, seeing a fingerprint in the clouds. I am afraid that I did not look at the examples to see what they would show me: I construed the examples as the theory would dictate. I used the examples as part of an exposition of the theory, which I thought must fit the examples since its opposite clearly would not. The examples gave me no insight because I read them with all the metaphors of the philosophical picture.

I must try then to do better. I shall try to think of other examples: one involving a word like "pencil," another like "arch fingerprint." I shall try to give these examples in greater detail and to test the "theory" against them without jumping to a premature interpretation. In "testing" the theory I shall try to use the examples to formulate the theory in a less metaphorical way.

The name of a bird, say "towhee," is like the word "pencil" in the relevant way. It is quite clear that not all towhees have common and peculiar observable characteristics: nestling towhees, immature towhees,

84

male and female towhees, dead and rotten towhees, four and twenty towhees baked in a pie. Suppose that I am a bird watcher of some years' experience, and that my friend Clive knows next to nothing of birds. One day Clive and I walk together through a brushy woodlot, and two medium-sized birds flit across our trail and perch nervously for a moment in the lower brances of a small cedar tree. I stop and watch them briefly. Clive, who is one step behind me, also stops, and he too watches the birds as they disappear into a tangle of bushes. When we return from the walk, someone asks us, "Did you see anything interesting while you were walking?" I shall say, "I saw two towhees." Clive, of course, will not say that. Why will he not say "I saw two towhees"? Isn't it just the fact that it is not true? He did not see two towhees. How could he have seen two towhees when he knows nothing of birds? He may never have heard the word "towhee." It is certainly no part of his working vocabulary. He cannot recognize a towhee when he sees one; he cannot point out one or describe one; he cannot comment on its habits or its song. I saw two towhees; Clive did not. Is that difference in what we saw a function of the fact that the word "towhee" is part of my working vocabulary, whereas it is not part of Clive's? Does Clive's language simply have no place for seeing a towhee?

Isn't seeing two towhees the same as seeing an arch fingerprint in the clouds? No, now I can see that it is not—it is certainly not at all the same as seeing an arch fingerprint in the clouds. Clive will not say "I saw two towhees," but he did see the two towhees. I, of course, can say of Clive that he saw two towhees, even though he did not know that the birds he saw were towhees. Not only will I not say "I saw the arch fingerprint," I did not see the arch fingerprint. No one will say that I saw the arch fingerprint in the clouds. After I have told Clive what he saw, perhaps he will then say that he saw two towhees. I will never—regardless of what anyone tells me—say that I saw the arch fingerprint in the clouds at the time when Kleinmetz first pointed it out to me. If someone tells me that I did, he will be wrong.

Many things can happen later which will change Clive's appraisal of what he saw. (1) I tell him that the birds he saw were towhees. Later, if someone asks him, he can say "I saw two towhees." Chances are he will add "--at least that's what I was told they were" or "--at least I learned later that that is what they were." (2) Later he might take up bird-watching himself. He might soon become an expert and become familiar with the towhee and its habits; he might be able to identify it readily under any sort of condition. Now he will say, "On that walk with E. I saw my first towhees." He may not remember seeing the relevant details of the birds on that first sighting, but everything he can remember fits the towhee, and nothing of what he remembers clashes with what he now knows. He will now be less inclined to add "...at least that is what I was told." (3) Again he might become a bird expert and have such a clear and detailed memory of those birds that he can now identify them as towhees—completely on his own. Clive may have been an acute observer, and the salient details may have recorded themselves vividly on his memory. He may even be able to close his eyes and visualize the details of those two birds we saw. And from his memory of the details he may now be able confidently to look up the bird in the field guide. He now says, "On that walk with E. I saw two towhees. I did not know what they were at the time but I can identify them as towhees." (If such memory for details is unimaginable, then this isn't: he could have made a drawing of the bird, with notes on coloration. Now he can identify the bird from his drawing and notes.)

There are three different possibilities:

(1) Clive saw the birds, and someone else made the identification and told him what they were.

(2) Clive saw the birds, and someone else made the identification, but he is now equipped to make it himself.

(3) Clive saw the birds. He is now equipped to make the identification. He remembers the salient details, and now makes the identification.

The fact that the first of these is possible shows that even though there is a language difference between us Clive can still see two towhees. And the fact that the third is possible shows that what he saw when the language difference existed did not differ from what I saw in the way I thought it would. When he first saw the birds, the fact that he did not know the word "towhee" or the fact that he did not know the basis of classification of birds did not rule out the possibility of his seeing a towhee. After he sees the bird Clive can remember the details of the bird he saw and at that later time he can recognize the bird he earlier saw as a towhee. That possibility shows that my first idea was wrong: that is, my idea about the difference in what we saw. I thought that one could not see a towhee unless the word "towhee" were part of his vocabulary in the proper way. I now see that Clive could have seen all the details necessary for the identification of the bird at a time when he did not have the vocabulary used in speaking of its identification. If he saw all of those details, surely then he saw all there was to be seen. When he learns that a bird with those details is a towhee, this does nothing to change what he saw. What I have in mind when I think that language enters into and molds what we see is more than this; I do not mean that language comes in to merely name or sum up the details we see; it is directly and formatively involved in the thing we see itself.

Seeing an arch fingerprint in the clouds is different. There, language seems to enter into the very object seen. Although I now am familiar with fingerprints and can see the arch fingerprint in a photograph of the sky, it is still not true that I saw the fingerprint in the clouds when Kleinmetz first said that he saw it. At that time I saw the cirrus clouds scattered across the sky. And even if the pattern of those clouds had engraved itself on my memory in such a way that in the image of the clouds in my mind's eye I now see the fingerprint, still I shall not say that I saw the fingerprint when first Kleinmetz pointed it out to me. Why is this? Surely there are no details which I didn't see. The pattern in the photograph or in my eidetic image I now "see" as an arch fingerprint. And before that I saw the clouds that were photographed or which I can revive in an eidetic image. In one very important way this is unlike seeing the towhee. The objects seen are unlike each other in an important way: the pattern of a fingerprint is far more subtle and elusive than the observable features of a bird. If I observe the right details, I can identify a bird as a towhee. What are the details of a cloud pattern that I might be supposed to observe? When I have a photograph before me--or an eidetic image--there is no guarantee even then that I shall see the pattern. I may have to stare at the photograph as blankly as I stared at the clouds. Then suddenly the fingerprint may emerge. Suddenly I may see the pattern. Seeing a pattern like an arch fingerprint involves this sort of phenomenon. Even when I see it instantly, it is always possible that I might not. There is no guarantee. It is not something which is right before my eye and which I cannot miss. This may explain why I do not say "I saw it." When this sort of thing is involved in my vision it would, of course, be inappropriate to say "I saw it".

Thus there seems to be an important difference between "towhee" and "arch fingerprint." I may observe the characteristics of a towhee one at a time: size, shape, habits, coloration, style of flight. I can make notes on each. But I cannot do this for an arch fingerprint. The requisites for recognizing something as an arch fingerprint cannot be similarly broken down into separate characteristics. It must be seen in its peculiar entirety. Or else not seen. Care in observation has nothing to do with it: the most careful and acute observer of the sky might miss it altogether.

The idea I have is that language enters into the object seen. I mean of course that with the right bit of language one would see something and without that language he would not. But that is not enough. The language must be, or become, an integral part of the thing seen. It must be inconceivable that one should see the thing without the right bit of language. There is no seeing it while not knowing its name. There is no seeing all the details or features, and just not recognizing them for what they are. There is no way one can preserve the thing in memory or on a photograph, and then later learn the purely adventitious vocabulary with which he refers to it. These are mostly negative things that I am saying, and it seems very hard to say positive things and to be clear about them.

Yet why should that be? Isn't it because I am blinded by these metaphors of language "entering" or "molding" the objects I see? Yet I have already determined the cash value of these metaphors. When I say that someone does not see something without the right bit of language, or when I say that language molds what he sees, I must mean only that there is no circumstance in which he would say "I saw..." when referring to a time when he did not know the relevant bit of langauge. If I do not want to become lost again in pictures of perception and their associated metaphors, I had better take this as my test: a person sees something, even though he does not have all of the relevant language, if he says, retrospectively, "I saw." And I shall take it as a test that he did not see something if he will not say "I saw." Thus Clive did see a towhee when he did not know its name. And I did not see the arch fingerprint in the clouds before I learned the phrase "arch fingerprint."

I shall try to find another example involving a word or phrase like "arch fingerprint." And I had best avoid the complications which come in with seeing something in the clouds. After all, I want to talk about seeing something in the world, the plain, ordinary, lower world, not seeing something in the clouds. Color words are certainly like "arch fingerprint" in all important respects. There are no details one could observe and then later learn that anything with those details was red or blue or yellow. If one is to see a color he must look directly at it. It is also true that with some colors, their character is not

88

immediately revealed. I may have to stare at such a color, and then suddenly its character may dawn on me. It may be just a little yellowish or just a little grayed or barely reddish. One could not learn color words without direct acquaintance with colors. If I imagine two people with differences in color vocabulary, then I shall have the makings of the genuine kind of perceptual difference I have in mind. Surely one's color vocabulary will enter into and help form the color phenomena he sees. Consider, then, the word "blue" and the phrase "shade of blue." We speak sometimes of tints of blue and shades of blue: a tint being a "light blue" and a shade being a "dark blue." However most of us most of the time speak of both "light blue" and "dark blue" as "shades of blue." So there are light shades of blue and dark shades of blue. Suppose that my friend Tate, who is an amateur botanist, has gone to collect flowers on a tropical island. After he has been there several weeks I go to visit him, and I decide to begin a flower collection of my own. Together we go on a collecting expedition, and at the end of the day I sort over the flowers I have gathered and straighten them out for pressing. Tate says, "On this island I've discovered that nature is most sparing of one color in her flowers. Have you noticed it?" After looking over my specimens, I say "Yes. Here is one which is light blue and here is one which is dark blue. And these are the only two blue flowers we have seen. You mean, of course that nature here is sparing of blue."

I set two flowers side by side and I notice something about them: both are shades of blue. Here surely is a feature of the world which I can see in the most direct and immediate manner possible. It is a visible fact about the color of the flowers. There is no way I could see that it was present by first seeing its component features or characteristics. Can I imagine a person whose color vocabulary does not permit him to see this fact? If I can, then my philosophical thesis will have been established; then I shall see that what we perceive is in part a product of our language. It is not necessary that I find the relevant difference in vocabulary in the language of two people or of two tribes. It is quite enough that it be imaginable, conceivable. Even though I have never heard of any person whose perceptions deviate in the relevant way from my own, the fact that I can imagine such a person will show that my perceptions are partially dependent in my language.

Imagine, then, a man named Duffy: he is born blind and he suddenly gains his sight when he is an adult.

Imagine, also, that during his many years of blindness he learned absolutely nothing of colors. Everyone around him carefully avoided talking of colors, or talking in color-language. His reading, recordings, radio-listening, are carefully arranged so that he remains completely innocent of any knowledge of or questions about color. Now, after Duffy has gained his sight, suppose that we hire a color-expert to give him his only training in colors. The expert will teach him only the names of fairly specific shades and tints and hues. Thus he will come to have a rich color vocabulary consisting entirely of words such as "puce," "magenta," "gamboge," "chartreuse," "cerulean," "vermilion," "fuscia." Duffy is carefully prevented from knowing such color words as "red," "yellow," "green," "blue." He never hears such words, either alone or in combinations such as "yellow-green" or "reddish-blue." He knows absolutely nothing of shades or mixed hues of colors.

As I try to think of such a person as Duffy, I realize that it is very hard to imagine someone in the state in which I have put him. He knows only the names of colors such as puce, gamboge, cerulean. What will he think when he comes across a new color, one for which he has no name? Surely he will be prepared to describe it, right off, as "like chartreuse," or "similar to vermilion" or some such. He must already have his vocabulary of the words which Austin calls "adjuster words," and although he has never had occasion to use them for colors, surely he will be able to do so. Perhaps I must imagine that he does not become very interested in colors, or in the colors of things. In any case, it is all right if he talks about colors as "much like indigo" or "similar to puce," so long as he ventures no further in an effort to describe them. When he becomes interested in a new color, I shall imagine that he goes to the expert and asks for the name of the color, and the expert will carefully avoid the words "red," "blue," "yellow," and he will never talk of colors as "yellowish-green" or "reddish-blue."

Now one day I go to Duffy with my flower collection. I carefully arrange my specimens so that the light blue flower and the dark blue flower are side by side, on the same page. I ask him to comment on these two, and he says that one is cerulean, the other lazuli. I cannot ask him whether he sees that the flowers are both shades of blue. He could not understand my question. He has heard nothing of "shades." He does not know the word "blue." Surely here is a case where one can see that perception is directly

90

shaped by language. There is a color-fact which I
readily see, namely that these two flowers are shades
of blue. Duffy does not see this fact, and only because of the language difference between us.

This case seems to be like the case of seeing an
arch fingerprint in the clouds; and, in all the relevant ways, it seems unlike the case of seeing two
towhees. I could see the arch fingerprint only after
the phrase "arch fingerprint" had become part of my
language. And after I do make the phrase part of my
language this does not lead me retrospectively to say
that I saw an arch fingerprint at a time before I had
mastered the use of the phrase. This shows that a
change in my language brings about a change in what I
see. The case of the two towhees is quite different.
As soon as I know that the birds I saw were towhees, I
can say that I saw two towhees. After I have learned
the word "towhee" so that I can point out and talk
about towhees, I can say in retrospect that I saw two
towhees. That is, I can say that I saw two towhees,
provided my memory is sufficiently accurate and complete.

Will his acquisition of the necessary color vocabulary lead Duffy to say "I saw that the two flowers were
shades of blue"? Suppose that I now teach Duffy all
that he has been prevented from learning about colors.
I teach him the colors red, orange, yellow, green,
blue, violet, and I teach him about shades and inter-
mixtures so that he learns to speak of colors as "dark
blue," "light green," "light reddish-yellow" and "dark
yellowish-green." I must also suppose that he has unusually good color memory. He remembers clearly looking at the two flowers I showed him and he remembers
the colors of the flowers. Will he now say, "I saw
that they were two shades of blue, one a light blue,
the other a dark"? I should think he would not say
that. And this seems to show that at that time, when
he would not say that. And this seems to show that at
that time, when first he saw the flowers, there was
something he simply did not see. If the occasion
arose, he could see it now--now that he has the color
vocabulary to form that fact--but at that time, when he
first saw the flowers, he simply did not see it. And
the reason he did not see it must be that his language
did not admit it as something which could be seen.

Now that I have the details before me, I feel most
uneasy about this result. I wonder whether I have not
again concocted an example to reflect the theory I seem
so anxious to find reflected. The example involving
the blue flowers and the example involving the towhees
are suspiciously unparallel. The question about Clive

91

and the towhees is whether he saw towhees. The question about Duffy is whether he saw that two flowers are both shades of blue. Clive is concerned with seeing "things," Duffy with seeing a fact about the colors of things. Because of that it is natural to ask whether Clive saw the towhees, and it is natural to ask whether Duffy saw that the colors were shades of blue. That is, I say that someone saw a thing. I do not say that someone saw a certain fact about colors. I say that he saw that there was a certain fact about the colors. Seeing that something is the case does not involve the same things as seeing something.

I can, however, rework the examples slightly so that they will become parallel in this one way: each will involve the same idiom, either "saw" or "saw that." Clive has now become a bird expert, and he can remember every detail of those two birds we saw on our walk through the woods. He can now identify--on his own and from memory--those birds he saw as towhees. Suppose I now ask him, "Did you see at the time that those birds were towhees?" To this, he will certainly say "No." He will not say "I saw that those two birds were towhees." What shall I conclude from this? He denies, of course, that he was able to identify the birds at the time we saw them. Of course he will deny that. At that time he did not know anything about birds; he had never heard of a towhee; he did not know the word "towhee." It does not follow from this that there was something he did not see. He saw (and remembered) every relevant detail. He saw everything there was to be seen. The test is whether he saw, not whether he saw that.

Similarly, I can redo the example involving Duffy and the blue flowers, so that the question is, "Did he see...?" not "Did he see that...?" Duffy saw the blue flowers, but at that time he had no color vocabulary other than names of fairly specific colors. Now he has learned our entire color vocabulary. He has amazingly accurate color memory: he can vizualize the colors of the two flowers he once saw. Now, of course, he realizes that those colors were shades of blue. Imagine that a stranger who has heard Duffy's story comes to him. "I understand that you saw two colors on that day when you were shown the flowers and that you remember those two colors vividly. What were the colors that you saw?" Can't his answer be, "I saw two shades of blue--one was light, one dark"? Or, suppose that the stranger merely wants to see how Duffy will talk about his experiences. He says "Tell me how it was." Duffy says, "I saw those two flowers. I saw their colors clearly, and I remember them as clearly as if they were before my eyes now. They were shades of blue--one light, one dark. Of course I didn't know how to talk of them at the time." Isn't that a perfectly correct thing for Duffy to say? If Clive is asked to comment on his experience, surely I can imagine him saying things of exactly the same sort: "I saw two birds. I saw the important details clearly, and I remember the details of those birds as if they were before my eyes now. The birds were towhees, but of course I didn't know what they were at the time. I didn't know anything about birds."

Now I see no important difference between the two examples. If Clive saw everything there was to be seen, then I do not see why I should not think that Duffy, too, saw everything there was to be seen. It no longer seems to me that his color vocabulary affected his vision of colors in the way I thought it would-- that is, in a way that gives support to the idea that language makes a difference in what is seen, or in a way that gives support to the idea that language enters into and molds the object seen.

However, I still have the example of my seeing the arch fingerprint in the clouds, and that is a case in which I see something, not a case in which I see that something is the case. Or is it? If I say "I saw that those two birds were towhees," I imply that I recognized them as towhees when I saw them. If I say "I saw that the colors were shades of blue," I imply that I knew or realized that they were shades of blue at the time I saw them. And what of "I saw an arch fingerprint in the clouds"? This is "saw" and not "saw that," but doesn't it imply that I recognized what I saw as an arch fingerprint? If I say "I saw an arch fingerprint in the clouds," isn't this much the same as "I saw that the clouds formed an arch fingerprint"? Either conveys the idea that at the time I was aware of, was cognizant of, the arch fingerprint in the clouds, and if called upon I could have pointed it out to someone. Of course there is a difference between them, but it is not a difference that is relevant here, that is, it does not have to do with whether I was aware of, alert to, or in a position to point out the arch fingerprint.

Perhaps this would be clearer if I took a humbler example. I have never seen a dolphin, never heard of one; I have never heard or seen the word "dolphin." Then I take a trip to Marineland; I see dolphins, and learn much about them. After that, while idly looking at cumulus clouds, I sometimes see a dolphin in the clouds. Suppose now that I remember seeing that very shape in the clouds once before, before I had ever

93

heard of a dolphin. Suppose also that I have a photograph to confirm my memory; I look and sure enough there is a dolphin in the clouds in the photograph. What do I say of that former experience? It seems to me that I will not say "I saw a dolphin in the clouds." Instead I shall say "I saw a figure in the clouds which was just the shape I now know to be a dolphin."

Suppose that after I have learned what an arch fingerprint is, I remember that one day while looking at a mackerel sky I saw exactly that pattern in the clouds. I think that I shall not say "I saw an arch fingerprint in the clouds then, long before I knew anything about arch fingerprints." Rather, I shall say "I saw a pattern exactly like the pattern I now know is that of an arch fingerprint." I think I shall not say "I saw an arch fingerprint in the clouds" unless at the time I thought of it as the pattern of an arch fingerprint.

Though I shall not say "I saw a dolphin in the clouds" or "I saw an arch fingerprint in the clouds," surely I saw everything there was to be seen. If it is conceivable that I should remember all of the details, and later learn that that is the shape of a dolphin or that that is the pattern of an arch fingerprint, then surely I saw all of the details that could be seen. Why then did I not see a dolphin in the clouds or an arch fingerprint in the clouds? If I had seen and remembered all of the details of a sea-mammal following my boat or of a fingerprint on a piece of paper and had later learned to identify them as a dolphin and an arch fingerprint respectively, those would be different matters. Then I should say, "I saw a dolphin," or "I saw an arch fingerprint." The difference has to do with the peculiarities of seeing things in the clouds. Seeing a dolphin in the clouds is seeing a form or pattern and thinking to yourself or aloud "That's a dolphin." That's not quite right, but it's close enough. What can one say? Seeing a fingerprint in the clouds is not like seeing a varied thrush on the lawn or a stone house on the hill. The fingerprint in the clouds can be clearly before my eyes, and I may not be able to see it. I may see the clouds and still not see the fingerprint. And then suddenly I may see it. When I later report in the past tense that I saw it, I can only report the fact that I recognized it: the fact that I saw it can be nothing less than the fact that I was aware of it at the time. Isn't this just the way one would expect it to be if the object seen were the result of having acquired some new part of language, some new word or phrase? I did learn what an "arch fingerprint" was, and only then did I see the fingerprint in the clouds. But it is now clear that learning what an arch fingerprint was did not play the part in my seeing the arch fingerprint in the clouds that I thought it did. This is what I thought: I saw the strands and wisps of cirrus clouds woven through the sky, and when I learned what pattern an arch fingerprint was, I saw that pattern emerge out of the very strands and wisps I had seen. The potential was there in the clouds and the presence of that pattern or concept in my mind made the pattern actualize out of the potential, right before my eyes. Of course it is true: the knowledge of that pattern helped me see it. Without that knowledge I did not know what I was to look for. But I could have seen that pattern without knowing what to look for. I could have said to Kleinmetz, "Do you mean that pattern there?" and then described it or drawn it on a pad. And he might have said "Yes. That is exactly the pattern of an arch fingerprint." So I could have seen the pattern and not known that it was the pattern of an arch fingerprint. And unlikely as it is, I might even remember having seen that pattern before. I could have seen it just as I might see a bird and not be able to identify it. Or as Duffy might see two shades of blue and not know how to talk about them.

The fact that I suddenly saw the fingerprint, that it "emerged" out of the clouds, is not explained by the fact that I learned what an arch fingerprint was—that is, it is not explained in the way I thought it was. "Why did you suddenly see it?" is sometimes answered by "I found out what to look for." But even when I know what to look for, I may not see it. A little later I may suddenly see it. Then if I am asked "Why did you suddenly see it?" what answer can I give? There is no one answer; sometimes I give one answer, sometimes another. "I relaxed," "I turned my head to the side," "My eyes tired," "I was just going to give up. The fact that I stopped thinking about it seems to have made me see it." "At first I was looking for something smaller and then suddenly it appeared." "I don't know. It just appeared, that's all." Knowing what to look for is just one of many things which can explain why I see a fingerprint in the clouds. And even when it does explain why I see something in the clouds, it does not "enter into the object seen" or "form the object." Its status does not seem different from any of the other possible explanations. I should never think of my relaxation as "entering into the object seen," or of my eyes becoming tired as "entering into the object seen."

I now realize that I thought of the example of seeing a fingerprint in the clouds while under the influence of a certain picture of vision, and I must have designed it and construed it in such a way as to show forth the picture that possessed me. I was thinking that my eyes presented me with only incompletely formed objects, and that the categories of my language somehow entered into and completed the objects which I see. I naturally thought of a sky full of wispy clouds, the partially formed objects of perception--full of lights and shadows, lines and projections. These were to provide the matter for vision; then my eyes, guided by the categories of my language, were to form these disconnected materials into the complete object which I see. I must have been thinking that an object which I see results from processes involved in my vision as a photograph results from processes in a camera and film. And more particularly, I must have been thinking that the object seen was like a photograph which resulted from double exposure. Part of the picture is the image focussed by the camera lens, part of the picture is already on the film. The lens produces a vague cloud-like image. The film has a familiar pattern already recorded on it. Then the image from the lens fills in the pattern already on the film, and the two together form one complete picture. Thus I will not get a picture of a towhee or of a fingerprint unless there is already on the film an outline or sketchy indication of a towhee or a fingerprint--which will be filled in by the materials from my animal perception. The outline on the film, of course, represents the part which knowing the word "towhee," or the phrase "arch fingerprint" plays in vision.

As a model in terms of which to understand seeing a towhee, or seeing two shades of blue, this is completely unsuitable. I can see all of the relevant details of a towhee and not know what a towhee is. I can see two shades of blue without at the time knowing the words "blue" or "shade"; and if I have sufficiently complete and accurate color memory, I can later recall those two colors and then characterize them as "shades of blue." And, what is worse, the picture does not even fit seeing patterns in the clouds. I can see a pattern in the clouds without having seen the pattern before or without knowing its name. The most one can say about seeing things in the clouds is that knowing what to look for plays a more important role than it does in seeing things in the trees, or on the lawn, or in the street. And that fact seems the only thing which determined my choice of the example, and it dictated my misinterpretation of it. All the rest came from the picture of vision.

According to my picture, a formative part was to be played by words and phrases. One who knows some word or phrase was to see something which, before he knew that word or phrase, he could not see. The word or phrase was, in some mysterious way, to "enter into" and "form" the object seen. There is obviously nothing like this involved in seeing a towhee. One can see a towhee and later learn to identify it. On careful examination, there does not seem to be anything like this in seeing two shades of blue. One can see two shades of blue and later learn how to talk about them. And there is not anything like this in seeing a pattern in the clouds. One can see a pattern and afterward learn what such a pattern is called. It would be odd, though, to learn the name of a pattern from seeing it first in the clouds (say a name like "trigonal" or "Japanese fret") unless, of course, it was the name of some pattern of the clouds themselves (such as "cirrus" or "mackerel sky" or "thunder-head").

Where did I ever get the idea that words and phrases had anything to do with vision? I have had it from the beginning. In the beginning I thought that visible things were marked by visible characteristics. By their visible characteristics they were made known to me as this thing or that: agaric, ragweed, sugar maple, whimbrel, telephone pole, fire hydrant, mailbox, watch chain. When I saw a thing I saw the characteristics by which it is recognized as just that thing and not any other. And to the thing I assigned a name, or, as is usually the case, I found that speakers of my language had already assigned a name; and so I learned the name which was already assigned.

And then I came to realize that the many things called by the same name do not share common and peculiar, visible, identifying characteristics. From this I drew the following conclusion: whenever I say "This is a pencil" or "This is a towhee," the fact that pencils and towhees are each grouped together only by "overlapping similarities" enters into what I say. So if I truthfully say "I see a towhee" or "I see a pencil," then that fact also enters into what I see. If what I see is what such a word refers to, then what I see involves my recognition that the thing I see is one of various kinds brought together by "overlapping similarities." Thus language, I concluded, "entered into" the objects I see.

I see now that these are extremely paradoxical things to think. The word "towhee" refers to males, females, immatures, nestlings, albinos, and others--and all of these do not share common and peculiar identifying characteristics. It follows from this that I cannot see a towhee unless I can recognize a towhee by name, regardless of which sort it is: immature, nestling, pickled, plucked, and so on. Of course this is ridiculous. Somehow I have confused the abilities required in order to have the word "towhee" in one's vocabulary with the abilities required to be an expert on towhees. I may know what the word "towhee" means in the sense that if anyone were to ask me what it means I could tell him, and in so doing I should answer his question. Of course I should not have to know much or to tell him much: only that a towhee is any one of several medium-sized sparrow-like birds. I can do better than that. I may be able to recognize towhees at my bird feeder and talk about them and ask questions about them. I may know their song and most of their call notes. I may know where they nest. When I speak of learning all of those things I do not speak of learning more about the meaning of the word "towhee." Well then, not "meaning," but the word does figure in my learning somehow. I am able to use the word in all sorts of ways and circumstances where before I could not. Yet I am still not an expert, and I may be unable to recognize an immature towhee when I see one. Yet this does not affect my ability to say, correctly, "There's a towhee"; it does not affect my ability to say, correctly, "I see a towhee there."

Then when I see a towhee the "overlapping similarities" business does not come in. It does not come into what I say I see or into what I see. If I become a bird-expert, then, the meaning of the word "towhee" is not changed by my acquisition of the ability to survey, classify, identify all the many types of towhees. Before I become an expert, my ability to say "There's a towhee," and my ability to understand what one says who says "There's a towhee" are abilities quite different from those an ornithologist develops who spends his life on the study of towhees. If this were not so I could not understand an expert who told me "That's an immature towhee."

Why do I have this picture, that learning the common nouns of my language is like packing my head with all the details of some identification manual? Why do I have the idea that learning words is learning which things they refer to, and learning which things they refer to is learning the identifying characteristics (or "overlapping similarities") of those things?

This picture must faithfully represent the way it is with simple words like "red" or "blue." Surely with words such as these the visible characteristics by virtue of which things are correctly denominated "red" or "blue" must stand out; and only when I learn to

98

recognize those characteristics have I learned the words "red" or "blue." Haven't I just determined that the alternative picture will not fit the facts? Duffy's lack of the words "blue" and "shade" does not make it impossible for him to see two shades of blue. Doesn't that mean that the visible details are there to be seen, waiting for the proper language to describe them? I am not concerned with whether the two shades of blue were "there to be seen." I was concerned with whether the difference in language between us, that is, between me and Duffy, would show that what I saw was something Duffy would not see. I should see two shades of blue and Duffy would not--I supposed. And that expectation turned out not to be so. There is certainly nothing in this to justify my thinking that all the multitudes of blue things with all their many shades of blue stand out in the world somehow, waiting for language to come along and thereby enable language-speaking animals to say that they are all shades of blue.

Here my picture of "simple words" and the way they work leads me to generalize with mad abandon. If we take the words "red," "blue," "yellow," and other similar color words from Duffy (and the attendant word "shade" also), and this does not affect what he sees, then if we take his language away from him entirely this will not affect what he sees. Duffy as a normal child, or anyone as a child, or any higher animal, will find in the world all the visual distinctions which we remark on with our color vocabularies. Now what am I trying to think? Does that mean that an animal will respond in the same way to all the shades, hues, and tints of blue, and all the kinds of blue too, such as phosphorescent, florescent, iridescent, surface, depth, and so on? If he does, do we know why he responds in the same way? Does it mean that an animal can be taught to respond in the same way to all of these? And, if so, do we know what we have taught him? Once again, all these questions seem to merge into a great mystery. It is surely not necessary that a small child respond naturally in the same way to every blue thing in order that he may learn the word "blue." He does not have to respond naturally in the same way to every pencil in order to learn the word "pencil." Sometimes I may have to say to the child "This is a pencil, too." Also, sometimes I may have to say "This is blue, too--a light shade of blue" or "This is blue, too--a slightly greenish blue." Are the two things "pencil, too" and "blue, too" different? Is "pencil, too" used to inform the child that he must count as a "pencil" some new and unexpected things on the basis of some similarity? And is "blue, too" merely an encouragement to the child to let his natural reactions run free--to count as "blue" everything he naturally responds to in the same way?

Even if the child does not realize how many kinds of pencils there are, and he would not yet call some of them pencils, is this any reason for thinking that he does not quite know the word "pencil," or that he does not know its meaning? And suppose he does not call "blue" everything that is blue, and he has to be told (or encouraged). Does that show that he does not have a grasp of the word "blue"?

There are three things here (or five): (1) (a) knowing a word or (b) knowing the meaning of a word or (c) having the word in one's active vocabulary; (2) learning to recognize and identify when there are no common and peculiar identifying characteristics; and (3) one's natural reactions. I do not now see how these three things can be separated in such a way that a grand picture of langauge and its relation to the objective world can be supported on them.

I dismissed the towhee case as not showing what I expected, that perception was shaped by language. I now must dismiss the case of seeing shades of blue. My test has been this: if language has a role in forming the object seen, then one will not say retrospectively "I saw." If one says "I saw" this shows that language does not play the formative role I have imagined that it does. And I have used this test because it brings down to earth more difficult ideas. There is no reason, though, why my test should require the exact words "I saw." Surely there are other things I can imagine Duffy's saying which would show just as well that his language does not form what he sees.

Suppose that when the color expert taught Duffy the many specific color names he gave Duffy a cardboard color-chip for each one. Suppose that Duffy leafed through his pile of cardboard color-chips and laid them out before himself many times, perhaps at first curiously and playfully, and then more studiously. Could he not begin to group the colors, some in one group, some in another? If he had two color-chips which matched my two flowers might he not put them in the same group? That does not seem unimaginable. Later when he learns the rest of the color vocabulary, might not he remember putting the two together and now say, "I saw that they belonged together in a way. I know now that belonging together in that way is being two shades of blue"? If he could say that, then he perceived everything there was to be perceived, surely.

Perhaps the "complex things" I have been talking about (towhees, pencils, arch fingerprints) are not complex enough--or not complex in the right way. Some philosophers are inclined to think that certain highly complex or "institutional" facts are relative to a culture and a language, and hence that such things could not have been seen except by a member of the proper culture or by one who spoke the language.

Before the middle of the 19th century there was no game of baseball. Hence there did not exist such things as "stealing second base," "throwing a strike," or "beating out a bunt." Of course, at that time--say 1820--no one could see a person stealing second base or beating out a bunt, because people were not doing those things. But the important thing is this: People could not do those things; such things came into existence with the game of baseball, and they do not (could not) exist outside of that game, its rules, its practices, its skills and strategies.

Suppose, now, that I imagine a person (call him Leonard) who knows absolutely nothing of baseball. He has grown up on a small English-speaking island off the coast of Alaska, where--for some reason--he has never played baseball, never seen anyone play baseball, and has never even heard of baseball. Now I take him to a game between the Dodgers and Giants; and I tell him that we must not talk during the game. Later, I may say something like this: "I saw Ron Cey beat out a bunt in the last of the ninth." Of course Leonard will say nothing of the kind. He can only ask me questions about the game, its rules, what took place, who won.

Suppose now that he does come to understand the game, and in short order becomes a fan. What now if I remind him of the first game we saw together? I might say, "Do you remember the man with the funny legs who bunted in the ninth?" And he might, surely, say "Yes. I know now that that was Ron Cey, and that he beat out an important bunt." I think he would not say "At my first game, I saw Ron Cey beat out a bunt." Certainly not like that. If the listener did not understand, he surely would explain "I knew nothing of the game, but I remember that man with the funny, waddling run--who put up his bat and rolled the ball--and then ran.... And now I know that that was the Dodger third-baseman, Ron Cey, and that he beat out a bunt." He would certainly not think that his ignorance of baseball had prevented him from seeing something there on the field. Whatever the important "ontological status" of such "institutional actions," one's ignorance of them, of the social

101

order, the rules, the practices upon which they depend--this does not affect one's vision in the way I imagined that language affected one's vision. That effect upon vision would have to be brought about by simple words like "blue."

Consider another example of something I might perceive--which is obviously relative to the language I speak. Suppose that I hear somebody say something in a foreign language--one that I do not know. Someone else, Taylor, a man who knows the language, might report that he heard a person ask where to catch the bus. I cannot say that I heard any such thing. Taylor heard a man ask the way to the bus. He heard the man say, "Where do I catch the bus?" in language I do not know. I heard no such thing. Suppose now that I found the sounds of the man's speech so strange that they stuck in my mind. I mimicked them--over and over, amused by the sounds and the rhythm. Now suppose that I learn the language. And then when I repeat these sounds from memory I recognize them: as I repeat the sounds from memory I can hear myself saying in this language, "Where do I catch the bus?" Isn't there now something which I hear which I could not hear before I learned the language? I certainly shall not say that I heard the man ask "Where do I catch the bus?" No, I heard the man speak and I heard the strange sounds of what he said. Only one like Taylor, one who knew the language, could hear the man ask "Where do I catch the bus?" That is something I could now hear, now that I know the language, but I could not hear it before I knew the langauge. So here is something the hearing of which depends upon knowledge of the language. Of course it does: it is the things which are said in the language itself.

But this is also clearly not the sort of thing I was thinking of when I thought that language shapes my perception of the world. I was thinking primarily of vision, of course, as one so often does in philosophy. I was thinking of trees and rocks and birds and houses. And in so far as I might have thought of hearing, I was thinking of claps of thunder and songs of birds, and squeaks of hinges. I was thinking of sounds and the sounds things make. I was not thinking of what a person says. I was thinking of "things" and "happenings" and such which might be shaped by this segment of our vocabulary or that--not "things" which are dependent on mastery of a language--as a language. Here then may be the truth in the idea that language determines the perceptual world; but it is not the truth I thought it to be.

According to John Austin, "truth" involves both langauge and the world--in a complex interrelation. Austin thinks that "statements," which are "historical uses of sentences," are the bearers of truth, and a statement is true when it "corresponds" in a certain way to a "fact" in the world. Our language correlates words (or certain words) with "historic situations" in the world, and it also correlates words (certain words) with types of "situations," "things," and "events." A statement is true when the historic state of affairs to which certain words are correlated is of a type with which certain other words are correlated. Austin explains what it amounts to to be "of a type...":

> 'Is of a type with which' means 'is suf-
> ficiently like those standard states of af-
> fairs with which'. Thus, for a statement to
> be true one state of affairs must be like
> certain others, which is a natural relation,
> but also sufficiently like to merit the same
> 'decription,' which is no longer a purely
> natural relation. To say 'this is red' is
> not the same as to say 'this is like those,'
> nor even as to say 'this is like those which
> were called red.' That things are similar,
> or even 'exactly' similar, I may literally
> see--in calling them the same color a con-
> vention is involved additional to the con-
> ventional choice of the name to be given to
> the color which they are said to be.[2]

I take it that Austin is here saying that I can see ("literally see") that two things are similar to each other, but that I cannot see ("literaly see") that they are of the same type or kind. Similarities are found in the world: "sameness" comes in with language. And Austin seems to think that things are the "same" in the relevant way whenever we call them by the same name.

Austin most certainly doesn't wish to deny that I can see two barn swallows sitting on a wire or that I can see two horses grazing in a pasture. He obviously means to say that language enters into seeing such matters in a way that it does not enter into seeing that two things are similar. Without language I should see

---

[2]J. L. Austin, "Truth," in Philosophical Papers, ed. J. O. Urmson and G. J. Warnock (Clarendon, Oxford University Press, 1961), p. 90.

only similarities and dissimilarities in the world. "Literally see" must be "see without the influence of language."

I think there is a powerful picture at work here. If I could see the world with non-linguistic eyes--perhaps as a small child I do--then I should see things similar and dissimilar to each other, alike and different from one another, but I should not see kinds or types or species of things. I could see that two or several things were similar but not that both or all are x's. I could not see an x. That comes only when I learn how my tribe or culture classifies things as x's or y's or whatever. I can see an x only when I learn my native language. My language makes some similarities significant and others not. Similarities are recognized as significant when my language gives a common name to things which have those similarities to each other. They are then marked as of the "same" type. Austin says that this is a matter of "convention," but he does not mean "convention" surely: he means that my language need not have marked out the classes and kinds which it does. The types and classes and species marked by my language need not have been so marked. If my people had had a different history, they would have developed a language which groups and classifies differently; perhaps the languages of other tribes and other cultures do group and classify things in a different way. Whether other langauges do in fact classify things differently is not important: it is at least thinkable that they should classify in a different way, and this shows that being of the same kind is not a natural relation. It is not something I see with my animal eyes.

How can I bring this down to the facts? Does Austin mean that if I do not know the name "cedar waxwing" then I cannot see a cedar waxwing? Though I might see a similarity between that bird, say, and an eastern kingbird? Suppose that I went to a bird-man and told him that I saw a bird which was similar to a kingbird but different--and then I went on to explain the differences and gave a pretty good description of a waxwing. He might well say, "You saw a cedar waxwing." And I might later tell someone "I saw a cedar waxwing--but I didn't know its name at the time."

Does Austin mean that I cannot see that a bird is a cedar waxwing unless I know the name--although I can see that it is similar in certain ways to a kingbird? When I go to the bird expert I may say, "I saw a bird... and I could see that it was similar to a kingbird...." Then, after hearing my description, he tells me that I saw a cedar waxwing. In telling about the bird which I saw on that day I shall not say, "I saw that the bird was a cedar waxwing." Certainly I shall not say that, not if I had been completely unfamiliar with the bird I saw. And even if I had read about the bird and seen its picture, and even though the bird seemed to "register" somehow, ("Don't I know that bird?") still I shall say "I ought to have seen that it was a cedar waxwing," not "I saw that it was a cedar waxwing." But the reason I cannot say "I saw that the bird was a cedar waxwing" (and so I did not see that it was a cedar waxwing) is not that I do not know the bird's name: the reason is that I cannot recognize the bird. I may know the name, but having not seen the bird, or having not seen one for a long time, I may be unable to recognize this one when I see it. And I may have seen that it was a cedar waxwing and not have known the name. "I saw one of those crested brown birds with the black mask... but I can't remember its name." "It is the cedar waxwing." "Ah, yes. I saw a cedar waxwing."

There is clearly some connection, though, between my ability to see that a bird is a cedar waxwing and the name "cedar waxwing." I must know that it is one of the recognized species of birds and that it had a name. I must be familiar with much of the linguistic apparatus if not with the name. Without having knowledge of a certain bit of language--the idea of naming species--I cannot see that a bird is a cedar waxwing. But then, without that bit of language I cannot see that the bird is similar in some respects to the kingbird. Without that bit of language I should not be able to see that there were two things which were similar--this bird and the kingbird.

Of course Austin means I should be able to see that two, or several, individuals are similar and not see that they are the same species. It is hard to see what that is supposed to come to. Some individuals which are very similar are of different species. And some individuals which are not very similar are of the same species. A female Wilson's warbler and female hooded warbler are very similar. A female red-winged blackbird and a male red-winged blackbird are quite dissimilar. Living organisms are not classified entirely on the bases of similarities--certainly not the similarities which might strike an untutored observer. And even an untutored observer knows that the similarities he observes may not be significant.

Mainly we notice and talk about similarities and differences among individuals when there is an interesting or important variation among them. Suppose that a mother mountain quail and her fifteen young have come

to feed at my chicken feeder. I may notice that the
young are not all alike by any means. "That one is
very dark, and heavily streaked. There is another
which is very similar to him...." Obviously, such
similarities have nothing to do with the fact that I
use the same name for them both: they are both young
mountain quail. Now if a California quail and her
young joined the flock, I might notice that the young
of the California quail were generally darker. But my
two dark young mountain quail are more like young
California quail than they are like those of their own
kind. If I had only the young mixed together in one
flock, I could see which were similar to which--but I
should not be able to tell whether the similar ones
were of the same species or not.

When I notice such similarities and differences, I
certainly notice, too, in what the similarities and
differences consist. "Those two are similar in build
and manner." "Those two are alike in that their backs
are more finely barred." "Those two have short tails."
"Several have pink feet." And I suppose that Austin
would think of build, and manner, and backs, and tails
and feet as "types" or "kinds." I am certainly prepared to say that two birds are similar in that each
has the **same** build or **same** barred back. It is scarcely
thinkable that, without being familiar with beaks and
backs and tails, I should notice any of these similarities I have been talking about. Noticing these similarities presupposes that I am already familiar with
those parts of langauge wherein beaks and backs and
feet--and of course, birds--have been classified and
recorded. Of course Austin wants it that these are
denominated "backs" because my tribe has noticed and
memorialized similarities among them--and the same with
"beaks," and "feet" and "tails."

It is very hard to think about the similarities
among things which make them beaks or backs. It must
be for this reason that Austin has chosen a color-word
to illustrate his thesis. "I can 'literally see' [that
is, see without the influence of language] that red
things are similar but not that they are red." That is
certainly a lot easier to think about than this: "I
can 'literally see' that all backs are similar but not
that they are backs." But is it? The fact that two
things are similarly colored does not make the things
similar. I have a bright red tool box with black
fasteners. Someone called my attention to the fact
that it is colored in a way similar to a scarlet
tanager. Its colors and their arrangement are like
those of a scarlet tanager. If I said to someone out
of the blue, "My tool box is like a scarlet tanager,"

106

he would quite naturally think I was going on to explain a riddle. To be understood, seriously, I should have to say "The colors and their arrangement are like those of a scarlet tanager." But suppose my tool box was solid red--about the same shade as that of the male cardinal. Then could I say "My tool box is like (is similar to) a cardinal?" This, too, would be taken as the beginning of a riddle or a joke. To be taken as making a serious comment, I should have to say "My tool box is similar in color to a male cardinal," or "The color of my tool box is much like that of the male cardinal." When we note that things are similar in color, it seems we observe and comment on the similarity of the color. ("The colors of those two things are similar.") But two colors can be similar without that fact having anything to do with whether they are the same color or not. The color of a bottle of red wine and the sky are similar: they are "depth" colors; they have no surface. Of course they are not the same in color: they are the same kind of color. A blue and red may be alike in being flourescent or in being iridescent or in being highly saturated--or in any number of other ways. These two would be the same kinds of color: both flourescent, iridescent, saturated, muted, muddy or what.

When are two colors both red? That seems to depend. On an artist's palette all the colors with red in them may be called "reds." But if we are concerned with the color of a wagon or a tractor or a flag or a sweater, it will not do to say it is "red"--just that and no more--unless it is a highly saturated red. Other "reds" require description: "It is a soft brownish red (or shade of red)," or "It is a very light shade of red--nearly pink."

Are all of the reds similar? Hardly. If I am trying to mix a color to match another, I might say at some stage "They are similar, but hardly the same." But if they are not even close, then they are not similar at all, even though each might be some shade of red. Similarity in colors is not the sort of thing which Austin wants me to think it is. Any shade of red is not similar to any other shade of red. Well then, if not similar, what? Perhaps "They are alike in both being some shade of red." But that description requires that I recognize them as shades of red. I must already know the colors (and color names), it seems, before I can characterize the relationship between two colors as both being shades of red.

There must be something one could see about them without knowing anything about colors or the language of colors. He could see that they belonged together,

107

that they had some affiliation--or something--without seeing that they were shades of red. That is a "natural" relation; that is a fact about the colors. The fact that they are shades of red is imported into them by language; in that importation "a convention is involved additional to the conventional choice of the name...." How am I to think of this? My imaginary experiment with Duffy was designed to test whether, without the vocabulary of the common color names and the ideas of "shades" and "hyphenated colors," he could see that two colors were shades of the same color. And it seemed that he could see that they were alike or belonged together in some way; but, of course, not that they were shades of the same color. When he learns the color vocabulary he will say something like this: "I saw two shades of blue--but I did not know at the time how to talk about shades or the color blue." Or perhaps he will say something like this: "I saw that they belonged together in that way but I did not then realize that belonging together in that way was being two shades of the same color. The fact that he did not see that they were two shades of the same color seems much the same as the fact that Clive did not see that two birds were towhees--because he did not know how to identify a towhee--though he might later look it up from his memory of the details which he saw. If that is what it is to "literally see" a "natural relation," then I literally see flowers and frogs and insects which I can describe and draw but not identify; I can literally see all sorts of things--and certainly not just similarities and dissimilarities.

Duffy was an adult who spoke English. He knew how things of many kinds are distinguished and classified and related. He knew the names of many specific colors. He had just gained his sight and so he was intensely interested in colors, and undoubtedly anxious to talk about colors. He would naturally study colors carefully and with an eye to classification: he would notice "affiliations" and "relations" among colors. So he is quite prepared for the last step: to learn that colors are classed by hue and described as shades and mixtures.

Perhaps he is too linguistically sophisticated to "literally see" what there is to be seen--to see, that is, without the influences of language on his vision. Only one can "literally see" who has no language at all. A dog has no language and he can see a bone; he can also see the mailman coming down the road; he can see a rabbit running for the blackberry bushes. But what theoretical weight can one place on the way we talk about dogs? In the end I am thrown back on myself, and upon the question: what should I see if I had no language? I do not know how to approach such a question but this much, at least, seems clear: It would not be correct to answer "similarities and dissimilarities."

* * *

I have been occupied with views which lead us to believe that language determines what we see "in the world." The things we see are only in part the hard objective things we take them to be; in part they are soft and social: they are shaped, in part, by our language. In talking of "seeing" and the "things we see" I have meant to talk of the most ordinary of things. I see two birds or two towhees; I see that two colors are both shades of blue. And the way in which I have imagined language to determine vision of these things has been through specific nouns and noun-phrases: "towhee," "arch fingerprint," "shade of blue," "red"—so-called "concrete general terms."

There has long been on the philosophical scene another view about the way language determines what we see. This is the thesis of Whorf and Sapir.[3] And it differs from the views I have been examining in precisely these two ways. (1) It maintains that language determines what I see—but "see" now in quite a different sense: "see" the world as a reflection of the categories of language. (2) The way language determines what I see is through its grammar—not through specific words but through word classes such as noun, adjective, verb, adverb, as these are understood in their roles in forming sentences.

Whorf and Sapir have mantained that I—and any speaker of an Indo-European language—see the world as composed of things and characteristics of things precisely because my language forces me to see the world in terms of nouns and modifying adjectives. Presumably speakers of languages with different grammatical categories do not see the world as composed of things and their characteristics.

What does this amount to? Whenever I talk using a noun such as bird, cloud, rainbow, sunrise, shadow, sound, odor, pain, itch, echo, dream, I think of what

---

[3]Benjamin Whorf, Language, Thought and Reality, ed. John B. Carroll (Cambridge, Mass., M.I.T. Press, 1964), and Edward Sapir, Selected Writings (Berkeley, University of California Press, 1951).

the noun refers to as a "thing." I think of all these
many "things" as fundamentally the same. Whorf and
Sapir hold that I assimilate them all to the "type" I
should think of first if I were just to think of a
"thing." That is, I should assimilate them all to
"things" such as bricks, pencils, and cups. And
whenever I use an adjective in characterizing one of
these things--heavy, vaporous, imaginary, chronic,
beautiful--I assimilate this "characteristic" to the
type I might first think of if I were to think of a
characteristic of a brick or a cup: hard, heavy,
white, short, hexagonal. Because my language has a
very limited number of word classes, I see the world in
terms of a very limited number of categories. I am
blinded to differences and I assimilate the great
diversity of "things" with their "characteristics" to
the simplest model: "Bricks are hard." I force the
world's great diversity into the simple mould of my
language.
    If this is taken as a thesis about vision, it is
quite ridiculous. When I see a raccoon in a tree, or
an electrical spark in a motor, or a smoke signal on a
mountain top, or a ripple in the water, or a green
afterimage on a wall, I certainly do not make any mistakes in what I say about these very different things.
I do not get sparks, smoke signals, ripples, and after-
images confused and try to talk about all of them as
though they were pebbles or fence-posts. When I talk
of seeing something, my talk is determined by the
nature of the thing I see, the circumstances in which I
see it, who I am talking to--and so on. I do not see
all things in the same way; I am certainly not blinded
to obvious differences by the fact that I say something
about what I see.
    Of course, the philosophical view I am discussing
is not intended to fly so blatantly in the face of the
facts. It does not deny that I can and do distinguish
in all the proper ways between such objects of vision
as boulders, lightning flashes, and will-o'-the-wisps.
It is supposed that the grammar of my language leads me
in a more subtle way to see the whole world as a scene
of things with their characteristics. What is it to
see the world as...(something)? "I see the world as
the creation of a patient and benevolent intelligence."
"I see the world as the outcome of accidental and
indifferent forces." Such are the culminating pronouncements of metaphysical thinking. "I see the world
as a scene of things with their characteristics" seems
a lower-level pronouncement of the same kind. And its
opposite--or one of its opposites--I suppose is this:
"I see the world as an uninterrupted series of events

and changes." ("Everything is change: I cannot step twice into the same river.")

What can the thesis be--that I am determined to have some such outlook by my language? It is quite apparent that speakers of English can be either Aristotelians or Bergsonians. The thesis of Whorf and Sapir, I conjecture, amounts to this: when I engage in metaphysical thinking, when I try somehow to represent to myself the way the world is in its entirety, then my language makes the picture of static things and their characteristics come first to mind. Speakers of Navaho or Cree would find that another picture came most easily to mind. I suspect that this is what the thesis amounts to. Is there anything to it? I do not know--and I do not know how one would go about finding out.

3. THE CAUSAL THEORY OF PERCEPTION[1]

I

A philosopher once told me that the natural, pristine, naive philosophical theory of perception is the causal theory. Also, "When all is said and done," he said, "the causal theory may well be the correct one." What could he have meant by that? When philosophers think about perception they think primarily—almost exclusively—about vision. So, I suppose, he was thinking mainly of a theory of vision. When, as a philosopher, I think about vision, when I try to think about the nature of vision, do I first, naturally, think of it as causal in some way? There seems to be some truth in this.

I ask "What is it to see something?" Or "When I say that I see something, what do I imply about myself and that something which I claim to see?" These are the philosophical questions with which I begin. They are very hard to formulate clearly. I want to know what is involved in the idea of seeing something, and it does seem that the first suggestions which come to mind have to do with the object seen and the way it affects me. When I say that I see a tree I mean that there is a tree there before me, and that the tree somehow has made me visually aware of its presence. My vision has been brought about by the action upon me of the object which I see.

At this point, if I am not careful, I shall become lost in thinking of the details of the modern optico-physiological account of vision. I do not know much of this theory, but I know enough that some of the details quickly come into my mind. I think of light waves and particles striking an object and being reflected. I think of the reflected waves and particles striking the lens of my eye and being focussed on the retina. There they set up electrochemical impulses which pass along the optic nerve to the brain. And so on, perhaps: although at this point I have just about exhausted my knowledge of the details. This line of thought can lead me into the wonders of modern physiology and optics, but it puts me off my philosophical inquiry. The physiologist wants to know what processes are involved

---

[1] I began this essay on a cold winter night in Edmonton at the University of Alberta. I want to thank Thomas Bestor and John Bucklin who discussed the topic with me at that time, and on and off for two years thereafter.

113

in vision--all of them, and he finds them by experiment and dissection. I want to know what is involved in the idea of vision, the idea of seeing something, and it is perfectly obvious that not all of these details which the physiologist uncovers are involved in the idea itself. One has that idea by being able to talk of things he sees and to talk of what other people see and to determine when other people see, and why sometimes they cannot see. And one can talk in all the relevant ways without any knowledge of modern physiology and optics. The human race possessed the idea of vision for centuries before the modern scientific theories were discovered, and that idea of vision would remain unchanged if the modern theories were discovered to be wrong or inadequate in all sorts of ways.

When I seek an answer for a philosophical question about vision, it is easy to lose my way and to think of some of the details of various scientific theories. This should not be surprising. I want the idea or "concept" of seeing and the scientific theories have their foundations in that idea. They are efforts to explain what transpires when one sees something. The scientific theories are causal, and this should confirm me in my belief that the idea of vision is causal. The scientific theories fill in the optical, chemical, physiological details of a causal account of vision. Those details are not part of the idea, but the idea must be the gross outline into which these details may be fitted. A correct scientific theory and a correct philosophical account must have a common source--our conception of vision. It is vision they both seek to understand, but of course in different ways. A scientific theory seeks to fill in the details, a philosophical theory seeks to set out and make clear those features which belong to the idea of vision itself.

Thus one way to get clear as to what is involved in the idea is to begin with the scientific theory and then ask with respect to each detail, "Is vision conceivable without that?" It is surely easy enough to imagine vision without the functioning of an optical center of the brain or the workings of an optical nerve. The anatomists and physiologists could well be wrong about such matters. Also, surely they could be wrong about the structural and chemical details of the eye. But how about the eye itself? Is it conceivable that one could see without eyes? That is more difficult. Suppose that someone has had his eyes completely destroyed in an accident. His eyeballs and optical nerves have been completely destroyed, and nothing now remains but surgical scars where patches of flesh were transplanted across the eye openings.

114

Suppose now that this person claimed to see just as before his accident. He would tell us what was going on before him, and he could describe things accurately in all their colors. Suppose also that there was no way to block his "vision": we cannot place an opaque screen before any part of his body and interfere with his ability to report the facts and the details. Should we say that he sees--but without eyes and apparently without any organ of vision? I should think not. I think we should be most careful about describing this phenomenon. We might say that he seems to see or that he seems to have some strange kind of pseudo-optical perception or something like that. The presence of some sensory organ which can be blocked seems to be part of the concept of vision. Is light necessary? Can one see in total darkness? I should suppose yes to this. Can one see things at vast distances, say on the other side of the world? I should think not: that too would not be vision but something else. Also I should think one cannot now see things which happened in the past or are going to happen in the future. Perhaps these would be, respectively, "visual memory" or "visual precognition" but not vision.

Many of these are difficult questions, and many of the answers will doubtless be iffy and indefinite, but I think one can see that the answers tend to confirm the idea that vision is causal in nature. Surely it is necessary to vision that the object seen be before one--or at least in a fixed relationship to some organ of sense and that the organ not be blocked out. The object and its features must somehow bring it about through some action on an appropriate organ that the perceiver become aware of it and its features. When I see something, the thing seen must act upon me in some way: it must register itself upon my awareness. The general features of the causal situation seem to belong to the very idea of seeing. They will include the object seen and its visible features and the fact that the object produces my vision of it and its features--and by acting in a fairly direct way and along a straight line. Without these features, the object seen and its fairly direct causal influence, we should not think of any phenomenon as "seeing" --regardless of how like seeing it was in other respects.

But now the causal account runs into a difficulty. Even if there is an object to be seen and it is located in the right place and at the proper distance from me, and its causal influences--whatever they are--register themselves in the proper way upon me, still it does not follow that I see the object. Other factors are required and these are not causal. Suppose that I am

115

walking in the forest and say "I see a winter wren there in the bushes." Much more is present in that act of vision than that a winter wren is present and before my eyes. I have to be alert, I must pick it out from the difficult background, I must be able to recognize it. All of this calls for some experience and training. These elements clearly are not to be causally accounted for. In addition to causal influences in vision there is also much human agency. Those elements which result from human agency are simply not to be accounted for causally. But there must be something which can be accounted for causally. In addition to my activity in seeing something, there must be something of which I am aware just because I have been made aware by the causal influences of the object. In addition to the aspect of vision for which I am responsible, there must be a passive element--something produced in me by the influence of the object acting on and through my organs of vision. This, of course, is where the "sense-datum" comes into the causal account of perception. It is what is produced in me as the end product of the causal processes involved in vision. It is that of which I am passively aware before I exercise my powers as an agent upon it. The idea of a sense-datum has been a notorious stumbling block to philosophers. It is obviously impossible to characterize anything in our awareness which is absolutely free of the interpretation which comes from our active intervention. But the causal account seems to require that there be such an element. And we do seem able to give characterizations which come closer and closer to fulfilling the requirement of a sense-datum report, that is, a report which is free of active interpretation. Thus it is essential to the causal account that there be a purely passive ingredient in visual perception, and that the causal account be limited to the production of that passive ingredient. Of course, it must also leave a place for the active part. If the causal theory is to be regarded as a theory of vision in its entirety, it will have to run something like this. Seeing something, seeing that X is P, for example, involves these ingredients: a non-causal act of recognition or characterization of X as P, plus these causal factors: X is there and X is P, and X's being P causes me to have the relevant sense-datum.

This suggests that we may be able to characterize a sense-datum in a way which is free enough from interpretation that it can be understood as something which is causally produced. Consider an example. It is easy enough to show that "seeing" in its entirety cannot be given a causal interpretation. Suppose I am on a field

trip with a bird-watcher friend of mine named Hopkins.
I see a bird moving secretively in a thick bush, and I
stand watching for a long time until finally I make out
the bird. Hopkins sees me staring into the bush and
asks, "What do you see?" I say "I see a wrentit." How
am I to imagine a causal explanation of this? What
could the question be which would provoke it? Perhaps
it is: "Why do you see a wrentit?" What are the answers to this question? Perhaps this is one. Let us
suppose the wrentit is a very rare bird in this part of
the country. Hopkins says, "On our trips, you always
find the rare birds. Why do you see a wrentit?"
Perhaps I answer, "Beginner's luck I guess." That obviously does not give a causal explanation of why I see
a wrentit. Suppose I say, "Because a wrentit is
there." What does that come to? Surely it is just a
smart-aleck way of saying "I don't know. That's just
the way it is." Suppose I say, "Because a wrentit is
there--and that partially explains why I see a wrentit." At this point I think that Hopkins would have to
understand that I was making a philosophical joke. But
in so far as he could take this as an answer to his
question, it must come to no more than "I don't know.
That's just the way it is." I can think of no question
other than Hopkins' question which could be asked with
the words "Why do you see a wrentit?" and no other kind
of explanation than "Beginner's luck" or "That's just
the way it is." Quite naturally I suspect that there
is no other question and no other kind of explanation
which will fit. Certainly nothing like a causal
explanation will fit in here.

Suppose instead that I peer into the bushes and
look quite puzzled. Hopkins says, "Do you see something?" I reply, "I'm not sure. It seemed to me for a
moment that I saw a wrentit." Now, I am inclined to
think, a causal question is not entirely out of order.
Can't someone ask "Why did it seem to you that you saw
a wrentit?" Perhaps I soon learn that there is a wrentit in the bushes. Then surely I can answer the question: "It seemed to me that I saw a wrentit because
there was a wrentit there--right where I was looking."
And that sounds very much like the required causal explanation. If it is, then my report is at least close
enough to a sense-datum report that it can give me
something subject to causal explanation.

It seems to me that the most important and provoca-
tive insight in H. P. Grice's article "The Causal
Theory of Perception"[2] is this: he suggests that when

---

[2]H. P. Grice, "The Causal Theory of Perception,"

I see a red object, my report "It looks red" can be explained causally. In many respects "It looks red" is not even close to what a sense-datum report should be. Most notably the "It" in "It looks red' is a physical object. So, at best, it is something like a sense-datum report of one color-characteristic of a physical object. But if it can be given a causal explanation, then at least it will tend to show that there is some element in perception which can be given a causal explanation. It may suggest a way in which we can characterize that element more generally. And at the same time this will lend credence to a causal theory of perception in advance of our ability to solve all of the knotty problems which arise in trying to introduce talk about sense-data.

Suppose that I am peering at a barn on a hilltop in the distance. It is sunset and the air is hazy. I say, "That barn looks red." Now I may ask "Why does it look red?" And someone may answer "It looks red because it is red and nothing stands in the way of your getting a good view of it. In short, it is red, and the viewing conditions are perfect, and so its being red makes it look red to you." Now that explanation sounds strange. It is far too theoretical for the humble question which provoked it. But it does not sound absolutely wild or hopeless. Perhaps the difficulty is simply this: the situation is not that in which a causal explanation is a natural thing to give. I shall try to examine more carefully the idea that "It looks red" can be given a causal explanation. I had best, therefore, try to think of examples where a causal explanation might be more at home than in a casual conversation about why a distant barn looks red to me.

It is quite clear that a person cannot say that something looks red (or looks some other color) just anywhere or anytime and provide a candidate for a causal explanation. Suppose that I am returning to Oregon from an extended vacation in Arizona. I awake on the train as we are entering the Cascades from Klamath Falls, and look out the window. I may say, "My, the trees look green here." Surely this would not provide an opening for "The trees are green here...." Suppose this: As I stare at an old house, thinking that I might return to this place and make a painting

Proceedings of the Aristotelian Society, Supp. Vol. 35 (1961) pp. 121-68. Reprinted in G. J. Warnock, ed., The Philosophy of Perception (London, Oxford University Press, 1967), pp. 85-112.

of it, I mull over what my art instructor once said to me. He said, "Think how the thing looks--not how it is: imagine how you will get the look of it in the simplest way possible." I ask myself, "How does the barn look?" And I say to myself, "It looks gray--plain gray." "Three gray brush strokes will get the gable end." Here "It looks gray" will not provide a place for a causal explanation: "The reason it looks gray is that it is gray." "It looks..." does not seem always to come to the same thing.[3] I must not therefore think of myself as examining the idiom "It looks...," but only as examining the idiom as it is used on some particular occasion. I want to consider someone's saying "It looks..." in some one particular situation, a situation in which the fact that something looks some color is likely to be a candidate for causal explanation.

Suppose that a physiologist named Wilson is conducting experiments to test the effects of certain drugs on color vision. I am his subject. I have just been given a drug which is known to change one's color vision dramatically, and I am then led into a room and seated facing a wall which has been painted with many colored shapes. Wilson points to one of these patches and asks, "What color do you see here?" I say, "It looks red." A long silence follows, as Wilson paces around the room. I ask, "Is something wrong?" Wilson says, "I think the drug has not had time to take effect. That patch is red." This example does not contain everything I need. Wilson's remark "That patch is red" is not offered as an explanation of why it looked red to me. When might he offer such a remark as the required kind of explanation? Suppose the drug has had time to take effect, and as anticipated it has had dramatic effects. Wilson points and I say, "That looks red." "I know that patch is blue," I say. "Why does it look red?" Wilson says, "The drug you have taken has some specific effects on the visual centers of the brain. We don't know exactly what they are, but you have just experienced one of its standard effects; it makes blue things look red." Even though Wilson does not think he knows the explanation, hasn't he given me explanation enough? I asked "Why does it look red?" and I have the answer "That is one of the standard effects of the drug; it makes blue things look red." Of course the answer does not specify the color of the patch as part of the explanation, but isn't that

_____

[3]See Essay 4 of this volume, "Does It Look the Color It Is?"

119

just because I already know the color of the patch? Suppose I had forgotten what color that particular patch was. Could I still ask, "Why does that look red to me?" I think not. I don't understand what such a question could be. Perhaps this: I realize only that my color vision has been thrown off, and I am simply using this one case in order to ask for an explanation in general of what is going on. "Why does that look red to me?" I ask. Wilson says, "It's a blue patch, and all we know is that the drug generally makes blue things look red." Is this an explanation of the sort I want? I ask "Why does it look red?" only because I have every reason to suspect that it is some color other than red--and I should like to understand something. What is it I want to understand? What part does Wilson's specification of the color of the patch play in his answer? Couldn't he just as well have said, "As you suspect, the color of the patch is not red. And all I know at this stage in my research is that this drug changes one's color vision dramatically." What was behind my question, he acknowledges he cannot answer: he does not know what effects on blood or nerves the drug has. I was not interested in the specifics of that one patch. I do not know what the question could be about the specifics of that one patch's looking red to me--a patch whose real color I do not know.

Thinking, with good reason, that the patch which looks red is not red, I might ask "What color is it?" I might just be curious. I might just want to savor to the full the strange effects this drug is having. Then Wilson will tell me "It's blue." But of course this has nothing to do with an explanation of why it appears red to me.

Suppose that a certain patch looks yellow to me, and I ask, "Why does that patch look yellow?" Wilson answers, "That patch is yellow. As far as we know the drug has no effect on one's vision of yellow. We do not know exactly what effects the drug has, or why it should have no effect on vision of that one color." Couldn't he just as well have said this? "You suspected that that color was not yellow. In this case your suspicions are wrong. For reasons we do not know the drug has no effect on vision of yellow." Isn't this an accurate account? With good reason, I suspect that my color vision has been thrown way off by the drug. I want to know how the drug works. I take this occasion to ask my question, "Why does that appear yellow?" Wilson tells me that my presumption is wrong. The patch is yellow, and he does not know the answer to my question. In short, he can offer no explanation. If

120

no explanation is given, then the specification of the color of the patch, "That is yellow," does not play a part in any explanation.

As a subject in an experiment of this kind, I can imagine myself asking for no kind of explanation other than that which has to do with the effects of a drug on my eyes or on my nervous system, and that is not the sort of explanation I want my example to provide at all. The explanation which in part is to specify the color of an object, say "That is red" or "That is yellow," must be consistent with the possibility of my seeing the color patch even though I am missing a large part of my nervous system. It must allow for a gap which could be filled by specialists in any number of different ways. So there can be nothing more to the explanation than, "That is blue and in some way this drug makes blue things look red." The specification of the color must be the main part, or at least an important part, of the explanation. And so in most cases the explanation must run "That patch is red, and that makes it look red to you." Or at least that must be the form of the explanation--with whatever technical fillings a physiologist would be expected to make.

Suppose that Wilson puts the drug in my coffee. He does not tell me that I am taking a drug, nor that a drug has anything to do with the experiment. He now takes me to the room with the colored patches and asks, "What color is that?" I say "That is red." Naturally puzzled, I ask "What is this all about?" Wilson explains, "That patch is really blue and I have put a drug in your coffee which makes blue things look red to you." "Well," I say, "that patch certainly does look red to me." Now surely here is an explanation of the right kind. I am told the color of the patch as an important part of an explanation of why it looks red to me. I did not know I was asking for an explanation of why a certain patch looks red to me, but certainly I shall accept it now that it has been given to me. But something is wrong here. What shall I say about it? I did not know that the patch looked red to me until I was given the explanation of why it looked red to me. Once I knew the explanation I knew that it looked red to me. Then this is not the sort of explanation I want at all. I certainly was not thinking that I had to know the color of the object in front of me or that I had to know that I had taken the drug in order to know how the color patch looked to me.

The difficulty with the example comes out more clearly when I try to alter it so that the explanation of why the patch looks red is that it is red. "What color is that?" Wilson asks. I say, "It's red." I ask, "What are you up to, anyway?" Wilson says, "That patch is red, and although I gave you a drug which affects your color vision it apparently has no effect on your vision of red." As a test, I shall try to imagine that Wilson says this: "So you see," he goes on, "the reason it looks red to you is that it is red, and although I gave you a drug which affects your color vision, the drug apparently has no effect on your vision of red." What shall I say of this? Do I acknowledge that the color patch looks red? If I realize that the drug is known to have pronounced effects on color vision, and that even Wilson is not sure whether it affects one's vision of red--if I realize that I am the first subject Wilson has tested--then yes, perhaps I shall say, "It certainly looks red: if you say that color patch is red, then I guess the drug has had no effect on my vision of red."

Now, has an explanation of its looking red to me been given by telling me that it is red and that apparently the drug has no effect? No. I used the fact that it is red and the fact that it looks red to me to show that the drug has had no effect. There can be no pretense of an explanation of why the patch looks red to me. To what question was Wilson addressing himself when he said, "The reason it looks red to you is that it is red--and the drug apparently has no effect on your vision of red"? I cannot imagine what the question could be, and so, I think, there is no way to make heads or tails or his remark.

Instead of the fatuous words which I put into his mouth, what would Wilson really be apt to say? He knows he gave me a drug which affects color vision. He asks me what color the red patch is and I say, "It's red." Wilson might say to himself, "Why does the red patch look red to him? The drug must have no effect on his vision of red." Wilson reasons in this way: "Given that the patch is red, and since I know he had a large dose of the drug, why then does it look red to him? The drug must not affect his vision of red." This is an explanation of why the patch looks red to me, but the patch's being in fact red plays no part in it.

Compare this with Grice's example:

X is standing in a street up which an elephant is approaching; he thinks his eyes must be deceiving him. Knowing this, I could quite naturally say to X, "The fact that it looks to you as if there is an elephant approaching is accounted for by the fact that an elephant is approaching,not by your having become deranged."[4]

Grice offers X the same inane appearance of an explanation that Wilson tried to offer me. Poor X thinks he has become deranged: he must think that he is subject to hallucination. And this seems to substantiate his worst suspicions: "My God. I seem to see an elephant in the street." What would Grice really say? I suggest something like this: "There is an elephant in the street. So you are not suffering an hallucination."

Of course I can ask why I changed my attitude from my original confident pronouncement "That is red" to "It certainly looks red to me." The answer seems to be that I came to realize that I had been given a drug which affects one's color vision. I came to realize that I could no longer trust my vision of color, that I was no longer in a position to make confident pronouncements about the color of things.

A causal explanation of "It looks red" is not as easy to come by as I had imagined it would be. And yet "It looks red" seems the most likely idiom with which to report something in perception which might be given a causal explanation. That still seems to me to be one of the most important insights in Grice's article "The Causal Theory of Perception." Yet Grice sometimes blurs this insight. Although most of his discussion is about "looks red" or "looks (some other color)," he allows himself to jump from "looks red" to "It looks to me as if a cat were before me" (pp. 105, 106),[5] "It looks to you as if an elephant were approaching" (p. 106), and many others, as though these cases could be dealt with in exactly the same way as the cases which involve uses of the phrase "looks red."

It is easy to sympathize with Grice's desire to get on, because before the causal theorist is finished he will have to take the jump from color-look to thing-look and many more besides. When it looks to me as if an elephant is approaching in the street, Grice suggests that it is plausible to explain to me that an elephant is in the street--and that this is the kind of explanation which is part of the analysis of "I see an elephant in the street." Even if this is correct, it

[4]H. P. Grice, "The Causal Theory of Perception," p. 106.

[5]These and all following are page numbers from the reprinted text in G. J. Warnock, ed., The Philosophy of Perception.

only begins the analysis of the perceptual act into sense-data. It must also be the case that there looks to me to be a street upon which it looks to me as if an elephant were approaching. Also, perhaps, there looks to me to be a village in which it looks to me that there is a street upon which it looks to me as if an elephant were approaching. Before the analysis is complete it must dispense entirely with its references to physical objects and replace them with mention of sense-data encompassed within my visual field--and caused by the relevant physical objects. If the analysis can be shown to work for one physical object, the elephant, perhaps it will work in the same way for the others, the street, the village, and so on, in progression. But still there is a big initial jump from red (or some other color) to the first physical object.

Grice does not think the jump deserves any special consideration; but it seems a most questionable jump indeed. And in taking the jump in such a casual way I think that Grice leaves behind his insight that "looks red" is a likely candidate for causal explanation. I shall consider some idioms of the kind which seem to introduce the "appearance" of "physical object." Grice uses the idiom "It looks to me as if..." as though it will give the required "sense-datum statement." This strikes me now as an unnatural and unlikely idiom, and so I shall begin, at least, with a consideration of the expression, "I seem to see...." As a beginning, consider these lines:

a. "I seem to see a gerbil in the corner," I say. And then I ask, "Why do I seem to see a gerbil in the corner?"

b. "Because there is a gerbil in the corner," someone answers.

Just as with the case of "looks red," these sentences can appear to support the weight of a causal theory of perception. Yet this is strange, because when I try to think of circumstances in which one would say "I seem to see..." I can come up with only one kind of circumstance. I shall tell a story which illustrates it. A prominent breeder of gerbils named Horace has an irrational fear that his gerbils may escape from their cages. He worries much too much about it, and is forever taking elaborate precautions to make certain that his animals have no way of escape. One day he thinks his fears have become real: he "sees" a gerbil outside the cages, standing on the corner of a rug. He rushes up to capture it, but when he reaches for the animal he finds that there is no gerbil there. As he reaches for the gerbil, it disappears before his eyes.

(Perhaps at first he says, "Where did the little bugger go?") The same thing happens the next day and the next, and finally it begins to happen several times every day. He goes to a doctor who tells him that he is having a hallucination brought on by neurotic anxiety about his gerbils. The doctor tells him that this is not a serious abnormality; and believing the doctor, Horace eventually makes an adjustment to his condition--as good an adjustment as one could make, I suppose. He expects to hallucinate gerbils occasionally, and he does occasionally hallucinate gerbils, but the hallucinations always pass quickly. They never cause him to lose his balance, but they do cause lapses in his concentration, and so they produce disturbing pauses in his work. Yet he always recovers quickly and completely.

Suppose that I am Horace's best friend and that he has told me all about his hallucinations: he has shared with me all his fears of escaping gerbils which led up to his hallucinations. One day Horace sits in his living room having graham crackers and milk with me, when suddenly he turns his head and looks fixedly across the room at the floor. He is obviously distressed. "Why," he asks, "do I seem to see a gerbil there?"

Now what is this question? In thinking what it is, I think I must imagine his tone of voice. "Why, oh why" seems to give the force of it. Although he knows he is having an hallucination, although he has been having this same hallucination for a long time, still when it comes it must be startling. After all these repetitions, he still reacts as though it were the real thing. I suppose it is hard for one to imagine how discomposing this sort of thing is unless he has suffered it himself. And so Horace asks, "Why do I seem to see a gerbil there?" I think I understand what he says all right. Why then should I dwell so on it? Because I need a philosophical measure of it; and however I am to characterize it for philosophical purposes, it is certainly not a request for an explanation--certainly not a request for any explanation of the kind that I am led to expect by my preoccupation with a causal theory of perception. If an explanation is in order, it may be a theological explanation that will best fit. Horace's question may be something like Jeremiah's: "Why do the wicked prosper?"

Now suppose that the story begins in the same way, but that it takes a different turn. Everything is the same up to the point where Horace looks up in distress and says to me, "Why do I seem to see a gerbil there?" At this point I look at the place Horace indicates, and a gerbil **is** there--as small as life--sitting up in the corner. What now do I say to Horace? "The reason you seem to see a gerbil there is that there is a gerbil there?" That is ridiculous. In asking "Why do I seem to see a gerbil there?" Horace was asking, if anything, how he is to bear this frighteningly realistic hallucination.[6] What shall I say to him? Maybe this will do. "I sympathize with you, Horace: I think I understand how distressing your hallucinations are. But this time you picked the wrong occasion for your lament because there really is a gerbil over there in the corner. I'll try to catch him for you."

Even though Horace has no question which calls for an explanation in terms of the presence of a real gerbil, can't I ask a question and then address myself to it? "Why does it seem to Horace that he sees a gerbil?" But how am I to find out what this question is that I am asking myself without putting it in the only situation I have been able to think of, namely that of Horace suffering from his gerbil hallucinations? And then what question is it? Am I asking for a better understanding of what an hallucination is like? Am I suggesting that Horace could make these hallucinations disappear if he exerted some kind of willpower? Or am I asking, "Why should my friend Horace have to suffer like this?" Without losing track entirely of what I am talking about, I cannot construe this question as a request for an explanation in terms of the presence of a gerbil. I cannot make heads or tails of any such purported explanation: "The reason you seem to see a gerbil is that there is a gerbil there."

Perhaps the reason I cannot find the question I want in this situation is that Horace's question "presupposes" hallucination. Does it have to? Suppose that sometimes when Horace "sees" a gerbil there is no gerbil there; but then sometimes when he sees a gerbil there is a gerbil there. Suppose that these two occur with equal frequency, and that he can never tell which is which. When he sees or thinks he sees a gerbil, he cannot tell what will follow. When he walks up to the right place, sometimes he finds a gerbil there and sometimes he does not. Now imagine Horace on one of these occasions which puzzle him so much. He is peering intently, his forehead is wrinkled. What does he say? "I seem to see a gerbil"? Surely "seem to see" is not in place there at all. "It looks to me as if a gerbil were there"? That is wrong, too. He might say

---

[6]Again, compare with Grice's example of the elephant.

that if he had some visual cue which led him to believe
that in this case he was not hallucinating. Suppose
that Horace asks, "Why does it look to me as if a gerbil were there?" Then I imagine that these might be
proper answers. "There is a gerbil there. There must
be some way you can tell the real thing from an hallucination." Or, perhaps, "There is a gerbil there.
Maybe your hallucinations are not as strong as they
once were: maybe they are going to go away." Suppose
that he simply says, somewhat hesitantly--as I
imagine he would--"I seem to see a gerbil there," or
"It looks to me as if a gerbil were there." Then
surely the right reply is "You're right. There is a
gerbil there."

This comes as a philosophical surprise, because
this last situation seems the one in which I am most
likely to find what the causal theory leads me to expect. I want a perceptual state of affairs which can
occur whether an object brings it about or not. And
then I want to be able to explain that state of affairs
as due sometimes to illusion, hallucination--but of
course most of the time as due to the presence of the
proper object in the proper place and at the proper
distance, exercising the usual causal influence. An
occasion when the perceiver cannot tell whether he is
having an hallucination or whether he is having a normal perception would seem to give exactly what I want.
The perceiver in this case would be expected to report
on that perceptual state of affairs--which may not be
caused by an object. Horace is such a perceiver, and I
cannot now think of any remark he might make which
would fit the niche the causal theory makes for me--
certainly no remark using the phrases "seem to see" or
"looks to me."

As I suspected, the jump from color-look to thing-
look is not as easy to make as Grice assumes it to be.
And I think I can see why. For "looks red" I can find
examples where something looks red to me and I do not
have the faintest idea what color the thing is: it
might in fact be red--or it might be any other color.
Thus, in saying of an object that it looks red, I am in
no way characterizing the object, and I am not voicing
any hunches I have about its color. It is for this
reason that I have the temptation to think that "looks
red" is a fact of the kind which could conceivably have
a causal explanation.

There is nothing analogous for my seeming to see a
gerbil or for its looking to me as if there were a
gerbil. After taking Wilson's drug and looking at the
color patches, I may say of one of the patches "It
looks red." And Wilson may reply "It is red--the drug

127

must not be taking effect." Wilson will not say, "You're right: it is red." But when poor Horace says "I seem to see a gerbil there" or "It looks to me as if a gerbil were there," a proper reply is "You're right. There is a gerbil there."

Perhaps I have been too impatient. Maybe the trouble with Horace's remarks "I seem to see..." or "It looks to me as if..." is that I have imagined him to initiate the remarks. I simply put him into a certain puzzling perceptual situation, and then make him say these words to me. I quite naturally take him to be telling me that he thinks, "This time there may be a gerbil there: I think perhaps I am really seeing a gerbil." I should not remain satisfied with just this remark. I ought to put him into a more theoretical mood, and urge him to comment on his "perceptual experience." What then would he say? "I have this strange visual experience. I cannot tell whether I am seeing a gerbil or hallucinating a gerbil. Why do you suppose I have this experience?" And what is the answer? Perhaps his doctor has given the answer. It is because he has had a neurotic fear about his gerbils escaping. This answer has nothing to do with a causal theory of vision. What answer would? "Sometimes you have it because you do in fact see a gerbil, and sometimes you have it because you are hallucinating a gerbil"?

I do not see any way one can find a place for a causal explanation here. "Looks red" is a much more likely candidate. I had better return and give it another run for its money.

II

In the examples I have imagined where a color patch looks red, I find a place for the question "Why does that look red (or yellow)?" And I expect to find answers to that question which will confirm a causal theory of perception, such as "The fact that it looks red (or yellow) to you is brought about by the fact that it is red (or yellow)." But the answers to the questions are not of this sort at all. It is a dangerous thing to undertake, I know, but is there any way I can make a useful synopsis of the questions and answers shown so far by my examples? The job is made a bit easier than it might be by the fact that only two of the examples are close enough to my causal-theory expectations to be worth serious review. So I can ignore the others. The two which remain are these: (1) I know I have taken a drug which affects color vision. I say "It looks red," and I ask "Why?" The answer: "It is red. The drug has not had time to take effect." (2) Same situation: but I say, "It looks yellow. Why?" Answer: "It is yellow. The drug does not affect vision of yellow."

In each case I have good reason to think that my color vision is abnormal. I think that it has been thrown off by a drug which affects color vision. So I think that the color judgments I should make--if I were not held back by my knowledge of the circumstances-- would be mistaken. Therefore I do not say "That is red" or "That is yellow." Instead I say "That looks red" and "That looks yellow." In each case I ask my question "Why?" thinking that Wilson will tell me something about the workings of the drug. I expect that Wilson will tell me the color of the patch I am looking at and then explain in terms of the drug's effects why the patch looks some color other than the color it is. So, of course, my questions arise from incorrect presumptions, and Wilson is unable to answer them in the way I anticipate. Instead, his answers are intended to correct the presumptions on which my questions are based. In one case, he tells me that the color patch is red, and that the drug must not yet have had its expected effect. That is, he tells me that although I have good reason to think that my color vision is affected, it is not: the drug apparently has not had its usual effect. In the other case he tells me that the color patch is yellow, and that the drug has no effect on vision of yellow. Although I have good reason to think that the patch on the wall is some color other than yellow, he tells me that it is not. Clearly my presumption that my color vision is apt to be unreliable explains my use of the word "looks." "It looks red," I say, and "It looks yellow." But when correcting my false presumptions, Wilson does not round on what I have said or suggest that any correction of what I have said is in order. He does not say, "It doesn't just look red to you, it is red," or "It doesn't just look yellow, it is yellow." Of course he doesn't offer any causal explanation of the facts that the patches look red or yellow to me. He cites the colors of the patches in the process of establishing or telling me that the visual situation is not abnormal in the way I thought it was. Had the situation been abnormal in the way I thought it was, then I am inclined to think that Wilson would have cited the colors of the patches and given me a causal explanation, say, of why the blue patch looked red or why the green patch looked yellow to me.[7] He might have told me how the drug changes the chemistry of the retina or how it brings about other related and relevant changes.

Why should I think a causal explanation in order when the situation is abnormal, but not in order when the situation is normal? I think that in a normal situation one does not ask for a causal explanation, and that is because Wilson and I both take for granted the causal explanation in a normal situation. That is a tempting way to look at it, and it is exactly the way Grice does look at it. He admits that it is "unnatural" to speak of the causes of sense-impressions in perfectly normal perceptual situations. But though it is unnatural to speak of such causes, there are such causes to be spoken of, and in speaking of them one can say something which is "correct and true, even if misleading..." (p. 106). Thus the causal theorist can indicate the nature of the causal connection he has in mind by giving examples, and these examples need not be of abnormal perceptual situations.

> The best procedure for the Causal Theorist is to indicate the mode of causal connection by examples; to say that, for an object to be perceived by X, it is sufficient that it should be causally involved in the generation of some sense-impression by X in the kind of way in which, for example, when I look at my hand in a good light, my hand is causally

---

[7]Though I am inclined to think that the causal explanation which is anticipated here is the kind anticipated by the causal theory of perception, it is not.

sponsible for its looking to me as if there were a hand before me.... (p. 105)

So, couldn't Wilson have said, "Its looking red to you is brought about by the fact that it is red--together, of course, with the normal behavior of light, the normal working of your eyes and nervous system, and so on"? Of course I didn't ask for such an explanation, and Wilson didn't give one--but again isn't that only because I already know that explanation, and Wilson knows that he would be a bore to give it to me? The fact that such an explanation would be trite and boring does not show it to be incorrect. Of course not. But what was it supposed to explain? The fact that a certain patch looked red to me. But exactly what fact is that? It looks as though, when I turn away from the examples, some fact slips in, the fact of something's looking red to me, a fact to be causally explained. How did that fact come to be? What reason have I for thinking of some such fact? Is there any more reason than this: I said "It looks red..." and Wilson did not correct me? Does that mean that I have a fact, its looking red to me, for which Wilson (or anyone) can offer a causal explanation? I said "It looks red" because I thought some drug had deranged my visual organs, and therefore I thought my judgment of the color of the patch--the one I should make if I had not had the drug--was apt to be wrong. Wilson tells me that my naive and unqualified judgment in this case would have been right, that my suspicions about my color vision, though understandable, are incorrect in this case. In other words, he tells me that everything is just as it would be if, in a normal situation, he had asked me "What do you see here?" and I had said "I see a circular red patch." So, shall I say that in fact I did **see** a red patch? Wilson says, "It is red. The drug has not yet had its effect." What if I now reply, "Then I do see the actual color of the patch?" To this Wilson will surely say "Yes." If I did see the red patch, I do not expect a causal explanation for that. I made it clear in the beginning that no causal explanation of seeing (in its entirety) can be given. "Its looking red to me" is the only thing involved in vision that is to be given a causal explanation.

But the reason I thought that seeing red could not be given a causal explanation was that it goes beyond looking red in a certain way, a way which involves human agency, a way which makes it quite senseless to speak of the causes of seeing. It goes beyond looking red by being a claim to know that the object seen is red. When I say that I see the pennant is red, I say that I know its color. But when I said to Wilson, "Then I do see the actual color of the patch," I did not make any claim to know the color of the object. I merely acknowledged Wilson's explanation that I was in a position to make such a claim if I wanted to. I was in a position to make such a claim but I did not know that I was. When I exempted seeing from causal explanation I was not thinking of this kind of seeing. One might say of this kind of seeing that I saw but I did not know that I saw. Usually when one sees he knows that he sees, and it was only seeing where one knows that he sees that I meant to exempt from causal explanation. But now that I think of it, this kind of seeing red, too, goes beyond looking red in a way that would rule out any causal explanation. Here when I say "I did see," I go beyond "It looks red" by saying that I was in a position to claim "It is red" (but I did not know it). Surely "I am in a position to make a claim" is not more subject to causal explanation than "I hereby make a claim."

One can easily think of an example where "It looks" can be compared with "I see..." in the sense of "see" I was first thinking of. Suppose that I go to Wilson's laboratory and am marched promptly into a room which is brightly lighted by clear glass skylights. There he points to a colored circle on the wall and asks, "What color is that?" I ask, "What is this all about?" Wilson says, "Nothing really. Everything is perfectly normal: I'll explain later. Can you see what color it is?" I look again at the circle and I am just about to say "Yes, I can see that it is red" when Wilson blurts out, "I can't lie. I had a drug put in your breakfast coffee, a drug which alters color vision." As soon as that remark sinks in I shall change the words "...see that it is red" or "it is red" which were forming on my lips to "It looks red." What has changed? Nothing I can see before me on the wall. Nothing of which I am aware about the circle there or its color. Nothing in my "visual field." Nothing of that kind comes in with "looks red" as opposed to "is red." Where then is that fact of its looking red, which can be given a causal explanation, as opposed to my seeing that it is red, which cannot be given a causal explanation? The difference between the time when I claim to see and the time when I say instead, "It looks" is the difference between whether I am in a position to make a confident judgment on the color of the patch or whether I am not. The difference is in what I thought or believed about the situation or state I was in. The difference is not perceptual, that is, not perceptual in the way I was inclined to think.

132

Suppose instead that Wilson really does put the drug in my coffee, and that it alters my color vision, so that when I look at a blue patch I quite honestly say "It looks red." Now surely Wilson can offer a causal explanation for the fact that it looks red to me when it is blue. I may ask "Why does it look red when it is blue?" and Wilson can say, "The chemical output of the red sensors in the retina is changed by the drug: they produce the chemical normally produced by the blue sensors, and that makes the red patch look blue to you." But suppose that Wilson had lied to me. He said he put a drug in my coffee but he did not. So, after looking at the red patch I say, "It looks red." There, then, is a red patch which looks red to me. Now surely if Wilson can give a causal explanation of the fact that a blue patch looks red to me, he can give a causal explanation of the fact that a red patch looks red to me. That is the way I am tempted to think in spite of the fact that I have not been able in this example to isolate the fact of "its looking red" as opposed to "seeing that it is red." After all, I really did see the color of the patch, even though I did not know that I did. But now it is clear that the temptation rests on a mistake. This time I have not failed to find a fact which can be given a causal explanation, I have found the wrong fact. The fact which can clearly be given a causal explanation is the fact of something's looking red to me when it is blue. The fact for which I expect a causal explanation is the fact of its looking red to me. That the patch is blue is not part of the fact for which I want an explanation: that it is blue is to be cited as part of the explanation of why it looks red. The same with something's looking red to me when it is red. Even if the fact of its looking red when it is red can be given a causal explanation, it is not the fact I want. The causal theory of perception leads me to believe that a causal explanation can be given for the fact that a thing looks red to me: the thing's being red is to be part of the causal explanation, not part of the fact to be explained.[8]

---

[8] I have already tried to construct examples where an explanation of the required form is given, and I have failed (p. 119ff).

I look at a color patch, but I do not know (or I have forgotten) its color. Wilson asks, "What color is this?" I say, "It looks red." Now I am to ask, "Why does it look red?" I am prepared, one must remember, for the answer "It is red" or "It is blue" or "It is

133

But surely there must be some situation in which the fact that a patch is red will straightforwardly be used as part of a causal explanation that the patch looks red. There must be some example which will at least show the source of the idea of a causal theory of perception. Consider this. Suppose that I have a disease of the eye: let us call it Henderson's disease. When one is suffering an attack of this disease red things look blue to him and blue things look red. The attacks come at irregular intervals and when they come they last for an hour or so. As an attack of the disease comes on, a person afflicted by Henderson's disease first experiences an intense itching in the eye lids and then a slight blurring of vision. These symptoms quickly pass and the gross abnormality of color vision follows: red things now look blue to him and blue things look red.

Suppose that I have had Henderson's disease for some time, and Wallace, who is an expert on Henderson's disease, is my doctor and also my friend. Incidents like the following have occurred many times. Wallace is walking down Jasper Avenue with me in Edmonton, Alberta, and he sees me rub my eyes and blink repeatedly. Shortly we pass a mailbox and I say, "That looks blue." "Yes," he says, "I thought it would. I saw the attack of Henderson's disease coming over you." On a later day another incident occurs. I rub my eyes and blink and so I am sure that I am having an attack of Henderson's disease, but as we pass the mailbox I say, "Why, the mailbox looks red--have they painted it blue?" "No," Wallace says, "the box is red--just as red as ever." I ask, "Then why does it look red?" My purpose, of course, is to put a causal explanation in his mouth: so suppose that he says, "The bio-tonic chemical transfusors in the D-cells of the retina must be again producing the usual D-oxyclino-pigment. We can confirm this at the laboratory by an infrared opthalmo-microphotograph of the retina." Suppose that Wallace later makes the photographs he mentions and from an examination of them he confirms that what he said is true. Now, surely, he has given a causal explanation of a red thing's looking red to me.

But is this explanation the kind required for a causal theory of perception? It is very technical and

---

yellow." I do not have the faintest idea what color it is; but I do know that my color vision is apt to be abnormal. In such a situation can I really ask, "Why does it look red?" Can I ask "Why does it look red?" without knowing what color it is?

134

full of specialist concepts. I do not expect the "concept" of vision to contain such technical details; I expect it only to allow a place for them--to contain the outline into which such details will fit. The concept of vision does not include details of what happens in the eyes or brain--or, for that matter, of what happens anywhere inside the skin. Suppose that Wallace's explanation of why the mailbox now looks red to me was wrong: the microphotographs did not show what Wallace thought they would. No repair or regeneration of my retinal tissue has taken place. All of the functional disorders associated with Henderson's disease are still there, and yet red things look red to me, as they ought not to. What would Wallace think? Perhaps that some changes have taken place elsewhere in the nervous system or in the brain, some changes which compensate for the abnormalities of my retina. Of course a physiologist like Wallace would follow this line of thought, but it is not forced upon him by the concept of vision. Yet something of the explanation must be forced on him. Regardless of how radically he may be wrong about the optical or physiological details, surely there is something he cannot be wrong about. He has said that the mailbox is red, and he has offered an explanation of why it looks red to me and in terms of something that is supposed to transpire between the box and my brain, namely in my eyes and optic nerves.

The explanation contains many extraneous details, but it is a causal explanation, and a causal explanation of the fact that a red thing looks red to me. So it gives me part, and the most important part, of what I have been looking for. But does it? What, after all, does it explain? It explains the fact of a red thing's looking red to me. And I attach importance to this because I think that looking red to me is something which is involved in my vision of red things generally. I think that when I see any red thing that the thing I see looks red to me; and I think that I can give a causal explanation of its looking red to me--but not, of course, of my seeing the red thing (for seeing a red thing goes beyond its looking red to me in ways that make a causal explanation out of order).

Consider another related example. Everything begins as it did before. I have Henderson's disease. My doctor and good friend, Wallace, is an expert in Henderson's disease, and he knows all about my case. But now I am alone as I have the symptoms of an impending attack, and I look with surprise at the mailbox I am passing. "Why, it looks red," I say to myself. I quickly look at the sky and find, also contrary to my

135

expectations, that it looks blue. Of course I think, and hope, that the disease has at last run its course and I am now back to normal again. I go about looking at familiar objects: my red ties, my blue jacket, my red sweater, my color slides of Crater Lake, of the cardinal flower, and of the blue Pacific; and in all of this my vision seems to be perfectly normal. The itching eyelids and blurred vision still come occasionally, but I learn that they are no longer followed by abnormal color vision. I notice, too, that the itching eyelids and blurred vision are less severe. I plan a demonstration for Wallace. I cut some red, blue, green, and yellow cardboard into small cards, and I take them to Wallace's office. I tell him truthfully that I have just had itchy eyelids and blurred vision. "Here," I say, "shuffle these cards and hold them up for me to see." So he holds them up one by one, asking "What color do you see here?" or "What color is this one?" And I get them all right: "That's blue, that's green, that's red," I go on. What does he think of this? I suppose he will say, "I'm glad to see that I can close the file on your case of Henderson's disease." Suppose now that I ask this question: "What happened?" or more explicitly, "What happened so that now when I look at red things I can see that they are red?" I imagine that Wallace will give the same answer he gave in the former example to the question "Why does the red mailbox look red to me?" His answer will be in terms of changes which have taken place in my eyes--the changes that apparently explain to a physiologist the return to normal after a bout with Henderson's disease.

Again, when I compare these two examples, the visual fact which I thought was causally explained seems to have slipped away. It is most elusive. In the first case, the red mailbox looked red to me and I asked "Why?" In the second case I could see that the red cards were red, and I asked "Why?" Apparently the same answer can be given to both "why" questions. This is not the way I expect it to be: I expect there to be a causal explanation for something's looking red to me but not for my seeing that something is red. What is the important difference between the two cases? In one I say "That looks red" and in the other I say "I see that that is red" or simply "That is red." In the second case I have convinced myself that I have overcome Henderson's disease, that my vision is again normal and reliable. I have gained enough confidence that I am willing to say that I can determine by vision the color of the objects before me. In the first case I expect my vision to be abnormal and am surprised that it is not. I do not know whether the grip of the disease has been overcome or whether I am experiencing a temporary one-shot remission. On the basis of my having just looked at the mailbox, I certainly cannot say that it is red: in fact I suspect at first that it has been painted blue. I cannot say that I see a red box: I have none of the confidence that goes with such a pronouncement. Yet everything is as it once was before I got Henderson's disease, and at the time I should confidently have said "It is red" or "I see a red box" (except that then there would have been no question). In short, as far as my perceptual apparatus or machinery goes, I am in a position to say what color the box is, but I do not—could not—know that I am in such a position. When I compare a situation where something looks red with one where I see that it is red, I cannot find any difference in what I am aware of in the two cases. I mean I am not aware in one case of anything different about the object or my perceptual field or anything connected with my perception. In saying this, I mean to be making the kind of comment I might make to an eye doctor or a physiological psychologist: someone who is interested in visual abnormalities or in the details of visual phenomena. Suppose that I am having some visual problems: I have blurred vision sometimes. I go to an eye doctor. He shows me a chart with many drawings and asks me to comment on it, and I decribe some of the details for him. Then he says "Take off your glasses, and look again. Are you aware of anything about your vision now?" I say "Yes, the edges of the drawings are blurred and there are little white dots floating in the corners of my field of view." In some such manner I might be aware of something different at a time when a thing looks red as compared to a time when I see that it is red. It might have a color fringe. I might see light stars blurring my field as I do when my eyes are wet. When a thing looks red it may look transparent. But there are no differences of these kinds. I am not aware of any difference in the object or my visual field. I cannot in any such way distinguish an object which I say "looks red" from one which I see and about which I confidently say "It is red."

In one case I look at a mailbox; in the other case I look at a card. If I look carefully I can make out the nature of the surface of the mailbox and of the card. One surface is irregular; the other smooth. One surface "looks red," I say. The other "is red," or I say "I see that that is a red rough surface." Where then is the "looking red" in one—which might be causally explained, perhaps in terms of the action of light on my eyes as it is reflected from the surface? Seeing the red surface, I know, cannot be given a causal explanation. And since I am not aware of anything of a perceptual nature in "looking red" which is different from "seeing red," I am inclined to conclude that there is nothing in "looking red" which can be given a causal explanation. But Wallace does give a causal explanation of the mailbox's looking red--and he gives the same causal explanation of my seeing that the card is red. How am I to account for this?

This suggests that I am giving an incorrect interpretation of the facts--or the examples. (After all, summarizing or moralizing about examples is always a dangerous business.) This suggests that the proper interpretation of the examples is, after all, the very one the causal theory leads me to give. The difference between "looking red" and "seeing red"--if you like--is not perceptual. The difference is in the degree of confidence with which I pronounce on the color of the object. And this shows that two things are involved in both "it looks" and "I see": the "look" of the object, and the degree of confidence I have about the color of the object. Hence the same causal explanation can be given in each situation, but in each it is an explanation only of the look of the object. Specifically, it is an explanation of the object's looking red to me.

As it stands, that cannot be right: my confidence in pronouncing on the color of the object is not what distinguishes "seeing red" from "looking red." Suppose that I have suffered from Henderson's disease for years and am convinced that I shall never be cured. Suppose that I have had all the signs of an impending attack of the disease and am sure that I am now suffering an attack. Now I see a man's sweater which looks blue to me. If called upon, I shall very confidently pronounce it to be red. Now nothing of that kind is involved in my seeing that one of the cards held by Wallace is red. In pronouncing confidently that the sweater is red I first note that it looks blue, and then I conclude that the sweater is red because I know that my Henderson's disease makes red things look blue. When I see that the card is red, I do not note first that it looks red, and then conclude that it is red because my Henderson's disease has been cured. After I have recovered from the disease and regained my natural confidence, I do not think that it looks red at all; I should think that it looked red only if I still had fears that I might be having another attack of Henderson's disease. And when I say the card is red I do not conclude that it is red. I should conclude that an object was red only during the initial stages of my recovery from the disease--at a time when I am not quite sure that my vision has

138

returned to normal, but when I have some reason to think that it has. In such a situation I might tentatively conclude that the object I was looking at was red and then ask someone with normal vision about its color in order to make sure that I was right.

When, after looking at one of the cards, I say to Wallace that it is red, I have complete confidence in my ability to pronounce on the color of the thing. For a person who has just recovered from Henderson's disease, that confidence comes from his certainty that he has recovered from the disease, which is to say, it comes from his certainty that his vision is again completely normal. But for most of us--who have never had Henderson's disease and have never even heard of it or of anything like it--our confidence in pronouncing on the colors of things does not come from any certainty that we have recovered from such a disease. Our confidence comes from the fact that we have no reason at all to suspect that anything is abnormal. No, it is misleading to suggest that our confidence comes from anything. It is misleading to suggest that we have confidence in our ability to perceptually determine the colors of things. We simply do what we have always done: we do the usual, normal thing.

What makes these examples important, I think, is that they bring the causal theory of perception out into the open. When I consider the kind of examples I have been appealing to[9] I am tempted to think that when looking at a red thing I can say or think either of two things. If I am very confident and I want to express that confidence, I shall say "I see that that is red...." But if I am not completely confident or if I want to be cautious, I shall say "It looks red." I am inclined to think that saying "I see..." goes beyond saying "It looks...." To say "I see..." is in effect to say at least these two things at once: "It looks red" and "It is red." (Of course if the causal analysis is correct, it is to say more than these two things.) If I say of one of the cards "I see a red card" and it turns out that the card is not red, then I shall cancel half of my joint assertion and put in its place a weaker pronouncement. I shall say, "Well, it looks red." Of course. I do not generally lack confidence or feel that I should pull my neck in, and so generally I say "I see..." or "It is... rather than "It looks... to me."

But can this be right? When everything is

---

[9]These are the only examples, I think, which give the causal theory a chance for success.

perfectly normal, can I look at my red felt hat hanging on the wall hook, and think "That looks red"? Is it just a matter of being cautious, of not being confident? How can I lose my natural confidence? Perhaps I do not have to: I can imagine it away. I shall imagine that I am in the frame of mind of a person who has just been cured of Henderson's disease. Or I shall imagine that I am in the frame of mind of a person who has taken one of Wilson's vision-altering drugs. Then I shall say "That looks red." Of course that is not right: I shall not say "That looks red"; I shall only imagine myself saying "That looks red." I can say, that is, speak the words, but they have their home in my imagination--not here in my living room as I stare at my red hat. If someone overheard me speak the words, he would wonder why I had said such a thing.[10] And I should have to tell him that I was imagining myself saying those words in a story: that I had spoken them aloud from my imagination.

I ought to be able to look at the red hat and think, straight off, "That looks red." It should be easy. I look at that hat: I see that it is red. Now I have only to take away the confidence I have in seeing the color of it. Nothing will change in my field of view: nothing that I am looking at will be different. I shall just subtract the confidence I have that red is the color of the hat. Instead it is the color it looks to be "It looks red." It sounds as though it should be easy to subtract my confidence, but I cannot do it. My confidence--if that is what it is--does not seem to be the adventitious thing the causal theory represents it as being. It does not seem to be just an addition to "It looks," so that I can take it away and get to the pure and simple "It looks."

Perhaps, though, I am misrepresenting the requirements of the causal theory. Whenever I see that something is red it must look red. Seeing red must consist of a thing's looking red and something more. I have represented that more as confidence in my ability to determine the color of the object. And consequently I have represented "looks red" as expressing lack of confidence. And of course one cannot have confidence and lack of confidence at the same time. Natural confidence is not something which will go away at philosophical bidding. And if it did go away then I

---

[10]The philosophical significance of the fact that someone, in these circumstances, would be nonplussed by my words I consider at length in Essay 4, "Does It Look the Color It Is?"

could no longer say "I see that it is red." And I must be able to see that it is red and have it look red at the same time. "I see that it is red" surely implies that I am confident that it is red. But does "It looks red" imply in the same way that I am not certain of its color? The causal theory must have it that it does not. It must be because I have reason to be uncertain about the color of the object, because I am not sure that I can tell the color by looking, that I say (or think) "It looks red." The fact that I am uncertain makes me comment on the color it looks rather than the color I am sure it is. And if that is the way it is supposed to be, then I ought to be able to comment on the color it looks at any time at all. This, of course, is what Grice means by saying "the implication is cancellable" (p. 92). I ought to be able to say "It looks red, but of course I can see that it is red." I ought to be able to look at my hat and think "It looks red but of course I can see that it is red." I must confess that I cannot do this.

But can't I do this after I have been cured of Henderson's disease? Isn't that just what that example shows? I go before Wallace with my color cards and I pronounce confidently "I see that that is red." And so on. Couldn't I just as well have said "That looks red," "That looks blue," and so on, even when I was sure that I saw the colors? I should have shown Wallace that I was cured in either case. Does this show that whenever I see something I can always think "It looks red"? I do not see how it does. I can say to Wallace, "It looks red", because that is what he is prepared to have me say. I can say "It looks red," because that is what I have been saying in similar circumstances. I can clearly remember how it once was. But outside of the part I play in this very curious example, I have never heard of Henderson's disease; I have no doctor who has treated me for it; I certainly cannot remember what it was like. I cannot therefore say or think "That looks red" when I see that something is red. The best I can do is imagine saying or thinking "That looks red" when I vividly create in my mind the conditions of example.

How can I take the example of my recovery from Henderson's disease as showing what the causal theory requires? I walk down the street with Wallace and show all the signs of an attack of Henderson's disease. Then, pointing to the mailbox, I say, "It looks red. Has it been painted blue?" Wallace says, "No. It's as red as ever." Suppose I say now, emphasizing what I say, "It looks red." This is the start of my realization that I no longer have Henderson's disease, and

141

when I am completely convinced that my vision has returned to normal, I stand before Wallace and as he holds up my color cards, I say "That's red," "That's blue...." And I tell him that I am reporting the colors that I actually see. Is it quite clear that in the first case I report the fact of something's looking red to me, and that in the second case I report that same fact but also go beyond it? Or isn't it rather more nearly the other way around? The second is like one of the normal, everyday situations in which I find myself looking at something and pronouncing on its color. Then, depending on the situation, I say "It's red," or "I see that it is red." Then I am concerned with nothing relevant except the object I see, a card, a beetle, a flag, a bird--and I am aware also, but less sharply aware, of the surroundings of this thing and other things that may also be in my visual field. But I am not aware of anything else--the way things look to me. This is the starting place. Sometimes, when I have reason to suspect my color vision while looking at something, I say "It looks red." In saying this I am not adding something, I am holding something back. Nothing need be different in my field of view or in what presents itself to my eyes. Perhaps the words "I see..." or "It's red" come to my lips but I stop them before they come out. I suspect something connected with my vision of the object is not normal--perhaps my eyes, perhaps the light--something which prevents me from seeing the thing as it is. So I say, "It looks red" which comes to something like this: everything is just as it is when I should say "That's red" except that I suspect something is wrong-- something which affects my vision or my ability to see the color of the thing. There is no fact--"Its looking red" or "Its looking red to me"--which I now report on. There is nothing I am concerned with except the color of the object, and I am trying to report on the color of the object. I would report on the color of the object, too, except that I feel that something is amiss about the situation, something which affects my visual powers; and so I am not sure that I am able to make a correct report on the color of the object. Or perhaps I am sure that I am not in a position to correctly report on the color of the object.

Now, as I think it, this interpretation seems more plausible; but then when I am in another frame of mind, the other interpretation, though difficult, can seem a real possibility. Thus, for the same examples, for the same visual data, there seem to be two possible inter- pretations, either one of which will do equal justice (or equal injustice) to the facts. The first is this:

142

the judgment "It's red," when based on vision, is analyzable into three parts, "The object looks red to me," "The object is red," and "Its being red brings it about that it looks red to me." The second interpretation is this: the judgment "It's red," based on vision, is a simple unanalyzable perceptual judgment. Along with this view there goes a certain interpretation of "looks red." "It looks red" comes to something like this: "Everything I am visually aware of is just as it is when I correctly say (or think) 'It's red,' but I have reason to believe that something is perceptually abnormal, something about me or about the situation I am in."

On first thought one might be inclined to think that an appeal to the child's acquisition of visual abilities and associated verbal abilities would settle the matter in favor of the second interpretation. Surely in childhood we are able to talk of the colors of things before we are able to talk about the colors which things look to us. We come to say "That's red" before we come to say "That looks red to me." One might, therefore, be inclined to think that "It's red" is simpler than "It looks red."

But of course this fact does not show that "It's red" is simpler than "It looks red to me" in the right way. Undoubtedly there are many reasons why we come to say "It's red" before we come to say "It looks red," but none of these would weigh against the view that "It's red" has a great hidden complexity. A child need not be aware of the logical complexity of his utterances when he acquires them. Nor, in fact, need he ever—even in adulthood—become aware of the hidden logical complexity of his most commonplace judgments. Philosophers who give something like a sense-datum, causal analysis of visual judgments have almost always insisted that only philosophers become fully aware of this hidden complexity—and then only on rare occasions.

When presenting the second interpretation—that "It's red" is simple and unanalyzable—I have suggested an argument which might seem to be in its favor. When I am looking, say, at a red pennant, and when I am asked to pronounce on its color, I am not aware that it looks red to me. Rather, I say simply "It's red," and I think no more than "It's red." When I am philosophically inclined toward a sense-datum interpretation of "It's red," I will think that I have given an incorrect interpretation of my lack of awareness of anything which might be called "its looking red" or "its red look." I have been mistakenly thinking that the fact of its looking red to me was to be something I could be

143

aware of which is different from and distinct from its being red. Whereas--according to the sense-datum interpretation--what I am aware of when I see that something is red is just the fact that it looks red to me. This is all that is ever given to perceptual awareness. Because, in most circumstances, I could not say "It look red to me" without creating confusion, I incorrectly conclude that it does not in fact look red to me. Because I should not say "It looks red," I should also not think "It looks red"; and from this I reach the incorrect conclusion that there is nothing presented to me which is its looking red. Whereas--according to a sense-datum interpretation--there is, in most circumstances, nothing I am aware of when looking at a red pennant other than its looking red to me. Its being red, as opposed to its looking red, is not something a person can be perceptually aware of while looking at a red pennant. The judgment that the pennant is red goes beyond what is given to perceptual awareness.

Compare the content of your perceptual awareness in a situation where you see that a pennant is red with the perceptual content in a situation where the pennant looks red to you and you can see they are the same. This fact--the sameness of perceptual awareness--is no more an argument for the unanalyzability of "It's red" than it is for the sense-datum and causal analysis of it. In short, it is not an argument for either interpretation.

III

But I can observe this air of neutrality between the two interpretations only so long as I confine myself to the first part of the sense-datum or causal analysis. As soon as I consider the analysis as a whole, there are insuperable objections against it. "It's red" (as a judgment of vision) could not come to "It looks red and it is red and its being red makes it look red."

Consider the first two parts of the analysis. "It is red" is equivalent to "It looks red" and "It is red." One part of the analysis of "It is red" as a judgment of vision is "It is red." How am I to understand the "It is red" which is part of the analysis? Is it, too, a judgment of vision? Then, of course, it will have the same analysis. So "It is red" will become "It looks red and it looks red and it looks red and so on and so on." So if a visual judgment on the color of a thing came to something like this, we should never be able to determine the color of a thing by looking at it, because we could never advance past the look of the thing to the color of the thing itself.

The "It is red" as part of the analysis of a judgment of vision must, therefore, be understood in some other way. But that other way is most difficult. I do not believe that I am able to understand it; so I do not believe that I can expose it and think through this part of the causal theory. Therefore, I shall hurriedly do the best I can. I shall rush through it in order to see what is on the other side.

"It is red" cannot be a judgment of vision. Therefore, it must be understood in this way. It looks red and it is a fact that it is red, but the fact that it is red must be determined by bringing to bear on "It looks red" information which is not obtained by reporting on what one is aware of when the thing looks red to him. This may sound paradoxical. It may sound as though I could not just look at a thing and determine by looking that it is red. Of course the causal theorist does not want to deny that I can, by looking, determine the color of a thing. When I look at something, he thinks, I invariably bring some knowledge to bear on the object of which I am aware--knowledge which I do not obtain from my awareness.

Suppose I confine myself to what I learn just from my perceptual awareness. I look at a red hat and I report "That looks red." As soon as I say "It is red" or "I see that it is red" I have gone beyond what is based on my perceptual awareness. The question, of course, is: how do I go beyond? The answer of the

145

causal theory is this: I make an inference which is based on data other than those given to me in perceptual awareness.   This is not an inference in the sense that it is something I may at any time be called upon to justify.   It is an inference only in the sense that I make a judgment which goes beyond the data on which it is based, and it has a logical structure which I can reconstruct and represent.   It is part of the purpose of the casual theory to do just that.

How, then, do I make the inference from "That looks red" to "That is red"?   I know, as all of us do, that when things look red they generally are red.   And I know this as the logical converse of a causal principle: red things generally bring it about (causally) that they look red.   Thus from "It looks red" and this principle I conclude--without being conscious of any inference, of course--that the hat is red.

Immediately, I wonder how anyone could ever have learned this by looking at the things.   At this point the sense-datum, causal theorist will want to remind me that the sense-datum, causal analysis does not tell us something we learn from experience.   Being an analysis, it makes explicit what is involved in saying "It is red" and so, in some sense, it spells out what we understand in a compressed way in saying "It is red."   "It is red" means, in some sense, "It looks red and it is red and its being red causes it to look red."   Part of what is implied by the analysis is the general principle that red things generally bring it about that when we look at them they look red.   The principle on the basis of which we infer from "looks red" to "is red" is derived from this.   That derived principle is this: things which look red generally are red.   When we see something which looks red we infer--without being conscious that we make an inference--that it is red.   The point of the analysis is to represent this "unconscious inference" as causal: we infer from effect to cause.   And the principle on which the inference is based is not a principle we learn from experience, and hence it is not something we learn from awareness in perception.

The fact that I can make it seem plausible that we have such a general a priori principle comes, in part, from the fact that I have been concerned only with colors and with how colors look.   So it might seem that the general principle is "Anything which is $\emptyset$, looks $\emptyset$," from which we can get, by specification, "Anything which is red, looks red," "Anything which is yellow, looks yellow," and so on.   But, of course, this will work only for colors, and a few other visual, surface characteristics.   It will not do for "round."   One

thing I have learned well from sense-datum philosophers
is that round objects (like pennies, that is) generally
look elliptical. Of course elliptical objects
generally look elliptical also. Rectangular objects
look rhomboidal, parallel lines look convergent, the
curved edges of columns look straight. Etc. Etc. How
many such principles are required? Can I really
imagine that they are all to be unfolded from "the
concept of vision"?

But, even if we have the specific a priori principle that red things generally look red, it remains true
that not every red thing will look red and not every
thing which looks red will be red. George says, "Stand
right here beside me and look at the paint mark on that
dead tree. Something makes it look funny." I do as
George directs, and he asks, "What color do you think
it is?" I say, "It looks purple." George says, "Now
let's walk up and get a good look at it." So we walk
right up in front of it and now I say, "Why, it's red;
I wonder why it looks purple from over there?" How
does the sense-datum, causal theorist explain such an
example? In his terms the example must be characterized something like this. From the fact that the paint
mark looks purple I am inclined to say that it is purple, but I do not allow this inclination to voice
itself. I am impelled to make an inference; but I do
not make it. I do not say that it is purple because I
have been alerted that something may be abnormal about
the perceptual situation. Instead, I confine myself to
a looks-statement, but at the same time I am ready to
operate on the principle that a thing is generally the
color it looks to be. Now I approach the tree and find
that the paint mark "looks red." And I promptly and
confidently conclude that it is red. This time
presumably I give free rein to my inclination based on
the general principle, and without hesitation voice the
conclusion, "It's red," or, "Now I see that it is red."

What is the crucial difference? How does the causal theorist account for the fact that I give my inclination free rein now but not before? Well, before,
George alerted me that something might be abnormal.
But, of course, I do not always have to be alerted by
George or by anyone in order to know or to suspect that
something is fishy about the perceptual situation: the
light is strange, 1 have taken a drug, the object is
very distant, I am in the midst of a dust storm, it is
very foggy, my eyes are watering, and so on. I know
how to watch out for these and other things which
affect my vision, and I know pretty well how to recognize a situation where these factors which produce

distortions and aberrations are not present. How did I
learn all of this? I certainly cannot unfold all of
this from the causal analysis. The causal analysis may
imply some general principles on which I operate, but
how does it explain the way in which I determine the
colors of things in specific cases?[11] In spite of
the fact that the paint mark looks purple I can walk up
to it, look at it and confidently pronounce that it is
red. The voice of the causal theorist tells me that
even now, in this case where I am so confident, it
looks red to me and it is red and I determine that it
is red by bringing in something I do not get from my
awareness of things. His explanation of how I determine that it is in fact red is this: it looks red
to me and I make a causal inference sanctioned by the
general principle that things which are in fact red
generally look red. But this cannot explain how I confidently determine in this particular case that this
particular paint mark before me is in fact red.
    Grice comments on the general principle involved in
this inference by way of answering an objection to the
causal theory. An objection often made to the causal
theory of perception is that it makes it impossible to
infer from effect to cause because there is no way one
could establish the necessary connection between them.
One can infer from smoke to fire only because he is
acquainted both with smoke and fire and hence can discover the connection between them. But one cannot similarly be acquainted with a "sense-impression" and the
"physical object" which is its cause. Against this and
in defense of the causal analysis of perception, Grice
says:

> [The smoke-fire] model should never have been
> introduced; for whereas the proposition that
> fires tend to cause smoke is supposedly
> purely contingent, this is not in general
> true of propositions to the effect that the
> presence of a material object possessing
> property P tends to (or will in standard cir-
> cumstances) make it look to particular
> persons as if there were an object possessing
> P. It is then an objectionable feature of the
> sceptical argument that it first treats non-
> contingent connexions cannot be established
> in the manner appropriate to contingent

---

[11]For each specific case is to be a case where I
infer from "looks Ø" to "...is Ø" and the inference is
to be from effect to cause.

connexions as if they were contingent, and then complains that such connexions cannot be established in the manner appropriate to contingent connexions. (pp. 111-112)

But Grice nowhere explains how in any particular case I could know that an object's looking red was caused by its being red. If you like, the objection I am trying to make is this: The causal analysis does not give a correct understanding--or indeed any understanding--of the perceptual judgment, "It is red."

And, of course, Grice does not think that the general non-contingent principle will explain the particular cases:

The non-contingent character of the proposition that the presence of a red...object tends to make it look to particular people as if there were something red... before them does not, of course, in itself preclude the particular fact that it looks to me as if there were something red before me from being explained by the presence of a particular red object.... (pp. 111-112)

Here Grice is thinking that the particular explanation will be an empirical matter.

...it is a non-contingent matter that corrosive substances tend to destroy surfaces to which they are applied; but it is quite legitimate to account for a particular case of surface-damage by saying that it was caused by some corrosive substance. In each case the effect might have come about in some other way. (p. 112)

The fact that it looks red in this particular case might be brought about by the fact that it is red, but it also might be brought about by the fact that it is blue. In a particular case Grice allows for the fact that a thing's looking red can be accounted for by the fact that it is red, but he does not discuss the question of how I could ever be in a position to give that explanation. I cannot appeal to something I have learned from experience, for I do not understand how I could ever learn from experience that any particular thing is red at all. Neither could anyone else help me out. No one could tell me that the thing is red. Another person could look at it carefully but he could

149

only discover by looking at it that it looked red to him.

How exactly can I determine that any particular object is red? The causal theorist might want to argue that there is more to the general principle than I (following Grice) have so far allowed. The inference which it sanctions is a causal inference: I infer from effect to cause. The principle as I have stated it is to the effect that things which look red generally are red, which is based on the principle that red things generally bring it about that they look red. The principle should more accurately be stated in terms of the causal theory. The principle actually at work must be this: red things look red when the causal production of the fact that the things look red to me is normal.[12] This principle makes it out that I determine the true color of things by establishing that the causal conditions involved in my perception of them are normal. So I apply this principle to the particular case I have at hand (or rather, before my eyes). I determine that the paint mark on the tree before me is red by determining that the causal conditions of its looking red to me are normal. The general principle is derived from the causal analysis of perception, and so it will not contain any specific details as to the causal transaction between the thing seen and my seeing of it. It can contain no more than is a proper part of the "conception of vision." But in applying the principle to any specific case I may need to use causal details which are not part of the "concept." After all, the causal analysis does not preclude me from doing this. But when I see that the paint mark on the tree before me is red, I may know nothing at all about the details of any causal transaction. I know that the paint mark looks purple to me from over there where I first stood, but I do not know why. Now that I stand before it in clear light I can see that it is red--and I may know no more about any causal transaction now than I did in the case when it looked purple. (The causal theorist, of course, will say that it looks red even when I see that it is red.) In some cases, though, I do have to decide that the light is right, that an hallucinogenic drug has worn off, that I have been cured of Henderson's disease, that the colors surrounding a thing do not materially affect my vision of it, and matters of that kind. That is, I do know of

---

[12]Note that Grice's statement of the principle does include the parenthetical phrase "in standard circumstances" (p. 111).

many different things which affect my visual abilities, and when I suspect the presence of one of them I may have to rule it out. But, sometimes I shall know that something is wrong only because a thing looks different to other people from the way it looks to me. Everything may seem to be normal but other people make it obvious to me that it is not. In fact the only way I can discover what conditions significantly affect my visual abilities is to learn what conditions produce visual abnormalities in me. And by a visual abnormality I can understand nothing except that which makes my visual perceptions differ from those of other people. I do not understand "normal vision" to be that which is produced by certain causal transactions; I understand it to be vision which is the same as that of other people. The "concept of normality" (if you like to speak that way) is not causal.

The plain truth is that we do not determine that a thing is red by first determining that the causal conditions are normal. Rather it seems to be the other way around. If we suspect something is abnormal, we can determine that it is normal by noting that the thing looks to us to be the color that in fact it is. If we suspect ourselves to be abnormal, we can determine that our vision is normal by asking others what they see.[13]

At this point the causal theorist may want to say that "It is red" should be analyzed as "It looks red to most observers under normal conditions" and add that "normal conditions" is not meant to be understood causally, but is to include whatever conditions are relevant, both causal and non-causal. Then the first two parts of the analysis of "It is red" as a judgment of vision would become "It looks red (to me now)" and "It looks red to most observers under normal conditions." But this is not a possible way out for the sense-datum, causal-theory philosopher, for even though it might do for the first two parts of the analysis, it will

---

[13]Also I have learned that my judgments of colors may be thrown off by things that are not part of the causal generation of vision of all. I may have visual aberrations due to fear or I may believe that I see something only because I am overeager to see that thing. But surely these so-called psychological aberrations produce some physiological changes, changes in the eye or optic nerve or the brain—someplace in the causal genesis of vision? Well, perhaps they do; perhaps not. This question certainly is not to be decided by examining the "concept of vision."

certainly not do for the third, the causal part. The third part would then become: "The fact that it looks red to most observers under normal conditions brings it about that it looks red to me now." This is hardly what I (or anyone) had in mind when I thought of the causal analysis, viz. "Its looking red is brought about by the fact that it is red." So the sense-datum, causal interpretation of "I see a red..." or "That is red" is not, after all, a possible interpretation.

* * *

But Wallace did give me a causal explanation of the fact that the mailbox looked red to me, and after my vision had returned to normal he gave the same causal explanation of the fact that I said the true colors of the test cards I had prepared for him. These explanations suggested and sustained me in the causal interpretation of vision: in each case he must be explaining causally the fact that a red thing looked red to me. So I had best re-examine Wallace's explanations. Perhaps I should not have let them pass as examples of the kind of causal explanation needed by the causal theory of perception.

I had become used to Henderson's disease, and I expected the red mailbox to look blue. I was surprised--and pleased, too, I suppose--to discover as I walked by the mailbox with Wallace that it looked red. I asked Wallace, as an expert on Henderson's disease, why the mailbox looked red to me. And he explained that in all likelihood certain changes were taking place in my eyes. Later he confirmed that these changes had taken place. Did Wallace really offer a causal explanation of the kind the causal theory of perception leads one to expect? What kind of explanation is it? Perhaps I can better bring this out by asking, "How did Wallace reason?" From a knowledge of the literature on Henderson's disease, and from experience with many cases of the disease, Wallace must have known that recovery from the abnormality in color vision is sudden. He must also have known that once color vision has been restored to normal it remains normal--even though the other syptoms, itching eyelids, blurred vision and the rest, may persist for a longer time. In addition to these things, he knew what changes in eye tissue account for the peculiar visual abnormality associated with Henderson's disease, and so he knew what regeneration or repair of tissue would be required to restore vision to normal. Therefore he had good reason to believe that my vision had returned to

152

normal. I did not. I certainly did not have the kind of reason which would give me the confidence necessary to report on the colors of things as a normal person would. After many days I regained that confidence. At that time I could go to Wallace with the color cards I had prepared and say, as he turned them up, "That's red," "That's blue," and so on. Then I might ask "Why can I now see red and blue as they are?" or "Why is my vision normal now?" And he would give me the same explanation that he gave in answer to my question, "Why does that red mailbox look red to me?"

When I am under the influence of the causal theory, I am led to believe that he gives the same explanation in each case because in each case he explains only why something **looks** red. Now it seems clear that in each case he does give a causal explanation for the same fact; but it is not the fact that something looks red to me: it is the fact that my vision has been restored to normal after I have suffered from Henderson's disease. He is not at all concerned with explaining the fact that something looked red to me as opposed to the fact that I saw that it was red. He is surely not troubled by the necessity to isolate "the color-look of things" because that is the only fact he can causally explain. In short, he brings to bear some of the details of the optico-physiological account of vision in order to account for a certain kind of visual ailment and also in order to account for its cure. He explains the fact that my vision had been restored to normal; and so, of course, that fact had to be apparent to him. And he apprised himself of the fact that my vision was normal in the same way I did. I looked at colored things and told him what colors I saw. When I reported the same colors as he saw and the same as others saw, then he knew, as I knew, that my color vision was again normal.

He did give a causal explanation of why my vision was abnormal, and he gave a causal explanation of why my abnormal vision had returned to normal. And I have been tempted to conclude from this that he could give a causal explanation of normal vision, and that this causal explanation would fill in the form of the causal theory of vision. And of course he can give an explanation of normal vision, but it does not fill in the form of the causal theory. He might say "The reason you see red when there is a red object before you is..." and then go on to tell about the wavelength of red light and its effect on the retina, and so on, giving the relevant details of the optico-physiological theory. But surely he will not say "The reason you see a red object is that there is a red object which reflects light of a certain wavelength..." and so on. What is the curious beginning of this explanation: "The reason you see a red object is that there is a red object"? What could I make of it? Is it any more than a misleading way of saying that he is concerned here with the explanation of normal vision? He did not establish by any laboratory experiments that one normally sees a red object when there is a red object clearly before him. That is simply what we do when we are normal. He asks--if you like--why that is a fact, and he offers a causal explanation. But that fact stands outside the causal explanation.

At last, I am brought up to that question about the causal theory I have tried hard to avoid, namely, what was I thinking of when I thought of a causal explanation of vision? This suggests that I must raise and answer such questions as "What is a causal explanation?" and "What is causality?" and, quite naturally, I have tried to avoid these apparently hopeless philosophical dead-ends. I assumed that if I turned to the physiologist, I should find clear-cut examples of causal explanations. If a physiologist does not give a causal explanation of vision, where would I ever find such an explanation? There is no reason why I should risk becoming lost by trying to find some general account of causal explanations when I can turn to a paradigm case, and moreover just the case that is relevant.

The physiologist does give the relevant causal explanations; but guided by the causal picture of perception I seem to have an entirely false conception of the explanations he gives--or ought to give. What explanation does he give? If I have a specific visual abnormality, he will tell me the causes of that abnormality. If red things look blue to me he will tell me what causes that phenomenon. If I have grown to expect my vision to be abnormal in some specific way, and to my surprise it is not, a physiologist will tell me what causes the return to normal. If I expect red things to look blue because I think I have a disease which affects vision, he will explain what has happened to cure that disease. The physiologist is able to give these explanations because he knows what normally transpires when one sees that a red thing is red and he knows what changes in the normal occurrences can make a red thing look blue. He is able to give a causal explanation of why a red thing looks blue or why it suddenly--and perhaps unexpectedly--looks red again, because among other things he knows what takes place when a normal observer sees that a red thing is red. The physiologist has as the basic item in his repertoire of explanations a fairly complete account of what occurs in

154

normal vision. This of course is the account which I have read about in popular science books and Sunday newspaper supplements. It surely is the very paradigm of a causal account. It goes like this. Red objects reflect light of such and such wavelengths. (Other colors are other wavelengths, of course.) Red light is reflected from a red surface (other colors are not). The light is focussed by the eye's lens on the retina where light of this wavelength produces such and such a change in the structure of the retina...and so on, whatever the details may be. Once the physiologist knows what is involved in normal vision, he is prepared to investigate the causes of abnormalities. If he finds that red things look blue to me, he will naturally assume that something has happened to change the normal chain of occurrences. He will find out what it is. And so with other abnormalities. He will discover the causes of double vision, astigmatism, color blindness, and perhaps color exchanges of the kind I have been imagining. I do not know but I suppose that the relevant sciences, physiology, ophthalmology, and others are fairly well-advanced and have discovered the causes of most recognized visual abnormalities. Although I know nothing of the details, it seems to me that I understand well enough what the "logic" of the matter must be.

When trying to think through the causal theory of perception, I was obviously thinking of a causal explanation of vision in quite a different way. Of course I never supposed that the "concept" of vision contained all of the details supplied by a physiological account. I never supposed that the causal theory would contain details about the nature of light, the structure of the retina or the optic nerve. The philosophico-causal theory will contain only the object seen and its visible characteristics, the eye with no obstructions--and whatever other few details are contained in the idea of vision. But I supposed that the kind or style of explanation was the same as that given by a physiologist. I thought that they had to be the same in style or manner, because both were derived from the idea of vision, or more specifically, from the way we talk about "seeing."

And yet I was thinking of a causal explanation in an entirely different way. I thought of myself as a philosophical physiologist all right. I was standing in for the physiologist--but I had no knowledge other than that which comes from the ability to talk about "seeing." Then I thought that I could ask myself questions and give causal explanations in all of the usual perceptual situations of everyday life. My

155

explanations would, of course, be easy and routine since they are those I knew how to give simply as the result of having acquired the usual language of vision: I can say in the right way "I see...," "He says...," "It looks..." and so on. I imagined the usual question would be this: I would look at a red object and ask myself "Why does that look red?" I must then have thought that the answer I would quickly give myself was this: "The causal genesis of its looking red is that which is involved in normal vision, so it is red. (Hence its being red causes it to look red.)"

Starting with "It looks red" I want to determine that it is red. And I can only do this by finding that the causal occurrences are those of normal vision. I was thinking something like this. Suppose that I have Henderson's disease, but I no longer have any symptoms which intimate when an attack is coming on. Hence if I cannot see objects whose color I know, I can never tell whether my vision is normal or not. Suppose that I awake one morning in a strange room in which all of the objects are unfamiliar. I see a hat hanging on the wall. Knowing that I can never be sure of my color vision, I say to myself "That hat looks red." And immediately I launch my causal inquiry in order to decide whether the hat is red or not. Since the relevant causal conditions in this case fall outside the concept of vision, and also outside my rudimentary knowledge of physiology, I shall never be able to determine whether the causal occurrences are those of normal perception or those that produce abnormal color vision. Hence I shall not be able to determine whether the hat is red or not. That is, I shall not be able to determine whether the causal occurrences are those of normal perception or those that produce abnormal color vision. Hence I shall not be able to determine whether the hat is red or not. That is, I shall not be able to determine whether it is red or not by the methods I ordinarily employ. Of course I shall call in other people and ask them. If they say it is red, that will settle the matter for me. But that is possible only because they have presumably settled it by normal means. Or, rather, that is an exaggeration, since they have never had Henderson's disease and have no reason to suspect it. They will simply not have my question. But no. As the causal theory represents the matter they will have the question, but in their case it will be settled by considering causal matters which fall within the "concept" of vision and will not call for a specialist's knowledge or for the use of such extreme means as dissection.

How is it thinkable that I or anyone should be able

to make such a determination? Suppose that some wag tells me that something strange is going on in the world. Everyone's color vision is unpredictably thrown off. It affects some people at one time, others at another. Whatever it is, he says, it has nothing to do with vaporous drugs which affect vision, or any indetectable change in light: in short it has nothing to do with any matters which affect vision but which fall outside the "concept" of vision. Suppose that I am an avid science fiction reader and I am unusually susceptible to such stories, stories which suggest extraterrestrial influences. I remember his warning vividly and so as I look at things I say "That looks red," "That looks green".... And so I set about my causal inquiry in order to determine whether my vision is normal, or whether it has in some strange way been changed. I trust the storyteller: if there is any change it is in those details which have to do with the concept of vision. What do I do? I determine that I have eyes by looking in a mirror and by feeling with my fingers? I make sure the lids are open? I make sure that colored glasses have not been placed on my head? I establish that there is the required object to be seen, and that it is within viewing distance? This is, of course, fantastic. If I, unreasonably, suspect that something is wrong--I know not what--I shall ask others. And if I find that we always agree and that our agreement remains a stable thing, I have done all that there is to do in order to establish that my vision is normal.

The causal theory gives me a completely distorted picture of "normal vision." It is inconceivable that "normality" should be determined by a causal investigation. Of course, a team of physicists and physiologists might examine someone in order to determine whether his color vision was normal. They might, because of their occupational prejudices, begin by examining the light, the lens, the retina, and other things they regard as relevant. They might make electroencephalograms and take all kinds of tests, and determine that everything involved in color vision was in perfect order. But how would they report their findings? Surely in this way: "As far as we can determine, his color vision is normal." And then, I suppose they would want to add: "So, why don't we find out whether it is or not?" And then they would proceed with colored objects in much the same way as you and I would.

I think I have been led into my misrepresentation of the part normality plays in vision because, while trying to think through the causal theory of vision, I

have been thinking in terms of some picture: I have
been thinking of myself here with my eyes pointed
there. I have been thinking that the object seen is
over there. It sends its influences to me, somehow,
and they are registered, somehow, on my mind. And
then, of course, starting from this registration, the
"sense-datum," I must figure out what the object is.
This, of course, is a caricature of the causal theory;
but I do not see how one can think through it without
something like this picture to guide him.
     In the beginning, of course, I tried to avoid any-
thing which would suggest such a caricature. And I
think, therefore, that I did not properly represent the
"analysis" of vision which is proposed by the causal
theory. It should be this: "I see that X is P" consists in a non-causal component of interpretation, recognition or claim, plus these factors: X looks P, the
causal conditions produce normal vision, and hence X's
looking P is causally produced by X's being P.
     One last observation: Grice thinks that the only
difficulty in considering the parts played by normality
or abnormality in vision is that causal accounts are
pointless and hence puzzling when vision is normal.

> The causal theory of perception as I have so
> far expounded it, it may be said, requires
> that it should be linguistically correct to
> speak of the causes of sense-impressions
> which are involved in perfectly normal per-
> ceptual situations. But this is a mistake;
> it is quite unnatural to talk about the
> cause, say, of its looking to X...unless the
> situation is or is thought to be in some way
> abnormal or delusive; this being so, when a
> cause can, without speaking unnaturally, be
> assigned to an impression, it will always be
> something other than the presence of the
> perceived object.... (pp. 105-106)

Though causal accounts may be pointless or unnatural
for normal perception, Grice thinks they are still
true. The difficulty with invoking causality in explaining the normal is simply that we are not interested in an explanation of the normal. We want an explanation only when things go wrong.
     It seems quite clear that this is not the problem
with normality and abnormality. I am certain that I
have not misrepresented the physiologist when I represented him as giving a theoretically basic causal explanation of normal vision. The real problem for the
causal theory is posed by the fact that normality and

abnormality in vision are not determined causally. For normal vision, the physiologist has a master-schematic explanation. When vision is abnormal, he quite naturally assumes that something in the causal sequence has changed. He tries to find out what it is. As his science progresses, he is able to give more and more explanations for this abnormality and that. But never does he think he is in a position to make the distinction between normal and abnormal by invoking anything he has discovered. Does he then appeal to more general causal matters--those that belong to the very idea of vision? It seems perfectly apparent to me that he does not.

What does all of this prove? Some long way back there was a fork in the road. I suggested that the relevant linguistic facts allowed of two interpretations. One was this: "That is red" (as a judgment of vision) is simple and unanalyzable. "It looks red" comes to "Everything is the same as in 'It is red' except that the speaker lacks confidence in his visual abilities." The other was the interpretation posed by the causal theory: I now understand how to properly represent this analysis: "It is red" comes to "It looks red and the causal conditions are normal." The second, the causal theory, is certainly paradoxical. This suggests, but of course it does not prove, that the first interpretation is the correct one. The causal theory seems to be erected on an incorrect interpretation or understanding of the phrases "looks red," "looks blue" and such, even in those examples which are the most likely candidates for the interpretation it requires. It requires that whenever I see something red, it should look red. In circumstances where I see that something is red, it is puzzling and odd to say or to think "It looks red," but it must be true--that it looks red--even though it is not sayable or thinkable. Not only must it be true that it looks red, the judgment "It is red" must somehow "include" the judgment that its looking red is caused by normal perceptual occurrences.

Perhaps I have sufficiently examined the suggestion that "It is red" involves a causal-normal element. But I want to give more thought to the idea that whenever I see a red thing it looks red.

Of my examples, I have observed that I say "It looks red" or "It looks red to me" instead of "It is red" because I suspect that something is wrong, and I suspect therefore that I am not able to see the true color of the object in question. I think that is the right way to characterize "It looks" and "It looks to me" as they occur in my examples. And in such cases, I

cannot discern or make myself aware of any fact when I
say "It looks red" which is different from that when I
say "It's red" or "I see that it's red." The only difference seems to be in my doubt and my caution.

There ought then to be a shorter way to deal with
the causal theory of perception than the one I have
pursued. After all, it maintains that all cases of
seeing involve "looks to me"; and this simply is not
so. As is shown by my examples, seeing could involve
"looks to me" only if I had reason to doubt my ability
to determine the color of the object, and in most cases
I have no reason to doubt my ability at all. The only
cases of seeing where I have reason to doubt my ability
are those in which I see but do not know that I see.
Since the causal analysis is meant to be perfectly
general and to correctly characterize every case of
seeing, it simply will not do. At best it will apply
to only a few cases, and even those are not the ones it
was intended to cover.

It is against this short refutation that Grice de-
votes most of his attention (at least seventeen of
twenty-seven pages). He tries to show that this short
way with the causal theory is based on a miscon-
struction of the linguistic facts. And he offers what
he believes to be a correct construction of those
facts. This is his insistence that we do not say "It
looks red" when we are in a position to say "It's red"
only because we need to observe the principle of com-
munication that we must not say the weaker of two
things when we are in a position to say the stronger.
When we violate that principle we produce puzzlement in
our audience (including ourselves, I think one should
add). When I see that something is red it is true that
it looks red to me, but it is also true that generally
I must not say so.

How does Grice set out to show that his is the correct interpretation of the linguistic phenomena? He
tries to show that in "It looks..." my doubt of my
ability to make a correct visual judgment is "cancellable." By that he means that the implication carried
by "It looks" can be taken away. I can say "It looks"
and then deny the implication that I have any suspicions of my ability to make a correct visual judgment
of the color of the object in question. Although the
result might seem odd, Grice claims nevertheless to see
that it might well be true.

> ...it is surely clear that if I were now to
> say "Nothing is the case which would make
> it false for me to say that the palm of
> this hand looks pink to me, though I do not

160

mean to imply that I or anyone else is or
might be inclined to deny that, or doubt
whether, it is pink" this would be a
perfectly intelligible remark even though
it might be thought both wordy and boring. Indeed I am prepared actually to
say it. (p. 99)

If I am to follow the spirit of Grice's reasoning,
how shall I go about gaining his insight that my suspicion in "It looks..." is cancellable? First I shall
show that there are situations in which I can plainly
say "It looks..." or "It looks to me..." without creating confusion and where I have no doubt or suspicions
about my ability to make a correct visual judgment.
Although these are not the ones which Grice mentions, I
can think of many such situations.
   (1) After spending a long time polishing and buf-
fing my red car, I might well say "There, it really
looks red now."
   (2) I might report on someone's appearance by saying "You look pale and ashy today" or perhaps "You look
as white as a sheet."
   (3) I might say of the rufous hummingbird's back
that it looks green from one angle and brown from another. That is just the way it is with that kind of
color. It is iridescent: it looks green sometimes and
at other times it looks brown.
   (4) Imagine a man who had spent all his life on
the desert taking a trip to Oregon. He might well say,
"The landscape here really looks green." Or suppose
our desert man and a man from Oregon are commenting on
the appearance of one of the valleys of California.
Oregon man: "The trees here are not very green." Desert man: "They look green to me."
   I produce these examples because they show cases
where "It looks..." or "It looks to me" does not carry
the implication that the speaker has any suspicion
about the perceptual position or condition he is in.
And I want to conclude from this that when "It
looks..." does carry the implication, the implication
is cancellable. How does that follow? It would follow
only if I could show that the words "It looks..." or
"It looks to me" somehow always come to the same thing,
regardless of the situation in which they are spoken.
Or, in Grice's language, it would follow only if I
could show that the implication is carried not by what
is said but rather by the fact that the person says it.
And so I need to see that what is said is the same in
every case where one says "It looks..." or "It looks to
me." Now in what way is the same thing said other than

161

that if I were to tell what is said in each case, I should use the same words? I cannot see how one could show that "It looks" always comes in the right way to the same thing. The belief that it does seems to rest on some doctrine to the effect that when certain words are presented in a certain order, our familiarity with the language enables us to isolate and consider a "proposition," the "content" carried by the words. In one circumstance the proposition will be asserted, in another denied, in another doubted, in another questioned, and so on, but the circumstances in which assertions are made or doubts are expressed in no way affect the proposition. It remains the same in every situation.

Grice does not himself seem to think that this demonstration is conclusive. Or at least, he does not rest his case entirely upon it. What else is there to do? There is the direct test. One can simply say, "It looks red, and I do not doubt my visual ability to make a correct perceptual judgment," and see that, although it may be misleading, it is intelligible, and true--if indeed one is looking at a red object. Before this experiment would show what it is supposed to show, we should have to make clear the "implication" that he was in doubt about his ability to make a correct perceptual judgment. If the words are spoken in one of those many situations where there is no reason for doubt or hesitation, then of course, there is nothing to "cancel."

Suppose, as in my first examples, that I go to Wilson's laboratory and I am given a drug which radically affects color vision. I stand and look at various color patches which Wilson points out on the wall. Wilson, knowing that I will be curious about the effects of the drug on my vision, stations my friend Dale beside me. Dale has not taken the drug, and his vision remains perfectly normal. Wilson tells me to address all my questions to him. The experiment begins, and Wilson asks "What color is this?" "It looks red," I say. And turning to Dale, I ask "What color is it?" Now suppose that Dale, who can see the color of the patch perfectly well, says "It looks blue." How can I say that this is quite intelligible and true? Does he mean "It's blue"? Then why didn't he say so? Does he mean "It looks blue"? Then what is wrong with his vision?

But suppose he says instead, "It looks blue to me." That does not sound odd in the same bewildering way as "It looks blue." What does that show? Well, first, that "It looks blue" and "It looks blue to me" do not everywhere come to the same thing as I, following Grice, have supposed. Dale says "It looks blue to me."

162

What am I to make of that? Well, maybe the atmosphere of my visual abnormality has begun to have an influence on him. Maybe he is beginning to think that something is wrong with the room or with the light, and that he ought not to be too confident about his visual power in this situation. After all, Wilson is capable of almost anything in pursuit of his research. Then let us explain again to Dale that there are no tricks, and that he can see the colors of the patches here as well as he can see the colors of anything anywhere. Again I say, "It looks red: what color is it?" And Dale says, "It looks blue to me," and he adds, "I can see that it is blue." Now what am I to make of "It looks blue to me"? I find it hard to think that there is not a trace of hesitation left. Suppose that there is no hesitation, no suspicion, not the slightest doubt in Dale's mind. Wilson asks, "What color is this?" I say "It looks red." And turning to Dale, I ask "What color is it?" and he says "It looks blue to me." I need no more background for his remark. What does it come to? I know he can see that it is blue: he knows that it is blue; why doesn't he say so? Well, is there any more to the form of his remark than that he is joining in the game? If I had not been present and Wilson had asked him about the patch, certainly then he would just have said "That's blue." His saying "It looks blue to me" follows my saying "It looks red." It is an interesting and slightly wise-acreish way of making the contrast between his position and mine. That is the interpretation I am now inclined to make.

But I have tried here to construct an example where one who is in a position to say "It's blue" can say "It looks blue (to me)" and be understood. And I suppose I have been successful. So there is the other interpretation: the one which Grice gives. In saying "It looks blue to me" Dale is saying something weaker than "It's blue." And perhaps that is right: Dale is never quite committing himself to pronounce on the color of the patch. So does it follow that he is reporting on some fact which is a part of seeing that it is blue and which can be given a causal explanation? Why does it look blue to him? Is this the answer? "Because he has normal vision, and is in normal circumstances." That is not a causal answer. Suppose that I, to whom it looks red, ask the question, and that I do not know what color the patch is. Then is this the answer? "It is blue, and his vision is perfectly normal." Still, that is not a causal answer. Try this: "It is blue, and the fact that it is blue brings it about that it looks blue to Dale." I do not know what to make of this, but I am sure it is not an answer to my question.

The answer might just as well have been: "It is red, and the fact that it is red brings it about that it looks blue to Dale." By this answer I am not told who sees the color patch or whether either of us sees the color patch. Surely that is what I wanted to know, and I should be satisfied only by "Dale is perfectly normal," or "Dale's vision is abnormal, too." I have already seen that the proper account of normality or abnormality is not causal. One can only see if one is normal, and the causal theory is intended to account for seeing.

This, I'm afraid, is the very best I can do for the causal theory.

What is the conclusion? Sometimes "looks to me" is in order when there is no implication of doubt or suspicion of the visual situation or of the condition of the viewer. But it doesn't follow from this that "It looks blue to me" reports something different from and weaker that "It's blue." Especially, it doesn't follow that it reports some fact which can be causally explained. Why then does it sometimes seems to me that "It looks..." does report such a fact? I can offer only one suggestion. Sometimes I look at the examples with a certain philosophy of language in mind. And that now seems to me a questionable way to look at them.

4. DOES IT LOOK THE COLOR IT IS?

I

I am not concerned now with where I get the idea or why it keeps coming back into my mind; but I do have the idea and it does keep coming back into my mind. I have the idea that when I look at things and when I see things, I am aware of something more direct than the things I see: something immediate and private to my own sensory world. I am thinking, of course, of what some philosophers call "sense-data." I think that if the thing I see--a tree, a bird, a house--should be annihilated, then the immediate, private object of my awareness might well remain unchanged.

When I examine this idea it does not seem to fit the facts of vision, but I keep thinking this way all the same. And sometimes I find something which the idea does seem to fit, and I am prepared immediately to think, then, that there must be something to the idea after all. One of the things it seems to fit is this: suppose I look at something and note or remark on its color. It is a barn, say, and it is bright red. When I say that it is red (because I see it, of course) or when I say that I see it is red, then it is also true that it looks red to me. It might look red and not be red. And it might be red and not look red. But generally if it is red it will look red. Thus, the connection between being red and looking red is just the one I should expect to find between "physical objects" and "sense-data." Although sense-data are not always reliable indicators of physical objects, generally they are. If that were not so, my visual judgments would generally be wrong, and I should not then be able, guided by sight, to find my way through doors, along streets, among trees. I should be worse off than a blind man.

Thus, reports such as "It looks red," and "It looks green," and so on, seem to be very nearly what I expect reports on sense-data to be. Of course they are not reports on sense-data because the "it" to which they are addressed is a "physical object." But then the color in question is the color which a physical object looks to be; and if a sense-datum interpretation of the color which a physical object looks to be can be made to work, perhaps it will suggest some way of making work a sense-datum interpretation of the way a physical object in its entirety looks to be. "It looks red" seems related to "I see that it is red" in exactly the way a sense-datum report should be related to a physical-object report.

But immediately I can see an objection. For "It looks red" to be the required sense-datum report, it must always (or nearly always) be true that a thing looks red whenever I see that it is red. And that seems not to be the case. "It looks red" is an expression with very limited application: only in very special circumstances do we say of something that it looks red. Very often I see that something is red, and it would be most paradoxical to say "It looks red." That sounds right; but I may be misleading myself here. Why should I think that I can see that something is red when it would not be in order to remark that it looks red to me? Do I think that "It looks red" requires special circumstances, but that "I see that it is red" does not? Do I think that "I see that it is red" is in order in any circumstances whatsoever? If so, then that is not right. One says "I see that it is red" (or something like that) only in very special circumstances too.

Here is a story which will illustrate one set of those circumstances. I have been taking photographs of all the barns in this part of the country which are a century or more old. If a barn has been unpainted I take a color photograph--because this best shows the raised grain and weathered colors of the wood. When a barn has been painted I take a black-and-white photograph because this cancels the effect of the color and emphasizes the texture of the old wood. A visitor has seen my photographs and he tells me where I can find a beautiful old barn: it is just behind a motel in Drain. My friend Rollo and I load my photographic gear and start out to Drain. I have nothing but color film--but that is no problem because the visitor told me that the barn was well-weathered and unpainted. We arrive at the motel after dark and take a room. Rollo wakes early. I awaken and see him sitting by the window. "Is the barn there?" I say. He answers "Yes. It's on a hill right outside the window." I think and I say, "What color is it?" Rollo says "It's red." "Oh, no. I have no proper film. Are you sure?" "Of course I'm sure," "Rollo says "It's right there and I can clearly see that it is red." Perhaps one says "I see that it is red" only in reply to questions of a certain kind: "How do you know?" "How can you tell?" "Are you sure?" I was not thinking that a person could see that something is red only in such circumstances as these. But even if one can see that something is red only in such limited circumstances, they are not circumstances which provide a natural place for "It looks red." "What color is the barn?" a friend asks me. I say, "It's red." "How do you know?" he asks. And I reply, "It looks red." "It looks red" would be most puzzling here. Unless I made some explanation, my friend would not know what to make of my remark, "It looks red."

But, of course, one can see that something is red when he is not in a position to say "I see that it is red." One often sees that something is red, even when he has not been asked a question such as "How do you know?" The question might come up later. "Do you know the color of that barn on Mobley's hill?" "Yes. It's red." "How do you know?" "I walked by it yesterday, and I saw that it was red." So as I walked by the barn I did see that it was red even though there was no question at the time about how I knew what color it was. So one can see that something is red when there is no occasion to say "I see that it is red." If I have looked at something, and I am at any time prepared to answer the questions "What color is it?" and "How do you know?" then it is true that I saw that it was red (or green, or blue, or whatever). The questions need not actually be asked: it is sufficient that I could answer them if they were to be asked, and to answer them by saying, "It is red" and "I saw it."

Again, I cannot by any similar means show, after the fact, that the barn looked red. "Do you know the color of that barn on the hill?" "Yes, I walked by it yesterday and it looked red." Without some elaborate explanation, one will not be able to make any sense of this reply. But isn't this just because the question has to do with the color of the barn? Why not ask-- after the fact--about the way the barn looks? What question would that be? "Did you notice that barn on the hill?" "Yes." "What color did it look?" Without some explanation, how am I to take this question? Is there something tricky about the color of the barn? Does the questioner want me to tell him that it appears to be exactly the same shade as my uncle's barn?

What I am trying to say is this: the circumstances in which I see that something is red are far more common and less peculiar than the circumstances in which something looks red. Although the words "I see that it is red" have limited application, it is still usually true that I see a thing whenever I look at it or whenever if falls within my field of view and I am not too preoccupied with other matters. Although I should not say "I see that it is red," it remains true that I do see that it is red. Also, when I report on the color of an object which is (or was) within my view, there is usually no question about how I know what color it is. It is quite understandably taken for granted that if someone were to ask me "How do you know?" I should

167

reply, "I see it" or "I saw it." Hence I report the colors I see by saying simply, "That is red" or "The house is blue" or "The leaf is yellow."

I am trying to make clear my misgiving about a sense-datum interpretation of "It looks red" or "It looks (some other color)" and this is what it amounts to. If "It looks red" is to represent a report of a sense-datum, then it must usually be the case that whenever I see that something is red, it will look red as well. I see that a thing is red, in the simplest and most usual of circumstances: whenever it is within view, and I am not blinded, or lost in thought; whenever I can later report that I saw it, or later tell what color it is. But in these circumstances I do not know what to make of the idea that the thing looks red or looks red to me. Of course, I do not want to say that it does not look red--not just like that. I want to say that the question of whether it looks red or does not look red is out of place. It has no hold. I do not know what to make of the idea that it looks red, and I do not know what to make of the idea that it does not look red. If it is red, and I see that it is red, then it neither looks red nor does it not look red.

Another thing: when I think of all those many cases where I see that something, say a flag, is red, but where I should not say "I see that the flag is red" or even "It is red," then I must be thinking of cases where there is no question about my vision or the circumstances. There must be no question about whether my vision is normal, whether the light is strange, whether the color is a peculiar one, or anything of that kind. And in all of these cases, so the sense-datum story goes, the flag will look red. But it is in just such cases that it is most difficult to think that a flag will look red (or look red to me). That is, it is most paradoxical to think that a flag looks red when there is absolutely no question about my eyes, the light, or whether I clearly see that it is red.

Doesn't the fact that I have so much trouble formulating this objection indicate that it is not a genuine objection after all? It is true that the circumstances in which I can say of something that it looks red are more limited than those in which I can say that I see something is red. Still, these special circumstances may have to do only with whether I can say that something looks red. They may have nothing to do with the truth of the matter. It may simply be true that something looks red whether these circumstances are present or not. When these circumstances are absent, it may well be that something looks red, but I cannot **say** that it looks red without puzzling my

168

listener as to why I should say such a thing.

After all, there are circumstances in which it would be puzzling to **say** almost anything. I can't just say anything I have a mind to, just anytime and anyplace, without creating puzzlement. Suppose that I am walking down the street with my friend, Langley, and I say--without any provocation or preface--"That is a tree." Or "Salem is the capital of Oregon," or "George Washington was the first president of the United States," or "That barn is red." Any of these would certainly puzzle Langley, and he would doubtless ask me for an explanation. In a similar way I should puzzle Langley if I were to say of a bright red barn, "That barn looks red."

But then I think that Langley's puzzlement would not be the same with "That looks red" as it would be with any of the others. I must be very careful here because this is the point on which the whole thing turns. I shall set up an experiment in imagination in which I shall say--out of the blue--such things as "Salem is the capital of Oregon," "That barn is red," "That barn looks red." And I shall try to imagine what Langley's response will be. His ears will be my ears; or rather, my ears will be his ears. Langley and I, then, are walking down the street together. It is a perfectly fine summer day: bright mid-afternoon sun, clear sky. We pass a bright red barn standing on the back of a lot, about fifty yards away. Both of us look at the barn. Langley clearly sees it and, of course, sees that it is red. He has every reason to think that I also see that it is red. Then, quite out of the blue, I say "That barn is red." He will surely wonder why on earth I said that. Suppose that he asks me, "Why did you say that?" He wants an explanation. What explanation can I give which will satisfy him? It seems to me that my explanation will have to be one of two kinds. (1) I might address myself directly to the question "Why did I act as though Langley would be interested in that or want to know about that?" I might say, "I thought you were counting red barns and I wanted to make sure you counted that one." Or perhaps I know that red barns are very unusual in Langley's part of the country. So I want to make sure he sees this one. He will think that a red barn is worth looking at twice. An explanation along these lines, I shall say, supplies the conditions which make it understandable why I should tell something to somebody. (2) On the other hand, I could deny that I intended to tell him something. I might say, "I was just thinking to myself: what fun it would be to say something simple and true and obvious. And before I knew it I was saying

'That barn is red'." An explanation such as this supplies the conditions which make understandable my thinking aloud or blurting out a truism. As far as I can see there are only these two ways in which I could satisfy Langley's request for an explanation.

I am trying to think that "That barn looks red" will be obviously true even though I am not in a position to say it. My saying "That barn looks red" will produce bewilderment, but still what I say will be true. If that is so, then I shall be able to clear up the bewilderment by explaining why I thought my listener would be interested in why I blurted out this obvious truth from my private thoughts. Suppose now that as Langley and I walk past the red barn, I blurt out, "That barn looks red." Of course Langley will be puzzled by this and surely he will ask "Why did you say that that barn looks red?" I shall naturally give him an explanation. But how can I give an explanation which will be one of the two proper kinds? We stand before a red barn and I say "That looks red." Langley sees that the barn is red, and he thinks that I see it as well as he. How can I then explain "I thought you would be interested in that"? Langley asked why I said that the barn looks red, and my reply gives him no answer. How can I say "I was just thinking aloud. I just wanted to think something obviously true, so I thought 'That barn looks red'"? This also will not answer Langley's question: "Why did you say that it looks red?"

I realize that I am placing quite a philosophical burden on Langley and his part in this conversation. But that is the way I want it to be. I want Langley to be dead serious; I want him to listen carefully, and to take nothing for granted. I do not want just any old slice of any everyday casual conversation. That might go differently. Langley knows that I am a philosopher: I think and say queer things. And anyway, who pays very close attention to what his conversational partner says? We hurry on and chitchat and make bad jokes, and each of us half hears and ignores a large part of what the other says. I say "That barn looks red" and Langley asks "Why did you say that?" I say "I was just amusing myself. I was trying to say something obviously true." Langley will probably not think twice about this; maybe he will not think about it at all. He will say "Did I tell you about my experience last week in the pipe store?" When I say "That barn looks red," and when I add "I was trying to think of an obvious truth," I do not want to imply that anyone would be immediately taken aback. In an average, everyday conversation, he might not. But I am not interested in that. My

170

Langley pays close attention. If Langley--or anyone--paid close attention and was seriously involved in carrying on the conversation, he could not let my explanation pass. He would remain puzzled.

Well, what explanation can I give him? I shall try to think of explanations, and make them fit as best I can into something like these two categories. First, what could I say to explain why I thought of myself as telling him something? There are several possibilities:

(1) "I took some pills this morning for my hay fever, and they often have a strange side effect. They sometimes change my color vision in strange and unpredictable ways. Sometimes they make red things look brown, sometimes gray, sometimes almost anything. I never know what to expect. I haven't noticed any effects on my color vision yet today, but I can never tell. Of course I couldn't be sure about the color of that barn. It looks red--and it probably is red--but it may be brown." This isn't yet an explanation of why I said "That barn looks red" to Langley. So I shall add "I know you are counting red barns, and I thought that might be one. I can't be sure."

(2) Same story with a few differences. "My doctor gave me some pills for my hay fever this morning, and he told me to watch out because they sometimes have a radical effect on color vision. I thought of this as I looked at the barn. I was about to say 'That barn is red,' when I thought of the doctor's warning. So I said instead 'That barn looks red'."

(3) "The man who owns that barn is a chemist, and he claims to have invented an iridescent paint which has a color like that of a male hummingbird's throat. That is, it supposedly produces a surface of the color we call 'iridescent red.' The color you see depends upon the light and the angle. Sometimes it looks black, sometimes gray, and, of course, sometimes red. He has painted the barn with this paint. I've looked at that barn many times before, and it always looked gray or black to me. I thought maybe the owner was joking about his paint, or that maybe it was a failure, and he ought to go back to his laboratory for more work on it. But now for the first time, as we walked by it today, it looked glowing red. I was surprised, and I blurted out: 'It looks red'." So far, of course, this sounds like an explanation of how I came to think something aloud or to blurt something out (though it is not a truism, of course). But I could add this: "I know you are counting red barns, and I don't know whether you want to count that as a red barn or not." Or I might say, "I thought you would be interested in the

171

way it looks red." Either of these two additions could explain why I had addressed, or half-addressed, my remark to Langley. But, of course, he could not understand the addition by itself: it would have to follow all the preceding explanations.

(4) "I have Wembley's disease. It is a disease of vision, and it comes and goes. When I have an attack of the disease it makes green things look red, and red things look green. I can always tell when an attack is coming on because it makes my eyes burn in a peculiar way. Just a few minutes ago I had that peculiar burning in the eyes, and then as we passed the barn I was surprised that it looked red. I've passed this barn many times, and I know it is red; but I expected it to look green. I wonder whether that means I am getting over the disease. I said 'It looks red' in surprise and without thinking." In this case, too, it seems I have given an explanation for blurting something out. (And again it is not a truism.) I might add "Knowing that you are counting red barns, I was going to tell you that the barn is red." But this will not explain why I said to Langley "It looks red." I might add "I thought you would be interested in the fact that it looks red to me." But Langley could not understand this without the whole explanation.

(5) "I walk by this barn several times a day, and I know the barn is brown. In fact, I saw it just a few hours ago, and I'm sure it was brown then. Now look at it. There hasn't been time for anyone to paint it. Could it be a strange light--or something? It looks red." At this point, suppose that Langley tells me that barn is red. Of course, I shall conclude that it has been painted red within a few hours, or perhaps I did not really notice the color of the barn the last time I passed by. In this case I am telling Langley that the barn looks red because it is surprising to me, and of course I think he will be interested. But again, I must tell the whole story in order to explain why he might be expected to be interested.

(6) "I was about to call your attention to that red barn, and when I looked up at it, it looked brown. I was surprised. Then as we walked on a few steps, it looked red. It is red, I know: it must be the funny light back there that makes it look brown. I'm afraid I was thinking aloud. As we walked on and it looked red--as it should--I thought 'There now, that barn looks red.' I blurted out the words, 'That barn looks red'."

Here if I am calling Langley's attention to anything or telling him something he might be interested in, it is the fact that whereas the barn looks brown from there, the barn looks red from here. If he did not know the whole story, he surely could not understand my saying "The barn looks red."

(7)   "For several weeks it has been dark and gloomy. A gray mist has filled the air. Last night it began to rain and the rain turned to snow. This morning the sun is out and it is beautifully clear with the brilliant sun reflecting from the light cover of snow. Every time I look up I am overwhelmed by the brilliance of the colors. I thought to myself 'My, but the sky looks blue. The trees so green. That house looks yellow as I've never seen it before.' Then I looked at that barn lighted by reflections from the snow and I blurted out my next thought, 'And, oh...that barn looks red'."

(8)   "Because bright light hurts my eyes I sometimes have to wear these special sunglasses. They're new and I haven't gotten used to them yet, and I doubt whether I ever shall. I don't like them: they make everything look red. I put them on just a moment ago and I looked up at that barn. Then I grumbled 'That barn looks red.' I intended to go on and tell you about the way these glasses make things look." (At this point Langley tells me that I have no reason to complain about my vision of that barn, because it is red.)

(9)   "I was staring for a few moments at the sun as it came from behind a cloud. Then I noticed that I had a red after-image. I began to play with it: I turned my head this way and that, so that the after-image was first in the sky and then on the trees. Then I closed my eyes, and when I opened them the after-image was squarely on the barn. It made that barn look red. I was amazed and I thought aloud, 'That barn looks red.' I was about to tell you about this phenomenon when I turned my head, moved the after-image; and then I was surprised to see that the barn is red."

(10)   "It's a long story. I fell into a brown study. I was thinking about something my painting instructor told me last week. He said, 'When you paint, don't pay attention to the things you are painting: concentrate on their looks. A moving object may look like a streak. It may look elongated. It may look like it is trailing an image of itself. You must concentrate on how it looks to you.' He said 'Think how you might get the look with just a few brush strokes.' I was thinking that I might paint that barn and I asked myself, 'How does it look?' I thought, 'Its impression is that of a red, intrusive square. It looks like the only red thing in the world. It looks red. One red brush stroke here and one there.' I must have spoken

173

some of my thoughts aloud.   I said 'It looks red'."
(Here again I blurt something out, think aloud, but it
is certainly not a truism: I got it only after careful
consideration.)

Any of these, surely, would explain to Langley why
I had said "That looks red."   I suppose there are many
other explanations as well.   But these are not explanations of the simple sort I was able to give for "That
barn is red."   It does not seem that I have explained
why I said to Langley "That barn looks red" in the same
way I explained why I said "That barn is red."   In the
case of "That barn is red" my explanation had to do
with the situation or state of mind I thought Langley
was in: he was counting red barns, or he had grown up
never seeing a red barn.   That is, I gave the reason
for my expecting that Langley might be interested in
the fact that the barn is red.   For "That barn looks
red" I first had to supply conditions which have
nothing to do with why I thought Langley might be
interested in some fact.   What would the fact be?   The
fact that the barn looks red?

So perhaps I am able to explain why I told Langley
that the barn looks red only after I have explained why
I thought or said aloud an obvious truth, namely, that
the barn looks red.   But my explanations do not fit
that pattern either.   In order to explain why I say
aloud some truism like "That barn is red," or "George
Washington was the first president," I must say something like this: "I was just tickling my fancy.   I was
trying to think of something indisputably true."   If I
could think of "That barn looks red" in that way, none
of these elaborate explanations would be called for.
It might just be true that the barn looks red.   I might
simply be aware that it looks red, and find that fact
to be an indisputable truth which I could use for an
idle remark. My explanation, then, could go like this:
"I was just giving vent to a whim.   I wanted to say
something obviously true.   So I said 'That barn looks
red.'   I was thinking aloud."

This is the important thing.   I have been thinking
that "That looks red" is like "That is red" or like
"The capital of Oregon is Salem," namely that it is
something I can simply think when I want to think of an
interesting fact.   It is something I can think when,
for my own amusement, I want to think of something incontestable, something unmistakably correct, a truism.
If I blurt it out in the presence of Langley, he will
naturally want to know why I said it.   And one thing I
can do is simply explain that I was so caught up in my
own whimsical thoughts that I spoke them aloud.   For a
moment I was oblivious to his presence: I was alone in

174

the world. And what I thought came to my tongue.

Can I walk along, see a red barn, and then think to myself in this way: "I shall say something obviously true today: 'That barn looks red'"? That is all there is to it. Absolutely nothing else leads me up to the remark. I have not taken pills which affect my color vision. I know nothing of some chemist and his experiments on the barn with iridescent pigment. I do not have Wembley's disease; I am not surprised by the apparent color of the barn, thinking that it is brown and not red. I am in no way surprised by what I see. I do not think the color I see is produced by my sunglasses. I do not think that I see a red after-image superimposed on the barn. I am not amazed by the unusual brilliance of the color. I am not planning to make a painting of the barn. I am not as an artist thinking how I might capture the look of the thing. I just walk along thinking that I shall now tickle my fancy by thinking of something clearly true--and as I look at the red barn, this comes into my mind: "That barn looks red." It comes into my mind, I am trying to think, in the same way "I have shoes on my feet now" might come into my mind. I want an obvious truth and I might even be a bit amused that this one should occur to me: "That barn looks red."

Surely this is fantastic. What could I be thinking by "That barn looks red"? What could this mean to me? What is this that has come into my mind? Just these words, surely, "That barn looks red." I look at the red barn and then I say these words; but what am I saying when I say these words? I was looking for a truism and these words came. Surely I would be mystified not only by the fact that these words came into my mind, I would be mystified by the words as well. I was trying to think of something true. Are these words supposed to express something true? What is supposed to be true?

Suppose that I am walking down the street with Langley and I get the idea that I want to think of something indisputably true. At that moment I see a red barn and these words pop into my head: "That barn looks red." If I voice these words, Langley will certainly need an explanation. Don't I also need an explanation? Don't I equally need an explanation, even when I keep the words to myself? These words pop into my head, but what am I to make of them? When I do actually say "That barn looks red," and when Langley asks me his inevitable question, I can give one of several explanations. It now seems clear that those explanations are not what I took them to be. I do not explain why I told Langley something as I might if I had said

175

"That barn is red." And I do not explain why I happened to have this thought, or why I thought it aloud. The explanations I give Langley for "That barn looks red" are of a different kind.

They are explanations without which I cannot make heads or tails of my own words. They are explanations which I need as much as Langley does. They are explanations without which I have nothing but mysterious words which popped into my head and tripped off my tongue. They do not supply the "conditions for telling" or the "conditions for thinking aloud" --or rather, if they do supply these conditions they can do so only because they have supplied something else first. If I felt in a classificatory mood, I should be inclined to call that something else "the conditions for intelligibility." Unless one of these conditions is present and known to me, I cannot think anything which might be articulated by the words, "That barn looks red." Unless one of these conditions is known to me first, I cannot go on to explain why I blurted out the words; and I cannot go on to explain why I thought Langley might be interested.

If I were to walk down the street with Langley and these words came off my tongue in the way I am trying to imagine, he would not be as dumbfounded as I--at least he would not be as dumbfounded as soon as I should be. Nothing leads up to these words except that I have said to myself "I shall think of something obviously true." And then the words come, "That barn looks red." Langley will surely be mystified but not as completely as I. He will wonder what is up; he will wonder what to make of the words. Suppose that just after I say these words I am struck dumb, and say nothing more. Then if he is ingenious, he will begin to think of the conditions which might obtain. He will wonder whether I have some disease which affects my vision or whether the barn has just been painted. He will not immediately give up on my words. If later my voice comes back to me, he then may ask me many questions. "Did you think you were having an attack of Wembley's disease? Were you surprised by the color of the barn? Did you think something was wrong with your color vision? Does the barn have a peculiar--perhaps iridescent--color? Were you looking at it as the subject for painting?" I shall have to answer each of his questions with "No." "There is nothing like any of these," I shall tell him. "I just had the funny idea that I should think of a truism and before I knew it those words came off my lips." At this point, surely, Langley would give up. There would be no way he could make heads or tails of my words "That barn looks

176

red."

The sense-datum picture of perception leads me to think something like this. If I walk along on a perfectly ordinary day in a perfectly normal way and glance at a red barn, then I see that that barn is red. And at the same time it is also true that the barn looks red. It may not be entirely plain what is meant by saying that I see that the barn is red, but with a little work one can see that it is a right-headed thing to say. As I pass the barn I can think to myself or say aloud, "That barn is red." And I think or say this precisely because I am looking at the barn and am prepared to say, if questioned, "I see that it is red." I can think that the barn is red (because I see it) as I can think "I am now wearing a sweater" when I want to think of something manifestly true. This is surely what is behind my thinking that I can see that a red barn is red in the most ordinary of circumstances. But the sense-datum picture of perception also leads me to think that there is this connection between "seeing" and "looking": whenever I see that something is red, it looks red. If I have correctly exposed what is behind the idea of seeing that something is red, then there is no such connection. When looking at a barn I know to be red--in almost any circumstances--I can think to myself "That barn is red." But I cannot think to myself "That barn looks red." There is nothing here to think, except some words which cannot be made intelligible.

Some Expansions

1. I have imagined my saying, out of the blue, "That barn looks red." And I have supposed that Langley, to whom I apparently spoke, would be puzzled by this. He would want an explanation. I gave him this explanation: "I was thinking aloud. I was just trying to think of something obviously true, and I thought of 'That barn looks red'." This explanation would not do, I thought. Langley would still be puzzled. His question would remain unanswered: "Why did you say that the barn looked red?" Then I thought of several satisfactory explanations which I might be able to give him. There are many of them and they are very diverse. After considering these explanations I decided that Langley was puzzled because he did not know what to make of the words "That barn looks red": he did not know what it was that I was saying, that which I thought to be obviously true. I thought that I, too, should be puzzled by my own words, that I should really not know what to make of this "obvious

177

truth" which had come into my mind--unless, of course, I could give myself some explanation.

Could it be that I have been too hasty in taking this last step, that is, too hasty in concluding that there is a problem about the intelligibility of the words "That barn looks red"? After all, Langley could have been puzzled, not because he was unable to understand exactly what obvious truth I had spoken, but because that particular truth struck him as an odd thing for me to think of. I too might be puzzled as to why that particular thing should pop into my head. Why, after all, should I say (or think) "That barn looks red"? So Langley's question (and my question, too) might have been: Why should I say "That barn looks red" when I could just as easily have said "That barn is red"?

H.P. Grice[1] thinks that I should puzzle anyone if I tell him something which is weaker or less definite than the thing he thinks I am in a position to tell him. Similarly, I take it, I should be puzzled as to why something indefinite should come to mind when I am in a perfectly good position to think of something definite.

I am a citizen of the U.S.A. with at least an average awareness of the political scene about me. I know that Richard Nixon is president of the U.S., and Langley knows that I know. If, as Langley and I walk along, I blurt out, "Richard Nixon is president of the U.S.," he will be puzzled. He will want an explanation. Suppose I say "I was just trying to think of something true, I thought aloud." Surely that will satisfy him. But what if I say "Richard Nixon is president of some country or other"? This is clearly a weaker and less definite thing than I am in a position to say. Suppose Langley asks why I said that, and I tell him I was just trying to think of something incontestably true. Wouldn't that explanation do? He might wonder why on earth I had thought such a strangely indefinite thing. But also he might not. Surely he understands well enough what I said: he knows that it is true. And if I was just trying to think of something true and incontestable then that will do. If he has a further question, then it is an entirely different question: he now wants to know something about the

---

[1]"The Causal Theory of Perception," Proceedings of the Aristotelian Society, Supp. Vol. 35 (1961) pp. 121-68. Reprinted in G.J. Warnock, ed., The Philosophy of Perception (London, Oxford University Press, 1967), pp. 85-112.

curious workings of my mind. Why, indeed, should I think that Nixon is president of some country or other? Why not think straight out what I know about the matter and say that Nixon is president of the U.S.A.?

I think that I, too, might wonder why I had thought of such a curiously weak thing. But it seems clear to me that this question is very different from the one Langley and I have about "That barn looks red." When I know that that is supposed to be true, I still wonder exactly what it is that is supposed to be true. I am not wondering why I thought such a queer thing. I am wondering, it seems to me, what it is exactly that I have thought. And it seems to me still, that if I have no explanation in mind, then there is nothing I have thought.

What indeed was I thinking when I thought that "That looks red" is weaker or less definite than "That is red"? I was thinking only of the words "That looks red" as they might pop into my mind when I was looking at a red barn, and when I might have said "That barn is red"--when, that is, I was trying to think of something obviously true. But why "weaker" or "less definite" than "That is red"? I was thinking that if I were in a position to say "That is red," then "That looks red" would be weaker and less definite. As soon as I return to the details of my examples, this idea loses whatever plausibility it may have had. I am not, in all of my examples, in a position to say the "stronger and more definite" thing: "That barn is red." But I am in such a position in several of them: I am clearly in such a position in examples (4), (6), (7), and (10). In these examples is there any reason to think that "That looks red" is weaker or less definite than "That is red"? In (4) I have Wembley's disease and am surprised that the barn looks red: I expect it to look green. Should I have been saying something stronger if I had said "That is red"? I was not talking about the color of the barn, but about the fact that it unexpectedly looked red. In (6) I was calling Langley's attention to the fact that the barn looks brown from over there, and red from here. In what way would "The barn is red" be stronger? I am not talking about the color of the barn at all, but the way it looks from here. In (7) I was expressing amazement at the brilliance of the colors. I was remarking on the way the barn-color looked today. I could not remark on this phenomenon at all by saying that the barn is red. In (10) I was sizing up the look of the barn as a subject for painting. It was a matter of two wide red brush strokes. In no sense, surely, was my remark that the barn looked red a weaker or less definite comment to the effect that the barn is red. I was not talking about the color of the barn, but about its look in terms of a special interest.

When philosophizing on this matter, I seem to have a strong inclination to misdescribe it. Someone says "That barn looks red," I immediately take the words and the bit of context which has been supplied, and ask "What sort of linguistic phenomenon is this?" When the sense-datum picture of perception holds my mind, I think that when someone says "That barn looks red" in these circumstances he is saying something obviously true, as "That is a barn" would be obviously true. But if that doesn't seem right, and I am struck with the way in which the words "That barn looks red" cry out for some background or preface, I try to find another characterization of the "linguistic phenomenon." The one that comes immediately to mind is this: "That barn looks red" is like "I have stopped beating my mother"-- or something which philosophers say has a "presupposition." As I walk down the street with Langley I blurt out "My brother is sick." Langley says "I'm sorry, but I didn't know you had a brother. Is he younger?" I say, of course, "Oh no. I have no brother. No sister, either. I'm an only child." Langley: "Then why on earth did you say that your brother is sick?" I: "I was trying to get you to consider a philosophical puzzle. I said 'My brother is sick,' and now you know that I have no brother. Now I want to tell you that when I said 'My brother is sick' I was saying something obviously true." Langley: "But it isn't. It's not true that your brother is sick--if you have no broth- er." I: "Then is it false that my brother is sick? Is my brother not sick, but well?" Langley: "Of course not. Your brother can't be well either. You have no brother." I: "That is my only point. You can't straightforwardly ask whether 'My brother is sick' is true or false, unless I have a brother. There is something fishy about saying 'My brother is sick' when you have no brother."

Philosophers generally say that "My brother is sick" presupposes that I have a brother. Unless I have a brother there is no question about whether my brother is sick or not to which one can address one's self. So if, while walking down the street with Langley, who knows I am an only child, I said "My brother is sick," he would not be able to make heads or tails of this. He would ask "Why did you say that?" And I could only say something like this: "I don't know. It just popped into my mind. I can't make any sense of it all. Those words just mysteriously came to mind, and I blurted them out. This sort of thing has been hap- pening a lot lately: I wonder whether I should see a

180

doctor."

"That barn looks red" is not like "George Washington was the first president." I am inclined then to think that it must be like "My brother is sick." But it is not. When the words "My brother is sick" pop into my mind, I can think "That might be true--if only I had a brother." There is nothing of the same kind I can think for "That barn looks red." That might be true if only--what? That might be true if only I were thinking of making a painting, and were trying to size up the color-look of that barn? But what is "that" that might have been true? I do not know what to think of as "that" ("That barn looks red") until I have supplied the clue that I am to think of sizing up the barn for a watercolor painting. When I supply that background I make something of the words which I could not do without that background. When the words alone popped into my mind they did not come with any intimations of the way I was to take them. If I think of another background, I shall make something else of the words. "That might be true--if only I had Wembley's disease and expected that red barn to look green." "That might be true--if only I had just noticed that the red barn looked brown." "That might be true--if only the brilliance of the color were amazing today." And so on.

I am asking myself a dangerous philosophical question: "How to describe the linguistic phenomenon?" Is there one proper, definitive way to describe the "phenomenon"? I am putting myself up to this only because I have a characterization already at hand: it is like "My brother is sick." And, of course, I want to say that it is not. In what way is it not? Well, then, the difference is this. With "My brother is sick" I know what to think--if only.... "It might be true if only I had a brother." With "That barn looks red" I do not know what to think--if only.... "It might be true if only..." what? I do not have any "it" to think of--which might be true. This description of the difference comes to mind. The idea of the truth of "My brother is sick" stands still while I imagine that I have a brother. The idea of the truth of "That barn looks red" is not some single idea which will stand still while I imagine one thing or another.

If it is not one single idea which will stand still while I imagine a background "presupposition" for it, then it must be several different ideas. The words "That barn looks red" must contain several different potential ideas--so that I cannot fasten on any one as the proper one to be actualized. This suggests a different pigeonhole for the linguistic phenomenon. I am talking about the words "That barn looks red" as they might pop into my head without any preceding events or thoughts which lead up to them. There is no setting in which they fit. True, the words are not as completely alien in the circumstances as they might be--not as completely alien as "Tokyo is the largest city in the world" would be. I am within eyesight of a barn, and that barn is the subject of my remark. But there is nothing more than that to provide a background or preface for the words "That barn looks red." Although I am looking at and thinking of that particular barn, the words come into my mind as a complete surprise to me, and I cannot make heads or tails of them.

I am now inclined to think that the reason I cannot make anything of them is that I cannot make any one definite thing of them. The words are "ambiguous." There are different ways I might take the words and I do not know which is the right way. If there were a background it would enable me to resolve this ambiguity, but since there is no background I cannot resolve it. The one word that causes all the trouble, of course, is the word "looks." It has different senses, and I do not know which sense to give it in this sentence, "That barn looks red."

This linguistic phenomenon is one with which we are all familiar. Suppose that I run across an isolated group of words (a sentence): I find them left on a blackboard after all else has been erased or I find them on a torn scrap of paper. I do not know the context--the story or discussion or description or what--of which the words were a part, and so there are many things I cannot know about what was being said. But in many cases something pretty definite is carried by the words alone, and I understand it without the help of the missing context. Suppose the words are "Some lizards are viviparous." They might be words used to illustrate a certain combination of sounds and stresses in an English poetry class. Or, of course, they might have been written in order to impart a certain piece of biological information--a simple statement of fact. Regardless, though, of what the setting might have been--which would show me what the writer was up to-- there is something definite conveyed by the words. By themselves they are a purported statement of a certain biological fact. Sometimes the words themselves do not convey anything quite so complete. For example, "This is a lilac bush." I get from these words only the statement that something (whatever or wherever) is a lilac bush. From "My grandfather has malaria," I can get only the purported fact that the writer's grandfather has malaria at the time those words were written. With the words "That barn looks red," which pop into my head, I get just a little more help: I know which barn it is that is said to look red.

Sometimes, when the words are such that I might expect them to give me a statement of fact, I discover that I cannot tell what fact they give because one (or more) of the words has more than one meaning. Suppose that I find on a slip of paper only the words "John posted the letter which was written by his uncle." Then the words will tell me that someone named John (whoever he is) posted a letter which had been written by his uncle (whoever he is). But what do the words tell me that John did? Did he put the letter in a mailbox or did he fasten the letter to a bulletin board? I cannot tell which. If I had the introduction or background or setting for the words, it would doubtless show clearly which was the proper reading. But I have nothing but the words to go on, and so I have no way of deciding the thing. The two undecidable possibilities come from the fact that the word "post" has two different senses. It means either "to mail" or "to display in a public place." Such sentences are easy to produce. "He waved his hairpiece." Did he give it a curly appearance or did he take it off and wave it as a flag? "He priced the watch," "He dressed the chicken," "He pointed his pencil," "He recalled the witness."

I am inclined to think that the sentence "That barn looks red" is like one of these: the reason I do not know what to make of it is that it contains the troublesome word "looks." In fact the word "looks" is more troublesome than "post": "post" has only two relevant senses whereas "looks" probably has many. At any rate when I have the sentence "That barn looks red" and I have no background, no setting for the sentence, I am unable to determine what sense the word "looks" is to have. So quite naturally I cannot make heads or tails of it.

I am inclined to put the linguistic phenomenon I have on my hands into this pigeonhole: it is a case of "ambiguity" and the "ambiguous" word is "looks." But on second thought this does not seem the proper pigeonhole for it at all. In the case of a sentence like "John posted the letter which was written by his uncle" I do not need the details of context in order that I might get a definite statement of fact from it. I do not need to know who wrote it or for what purpose. I need only be told in what sense I should take the verb "post." The word "post" means mail: then John mailed the letter. The word "post" means "put up for display": then John put the letter up for display.

Suppose now that I have the sentence "That barn looks red." It pops into my head quite unexpectedly and I do not know what to make of it. What fact do those words, by themselves, purport to tell? I do not know what to think of as that fact, the barn's looking red. Would I know what fact to think of if I were told in what sense to take the word "looks"? How would anyone tell me in what sense I was to take the words "looks"? How many relevant senses are there? What could someone tell me? "Looks" has the sense of "seems to be." "Looks" has the sense of "has the look of." "Looks" has the sense of "appears." None of these would help me: they might make things worse. What could someone say? "'Looks' has the sense of 'looks' as when the atmosphere is clear and colors are seen in their purity." "'Looks' has the sense of 'looks' as when things are seen through colored glasses." "'Looks' has the sense of 'looks' as when one suffers a visual abnormality and knows that he judges things to be colors other than they are." These characterizations of the sense of "looks" are not like those I gave for "post." For "post" I gave the relevant senses without supplying any of the details of context or background for the words "John posted the letter." If these characterizations of "looks" are helpful to me, if with their help I can think anything definite for "That barn looks red," it is only because they supply a significant part of the background and context which I have supposed was missing. It is suggested that I am to imagine myself with a certain visual abnormality or to imagine myself to be an artist sizing up the look of things, or that I am to imagine myself remarking on the clarity of the atmosphere and the striking purity of the colors. These characterizations can help me make something definite out of the words only because they suggest a background for the words. And that they are not supposed to do. So, I cannot after all comfortably fit this linguistic phenomenon into the pigeonhole of "ambiguity."

One might reply to all of this in the following way: for the sense-datum theory we need only one sense of "looks" and it can be given by example. When I said that if a thing is red it looks red, I meant of course that it looks red in the way that the red barn looks red in your example (2). That is the only case which is relevant. In this case "looks" has the sense of "epistemological withdrawal" or "pulling one's neck in." In such circumstances as these I might say that the barn is red, but then anyone who knew the circumstances might ask me how I could be sure. His question would remind me of the fact that I had taken medicine

which is known to affect color vision. And when I was
reminded of that fact I should then say "It looks red.
I am not after all entirely sure that I can determine
the color of the barn by sight."

Of course this reply is misplaced. In this circumstance a red thing looks red all right, but I, who
look at it, do not see that it is red. If I told someone the barn was red and he asked me how I knew, I
could not say that I saw that it was red--not at the
time when I had uncertainties about the reliability of
my color vision. It is not true, in this case, both
that it looks red and that I see that it is red.

Roderick Chisholm thinks that certain verbs,
"seem," "appear," and others, have several different
senses, and that among these senses is a "descriptive,
phenomenological" one. When we use one of these verbs
in this sense we can give a description of the "directly evident" as it is presented in "sense experience."
That is, we can give a sense-datum description. In one
of their senses, the verbs are used to report a belief
and not a sensory experience: "'It seems to me that I
see light' could be replaced by 'I believe that I see
light.' Taken in this way, the 'seems'-statement ex-
presses... a belief statement." In another sense, these verbs may be used to provide the speaker with a
hedge. When I use one of the expressions in this way,
"I play it safe, indicating... that what I say carries
no guarantee at all...." When I use the verb in this
sense, what I say "cannot be said to describe what is
directly evident, for it cannot be said to describe
anything at all."[2]

Then there is a third sense, the "descriptive, phenomenological one." Chisholm says:

> When "appear" is used in this descriptive, phe-
> nomenological" way, one may say consistently
> and without any incongruity, "That thing ap-
> pears white to me in this light, but I know
> that it is really grey." One may also say,
> again, consistently and without any incongru-
> ity, "It appears white to me in this light and
> I know that, as a matter of fact, it is
> white."[3]

This is difficult to appraise as it stands. I must

---

[2]Roderick Chisholm, **Theory of Knowledge** (Englewood Cliffs, N.J., Prentice - Hall, 1966), p. 30

[3]R. Chisholm, **Theory of Knowledge**, p. 31.

assume that Chisholm has made a slip in his choice of verbs. Surely he wants "looks" and not "appear." "With the first flakes of snow the juncos appear as if by magic." Juncos may appear in that way. I'm sure Chisholm means to have his sentence read "That thing looks white...." With this correction, then, Chisholm says that one may say "That looks white, but I know that it is gray" and also "That looks white and I know that it is white." Also Chisholm has made it plain that there is a question about the light. "It looks white in this light...." Something then must be funny about the light. What are the examples to which Chisholm is appealing? I pass what I believe to be a brown barn. The light seems somehow strange to me and I say "That barn looks red (in this light)." And a brown barn might thus look red. But it may have been painted red just today. Suppose that I am told that it is freshly painted and is now red. I might say, "Well, that explains why it looks red: it looks red and it is red." How is this supposed to show that I have given a "phenomenological" or sense-datum description of the directly evident in sensation? I suspect that something is funny about the light, therefore I may not be able to tell by looking what color the barn is. I say "It looks red...." If I do not think that something is funny about the light I shall not say "It looks red...." If I did say that, a hearer would not know what to make of it. I could not make anything of it if I had said it to myself. In fact, I could not say that in any sense other than that those words might come out of my mouth. When I find out that the barn is red and hence that nothing is funny about the light, I still say "It looks red." But I add "and it is red." Surely no one could understand this who was not cognizant of the details of the story. "It looks red" is still appropriate because I had reason to think I could not tell its true color in this light. There is also a little word-fun in what I say. My audience will appreciate this. To the extent that I want to say "It looks red..." I imagine that I cannot tell its color by sight, and to the extent that I want to say "It is red" and to imply that I can see that it is red, then I do not want to say "It looks red." One who did not understand the position I was in could not make heads or tails of what I said. Nothing could be made of it. Surely a "phenomenological description" does not need a context of suspicious lighting in order to be comprehensible. No, but the point is this: in such a circumstance one can find an example of a "phenomenological description." But if there is this phenomenological sense of "looks" I ought to be able to say anytime, anywhere, "I am going to describe how that looks and then say such things as: 'That grass looks green,' 'That white house looks white.' If I did this, I do not believe that I could understand my performance. I should not be able to make anything of these words of mine. "Looks green?" "Looks white?" "How looks?" What does it mean to say that green grass looks green, a white house looks white? I do not know what it means to say that anything looks red or green--or some color--unless I have the details of the context or can pretty well guess at them.

2. I have been trying to bring up and make plain a certain objection to the sense-datum interpretation of "It looks red." That objection is this: it is not always the case that something looks red when I see that it is red. I had first, therefore, to think what is involved in seeing that something is red. It is obvious that I can see that a barn is red even when I am not in a position to say so. I may later be in a position to say "I saw that it was red." I can show, retrospectively, that I saw that it was red. So I can show that I often see that a barn is red when I should not say "I see that the barn is red." If, at the time, I had said "I see that the barn is red," I should have really puzzled my hearer.

Why, by the same means, can't I show that a barn looks red at a time when it would be most puzzling of me to say so? Suppose that I am walking along with Langley. We pass the barn and I look first at the barn and then at Langley, and I say in a puzzled tone, "Does that red barn look brown?" Langley says, "No. It looks red. It looks red--just at it always has." Now doesn't this show that the barn has always looked red--even though there was no occasion for saying so? And if that is true, then it looked red whenever I saw it and saw that it was red. And that shows that the sense-datum interpretation of "It looks red" is right after all.

Does this example show that a red barn always looks red? I look at the red barn, and I suggest to Langley that something is odd here: I suggest that the barn looks brown. He looks--perhaps moving his head back and forth to get a good look, or something like that--and says "No. It looks red." His tone must imply "No, I don't see anything wrong or strange." Then he says, "It looks red--just as it always has." Perhaps it would have been more natural to give Langley the line "It looks red to me" rather than "It looks red," but the important question is: how am I to understand the words "...just as it always has"?

I see that a barn is red, I decided, if I should be

187

prepared to say "It's red" and "I see that it's red" if I were asked the questions "What color is it?" and "How do you know?" By similar reasoning, the barn should look red to Langley at a time when he would not say so, if he were prepared to answer the relevant question. And what is the question? I should think it is this: "Is something strange here? Does that barn look brown to you?" Thus I am inclined to think that the words "...just as it always has" imply that had Langley been asked the same question at any previous time, he would have said that the barn looked red.

I was first inclined to take the words "...just as it always has" to mean "If I had been asked what color the barn looks I should have said 'It looks red'." Now I think that is not right. I think the words mean "If I had been asked whether the barn (strangely) looks brown, I should have said 'It looks red'."

If someone came up to me and said "Is something strange here? Does that barn look brown?" I should say, after taking a very careful look, "No, it looks red," or perhaps "No. It looks red to me." What, though, if someone said "There is nothing strange or irregular here. There is nothing odd about the way that barn looks. But what color does it look?" I should not then know what to think. I think I should not know what question he was asking me.

3. When I think of occasions where I see that the barn is red, and I think of occasions where the barn looks red to me, I can see that "That is red" and "That looks red" are not connected in the way the sense-datum interpretation suggests. And yet it is very easy to "forget" the details when I philosophize about vision. I can so easily imagine myself looking at the side of a red barn. Then I think somehow to myself, "That looks red." I imagine looking at a red barn and I imagine that I say these words to myself; and with the help of some philosophical expectations, I can make it seem true and obvious that a barn looks red when I see that it is red. There is the red surface. It is clearly before my eyes, and I can see that it is red. Surely it looks red. Surely if it is red and I can see that it is red, then it looks red to me. What could be more plain than that?

II

I have considered the expression "It looks (red, green, ...)" because I can honestly think, at times, that the expression functions in the way a sense-datum picture of perception suggests that it does. I can honestly think that it functions in that way when I stare at a brightly-colored object and say the words over to myself, without trying to put the words into examples where they belong. I considered "It looks (red, green, ...)" because, when I am unguarded, this expression seems to come the closest of any to supplying what a sense-datum theory needs. It does not supply it, I now see; but even if it did, it would only give a small part of what is required. If would give the "looks" of the color of a thing. And what a sense-datum theory needs is the "looks" of the thing in its entirety.

Sense-datum philosophers would obviously prefer some expression which would take them the whole way. And some have suggested that there are expressions which will do that--or at least very nearly do that. They have suggested "It seems to be ..." and "It looks like...," but these are unlikely candidates and could only be suggested as some how vaguely pointing in the right direction. Some philosophers have taken much more seriously the idiom, "It seems to me that I see...." At times A. J. Ayer[4] seems to think that this will give him reports of sense-data. This does not strike me as a tempting or likely candidate, but even so I should like to examine it--to try to determine why it might seem to some, at least, to give a full-scale sense-datum report.

When might one say "I seem to see (something)"?

(1) Coulter tells fortunes by looking in a crystal ball in a darkened room. I go to consult him. He dims the lights and says, "Let me try to see your future." He peers into the ball for a long time, muttering. "Nothing is clear," he says. "Ah, now I see something. I see you riding a horse. No. I see a horse. It is very vague. I seem to see an animal...." This example will not give anything like a sense-datum report.

Coulter looks into a crystal ball and then says something like "I see you travelling to Afghanistan in April." That is, he says that he sees something which he thinks you are going to do or something which he thinks is going to happen. That is the sort of thing

---

[4]A. J. Ayer, The Problems of Knowledge (Baltimore, Penquin Books, 1956), pp. 95-104.

he "sees in a crystal ball." But we can discuss with
him the workings of the crystal ball--the part the ball
plays in his fortune telling. He may say that he sees
vague, shifting shapes in the crystal ball and they
suggest what is going to happen. Perhaps he sees
nothing in the crystal ball--but looking into the ball
makes these "fortunes" come into his mind. When he
says "I seem to see..." he is saying that he is not
certain what the "fortune" amounts to which has come
into his mind. This is certainly not a report on
sense-data as they might occur in the perception of
some "thing" or "happening."

Perhaps Coulter sees in the crystal ball a tiny
moving picture--a detailed image in brilliant colors.
There is then no question of what it suggests to him.
He does not need to wait for something to come into his
mind to make up the "fortune." Now if he says, "I seem
to see..." I suppose he means that because the picture
is blurred or indistinct he cannot tell what the "fortune" is. Again, this is a way of saying that he is
not certain what the "fortune" amounts to; it is nothing like a report on sense-data.

(2) Jansen was the first to enter a room in which
a murder victim was found. He called the police.
Later a detective questions him, but he is so flustered
he cannot remember much. The detective says, "Relax.
Close your eyes and try to picture the room as you entered it." Jansen closes his eyes, tilts his head back
and says, "All right, I am now coming into the room. I
see a coat over the sofa--it is gray." "What do you
see on the coffee table?" "A cup--and--and--I'm not
sure--I seem to see a cigarette case." This, of
course, could not be a report on a present sense-datum.
But perhaps, in the historical present sense, it is a
report on a past sense-datum. Again, though, it is
partly a tentative report on a physical object, a
cigarette case. Jansen thinks he may have seen a
cigarette case, and he reports this by telling what he
can recall and he is trying to stimulate his memory by
closing his eyes and thinking how the room looked. In
particular, he is trying to visualize what he saw in
the room.

(3) Hoskins and I have been lost for some time in
an old coastal spruce forest. It is very foggy; and we
have been trying to hike continuously in one direction.
Finally we arrive at what appears to be the forest
edge; a screen of fog hangs before us. Hoskins climbs
up in a leaning tree to look around. I turn and shout
up to him in the tree, "What do you see?" Hoskins
says, "The fog is very thick. I can't make anything
out very clearly." He looks intently into the fog

190

bank, and he says somewhat meditatively, "It seems to me that I see a building not far away."

This certainly doesn't suggest anything like a sense-datum report. Hoskins undoubtedly sees many things: the fog certainly, and perhaps vague outlines of bushes and trees. The question is whether he sees a building. He can't be sure, but he thinks he may. Because of the thick fog he is in doubt about whether he sees a building. In the language of a sense-datum philosopher, a building is a "physical object" and Hoskins wonders whether he sees a physical object--in the ordinary way one sees a physical object.

(4) Henry is subject to spells of hallucination. He hallucinates large animals usually and he sees them before him at a distance of about fifty feet. He always knows when a spell is coming on him because just before the hallucination begins he gets a little dizzy and his eyes burn in a peculiar way. Henry and I have been sitting in the park, talking about salmon fishing, when a spell comes on him. He frowns, rubs his eyes, and stares intently for a few minutes; and then, as with relief, he turns and speaks to me again. "I just had one of those spells, you know. I saw a large moose looking right at me. Then it slowly faded away." "Do you always know when a spell is coming on?" I ask. And Henry says, "Yes, I do. I know when it's coming, and I've been through it a thousand times. I know I'm going to hallucinate an animal, and so I am quite prepared for it. Even so, when it first appears--and for a few moments--I am still surprised. I know it is not real--still, it seems to me that I see the animal--right before me."

This might be a better candidate. For one thing, the language of "visual experience" seems at home here. Henry might well say "It is a disturbing visual experience. I know I am not really seeing anything. For a few moments, though, it seems to me for all the world that I am." Henry is saying that if he did not know he was hallucinating, he would say that he saw a moose. There is nothing about the animal or its surroundings which gives it away as a creature of his hallucination. Then, I take it, the moose begins to fade or to shimmer, or to take on an aura which is peculiar to Henry's hallucinated moose.

The difficulty with this as a "visual experience" of the kind which is supposed to be the content of a sense-datum report is that the experience would have to be the same as it is in any ordinary report of what is seen. If Henry were to say on some ordinary Tuesday, "I see the mailman coming down the road," then that visual experience would have to be present, that visual experience which I am supposing he would report with the words, "I seem to see the mailman...." Of course, it is not. What makes Henry's vivid hallucination a visual experience is that it is unusual and strange. The experience is this: Henry knows that he is hallucinating, and even so he is inclined or half-inclined to think that he sees a moose. Nothing like this is present when he sees the mailman. He does not know he is hallucinating. And he does not almost believe that he sees the mailman in spite of that.

Yet there is the moose! Henry is hallucinating a moose, and he knows it. In spite of that, he is half-convinced that he sees the moose. What about the moose? Isn't that a sense-datum? Isn't that something which is the same in normal vision and in hallucination? Do we have two things here: an hallucinated moose and a real moose? Or do we have only one: a sense-datum which is present both in hallucinations and in normal vision?

I have been through this before,[5] so I shall now be short with it. It is only when philosophizing that I might think that there is only one object here, and that that object is a moose-ish sense-datum or something like that. Henry certainly will not think those things. When he sees a moose, he certainly thinks his "object"--what he sees--is a moose. And a moose is a far cry from a moose-ish sense-datum. When he hallucinates, what he hallucinates is a moose, too. So perhaps there is one object, but then in both cases it is a moose. Of course Henry can talk about the moose he hallucinates, and at times it is shimmery and semi-transparent. Henry does not believe that there are any shimmery and semi-transparent moose. So when he is concerned with the details--particularly the strange details--of the moose he hallucinates, he may speak of it as "the moose I hallucinate" or "my hallucinated moose." Then, of course, he does not think this is the same "object" as the moose he sometimes sees wading in the lake at the bottom of the hill.

I can think of many cases which would be variants of example (3). I need to imagine things which interfere with normal vision, such as heat waves, drugs, and others. Suppose that a person has had the pupils of his eyes completely dilated, and then he goes for a walk on the beach in the bright sun. "I can't see a thing," he says. "I keep trying, but everything is a

---

[5]"Seeing Things," in F. B. Ebersole, Things We Know (Eugene, Oregon, University of Oregon Books, 1967), pp. 18-49.

blurry glare. No. Wait. It seems to me that I see a person standing there."

Also, it is easy to think of examples like (4). Instead of hallucination, one could consider double vision, mirage, or illusion. Suppose a person to have double vision. He claims that he can always tell the real thing from the double and he shows that he can by always pointing to the real thing. Now, one time he knows that he is having double vision because he sees two pencils on his desk where he has just laid one, but he cannot tell the real from the double. He says, "It seems to me that I am seeing two pencils." Or someone might remark on how he almost took an after-image for a stain on the wall. "I know I was having a red after-image but for a moment it seemed to me that I saw a stain on the wall." I can also imagine cases similar to (1). Instead of looking in a crystal ball, a person could be attending to the images that float before his mind. He could be looking at tea leaves or ink blots, or such.

"It seems to me that I see..." could not be taken as a sense-datum report in cases (1) - (4). And because of the relevant similarities of these new examples to examples (1) - (4), "It seems to me that I see..." could not be a sense-datum report in them either. Where, then, can "It seems to me that I see..." be a report on "sense-experience"? Perhaps this passage from A. J. Ayer's Problems of Knowledge contains the required suggestion.

> ...The drawback to employing such a formula as "it seems to me that I now see a cigarette case" for the description of one's experience is that the phrase "it seems to me" most often serves to express a tentative opinion. One uses it in the cases where one is hesitant about the identification of what one is perceiving. It would be considered odd for me to say "it seems to me that I now see a cigarette case" if I had in fact no doubt that I did see one. But the **oddity** is not so great that **there need** be **excessive** difficulty in understanding what is meant.[6]

Ayer thinks it would be odd to say "It seems to me that I now see a cigarette case" unless the speaker was hesitant about identifying the thing seen as a cigarette

---

[6]A. J. Ayer, The Problem of Knowledge, p. 101. The bold type is my own.

case.

Ayer seems to be thinking that the words "It seems to me that I see..." would be out of place--and hence odd--except in a context like that supplied in my example (3). If that is what he is thinking, then his statement of the conditions necessary for one to appropriately say "I seem to see..." is not quite right, or at any rate, it is not complete. Suppose that a person drops his cigarette case while walking through a field of high grass. As soon as he becomes aware that he has dropped his cigarette case, he retraces his path through the grass looking for the lost case. He spots a bright metallic object--but it is almost hidden from view by the bent grass. What does he say? Surely he does not say, "I seem to see my cigarette case." This person's position satisfies Ayer's characterization of the required condition for saying "I seem to see...." That is, the person is "hesitant about the identification of what he is perceiving," but he does not say, "I seem to see...." Perhaps Ayer does not mean his characterization of the condition to be complete. At any rate it seems that a more complete characterization would include the condition that the speaker is hesitant because he thinks that something is wrong with his eyes, or something wrong with the atmosphere--that something is suspect about the organic or physical conditions which affect his vision of the object in question.

In my example (3) something is wrong with the atmosphere: it is so foggy that one cannot clearly see objects at a distance. Apparently Ayer does not think of any of the other contexts--such as examples (1), (2), and (4)--in which it is in order for a person to say, "I seem to see...." In any case, Ayer says, "The oddity is not so great that there need be excessive difficulty in understanding what is meant." How is Ayer thinking? He thinks that one can discern "what is meant" in spite of the fact that it is presented in an odd or bizarre context. This is a tempting thing to think.

I shall imagine a dialogue between two people, Lee and Herbert, in order to explore what may be behind Ayer's way of thinking, and to determine whether it is right. First let me supply a clear case where one of the characters--I shall call him Herbert--will say, "I seem to see...," and in which his saying this will be in perfect order--will raise no question at all. Lee has a deep but amateurish interest in the physiology of vision, and he has persuaded Herbert to become a subject of some of his experiments. Today he is testing to determine what Herbert is able to see while the pupils of his eyes are dilated with atropine. He puts atropine drops in Herbert's eyes, and after a suitable time, he leads him about through a strange house asking "What is that?" and "What is this?" "Can you see anything there?" and "Can you see that?" Herbert says, "There, I can see that. That is a clothes tree." Then he says, "I see something there on the table. No, I'm not sure. It may be just my eyes. I seem to see a cigarette case." In this situation Herbert's "I seem to see..." is quite unexceptionable. Here, then, is an example of an appropriate context for the words, "I seem to see...."

Suppose now that it is one day many weeks later. Herbert and Lee meet on Main Street. They exchange hello's, and as they are commenting on the weather Herbert takes out his cigarette case and offers Lee a cigarette. Then he takes one for himself and lights it rather affectedly. Herbert shows Lee his cigarette case: "See those initials? They were engraved by my uncle many years ago." Now he holds the case out at half-arm's length and while looking at it admiringly he says "I seem to see a cigarette case." That would be a very odd thing for Herbert to say, and as he begins to speak again Lee stops him short: "What on earth do you mean? You seem to see a cigarette case?"

Herbert: Surely you know what I mean. You just don't know why I said what I said.

Lee: No, not at all. It's a very odd thing to be saying--so odd I really don't know what to make of it. Were you reminding me of the tests I conducted on you when your pupils were dilated?

H.: No. No. I wasn't thinking of that or of anything else in particular. I just said "I seem to see..." because it's true and I wanted to say it.

L.: What's true?

H.: (Holding the case up again.) I seem to see a cigarette case.

L.: Are you having some trouble with your vision?

H.: No. Not at all. I see perfectly. I see my old silver cigarette case there as clearly as I have ever seen anything.

L.: I am flabbergasted.

H.: But why? You do not expect me to say any such thing, and so it strikes you as odd. Isn't that it? You wonder why I should say such a thing. Well, then the only reason I say "I seem to see..." is that it is true--or maybe more than that, it is also philosophically interesting and important. I say it because I think it's good to consider such a thing once in a while.

L.: Consider what thing?

195

H.: The thing I said.

L.: I know. But what is it? I mean, what is it that's interesting and important?

H.: It is what I said, and it is interesting because it is a description of the immediately given in sense-experience. It is what some philosophers call a sense-datum report.

L.: I am not ready yet to discuss what it is. I want to determine first that there is something-- something to discuss. You said something but I am quite puzzled by it. I can't make anything out of it. And so I am flabbergasted.

H.: But why? When I was having all that trouble seeing things--when you dilated my pupils--you were not puzzled when I said "I seem to see...."

L.: No, of course not: not then.

H.: Well, I'm saying the same thing now--only now I do not have the visual difficulty, the dilated pupils, the blurred vision.

L.: Same thing? Well, **same** only in that you spoke the same words.

H.: No. **Same** in that I said the same true thing. The "meaning" is the same--and it is a sense-datum report.

L.: Go back and consider again what you said when your pupils were dilated and you could not see clearly. Surely, you were not giving a sense-datum report then-- when you thought that you might be seeing a cigarette case. Under those conditions, when you say "I seem to see...," **that** is just what you report--the fact that you believe you see a cigarette case: you are far from certain about it.

H.: No. Now I see what our problem is. I do not think of that as **what** I report. That is the situation in which I make the report. I am in a situation in which I am uncertain: because of my blurry vision, I am not sure that I can see a cigarette case. I believe that I can; so I report on what is immediately given to me--sense-data.

L.: That seems a most implausible way to describe or interpret what I understand you to be saying when you say "I seem to see a cigarette case."

H.: It seems quite plausible to me.

L.: I suspect you do not find it so just by considering what you say in the situation when you have dilated pupils. I suspect you read that interpretation into your words--because of a philosophical theory you espouse.

H.: If so, I am not aware of that. As you know, I do hold a theory of perception--and I believe in sense-data. I need the example to illustrate and support the

196

theory, but I must not just read the theory into the example.

L.: Then how can you tell that the words "I seem to see..." are a report on sense-data?

H.: The form of your questions suggest the answer: I tell from the words. The words themselves are a description of what is immediately given. Hence in order to tell what one is saying who says "I seem to see..." one needs only to consider the words.

L.: Now you have quite lost me. If I have only the words and no context at all, I should not know what to make of the words. Think of the examples Ebersole supplied earlier in this essay. How would you know that the speaker was not telling a fortune, or trying to recall the scene of a murder, or telling how realistic some hallucination is?

H.: I was not thinking of the words "I seem to see..." in those situations, but only where the speaker is uncertain about the object perceived.

L.: Then you do not find your interpretation given by the words alone. You do consider the words in a certain context.

H.: Yes, but in that context, I consider the words alone. I start with a context in which the speaker is uncertain about the object. I am the speaker and I have dilated pupils. I cannot be certain about the object on the table so I say "I seem to see a cigarette case." I have described what is given in my perception—whether there is a cigarette case there or not. Now I use the words in that way—that sense—in other circumstances when I am not uncertain about the object I see.

L.: Your case, then, depends upon your words "I seem to see..." as used in the situation where you have dilated pupils. It must be quite clear that these words in that situation are a description of sense-data.

H.: Yes.

L.: That seems to me a most unlikely reading of the words "I seem to see...." You think of the words as describing something which may or may not be a phys-ical object—something given in "immediate perception." When you have dilated pupils, cannot see clearly, and are uncertain about the identity of the cigarette case, you are not uncertain about the fact that you see a "physical object." You see a "physical object" all right—indistinctly, in a blur—and you are uncertain about the identity of the "physical object." You think it is a cigarette case, but you can't tell for certain what it is. It seems a fantastic proposal, to inter-pret the words "I seem to see..." in this circumstance as you suggest, that is, as coming to something like this: "I have a vision-like awareness of something like a cigarette case, real or illusory or halluci- natory or something...."

H.: Perhaps that is an unlikely interpretation of the words "I seem to see..." in those circumstances. In those circumstances, though, one cannot report with confidence on the nature of the physical object he sees—and so he might take the occasion to make a sense-datum report.

L.: But his hearer would not take him to be making a sense-datum report.

H.: No, of course not.

L.: And he could not use those words in any other circumstance to make a sense-datum report—certainly not in any of the circumstances we have considered.

H.: That seems so.

L.: So he could not be using the words in any way that would allow them to be understood.

H.: No. He would simply have to say to himself "Now I am going to take the occasion to report on my sense-data" and then say "I seem to see..." in order to give an example of a sense-datum report.

T.: Now you are saying that a person can give a sense-datum report any time he wants to. All he needs to do is to tell himself that he is going to report on his sense-data—and then go on to do it.

H.: Yes. That's right.

T.: Have you changed your mind in this matter? Just a few minutes ago you had quite a different attitude. You agreed then that the words "I seem to see..." could be given a sense-datum interpretation only where the speaker was in doubt about the identity of the physical object he was talking about.

H.: Yes, I see that I have become quite confused.

5. THE ANALYSIS OF HUMAN ACTIONS

I have many times asked the question, "What is an action?" and now I want to ask, "What was I asking when I asked the question?" What kind of understanding did I have of the question, and how did I come to have that understanding? For one thing, I could not have asked the question without some philosophical tutoring. When one asks a philosophical "What is...?" question he needs to know where to turn for help. "What is vision?" is "What is it to see?" and so one turns for help to examples wherein someone sees, examples in which sentences such as these will appear: "He sees," "I see," "She saw." For "What is emotion?" we must look for help in examples where one would say, "He is sad," "He is pleased," "He is jealous," "He is sick of heart," and others. For "What is an action?" we must look to examples where one answers the question "What did you (he, she) do?" or "What was he doing?" by telling what a person did or is doing. The philosophical question, "What is an action?" is the question "What is it for a person to do something?"

It is easy to see that answers to the questions "What were you doing?" or "What was he doing?" will specify two very different sorts of things. First, such as these: "He was thinking of home," "He formed an image in his mind's eye of a soaring buzzard." And others, such as these: "He whittled a stick with his pocket knife," "He pointed his finger at me." The first ones, we are inclined to say, are purely mental actions: whatever is done is done in the mind. The second ones are physical actions: in those something is done in the physical world. As soon as I observe the distinction between mental and physical actions, I realize that philosophers have never been greatly concerned with mental actions; and when they have asked the question, "What is an action?" they have almost always meant, "What is a physical action?" And so, too, when I asked "What is an action?" I meant "What is a physical action?"[1]

---

[1] "An action must have the aspect of physical activity, either positively by way of doing or negatively by way of refraining. Thus purely mental acts done solely in **foro interno** cannot qualify as actions. Giving overt verbal agreement is an action, giving tacit assent is not; being worried is not of itself an action, though pacing worriedly is. Every action must have an overt physical component and involves bodily

So the question is "What is a physical action?" And of course part of the answer is "It is physical." But physical in what way? And what physical things are involved? For a long time philosophers tried to spell out the answer in this way: "An action is a movement of a human body which is caused by an act of will or it is a group of occurrences which includes at least one such movement of a human body." J. Austin in **Lectures on Jurisprudence** (1963) says, "Certain movements of our bodies follow invariably and immediately our wishes and these consequent movements are human volitions and acts...."

I ask the question while prepared for the answer, "An action is an occurrence or group of occurrences--among which is a movement of a human body caused by an act of will." I am thinking of an answer in terms of genus and differentium. The genus is "occurrence involving movement of part of a human body" and the differentium "caused by an act of will." Now I am prepared to re-examine this differentium and find it wrong in all sorts of ways, perhaps even nonsensical. But I am not prepared to revise or reject the specification of the genus. And this is not a unique attitude to take toward a philosophical question: it is not unlike the attitude philosophers take toward other questions. For example, philosophers often ask, "What is knowledge?" while taking for granted that the genus is "true opinion (or belief)." Their question is really, "How does knowledge differ from other true beliefs?" Grice in his article "Meaning,"[2] and John Searle[3] in comments on that article, ask the question, "What is it to say something and mean something?" They make it plain that their question is to be understood as the question, "What more is involved in saying and meaning something than the uttering of sounds?" It is taken for granted that meaning something is at least uttering sounds. The genus for the genus-difference answer is "uttering sounds." Likewise for "What is an action?"

---

activities of some sort. It is thus no accident that paradigm actions are done by persons--i.e., agents with corporeal bodies." Nicholas Rescher, "Action Descriptions" in **The Nature of Human Actions**, ed. Myles Brand (Glenview, Ill., Scott, Foresman & Co., 1970), p. 248.

[2]**Philosophical Review** (July 1957), pp. 377-88.

[3]John Searle, **Speech Acts** (London and New York, Cambridge University Press, 1969), pp. 53-9.

I take the genus as given, it gives me part of my understanding of questions. I think of occurrences, physical occurrences or happenings, and I think that actions are among them. My question is, "How do actions differ from other physical occurrences?"

What understanding, then, did I have of the question "What is an action?" Unless I know that something like that answer is to be given, I think I should have no way of understanding the question at all. Like many philosophical questions, I think I can understand it only after I know what the answer is to be. And knowing that "bodily movement caused by will" is an appropriate answer, I can see the frame of mind I am supposed to be in in order to have some understanding of the question. In short, when I ask the question, "What is an action?" I have a certain philosophical view or picture of things. The world is made up of physical occurrences or happenings and among these are human actions. Some occurrences are "mere" physical occurrences, others are human actions. The distinction is not to be found in the occurrences in so far as they are occurrences. Perhaps they are distinguished by their causes: actions have a peculiar cause such as an act of will. Whatever an act of will is thought to be, it cannot be just one more physical occurrence among the physical occurrences. An act of will cannot be found in the world of occurrences at all. It must be in a different realm or scene entirely--perhaps the mental or spiritual.

Thus when I look out upon the world of events, happenings, occurrences, the human actions which are found there are--as happenings--indistinguishable from the "mere" happenings which make up the physical, biological, physiological world. An action is in part a bit of the physical world; but also in part it is not. At first I think that the non-physical part is an act of will which acts as a cause of some physical occurrences, but it is impossible to think any such view coherently. What am I thinking when I think that an act of will is a non-physical thing? I must mean that an act of will is something in the mind, an idea perhaps, something of which I am clearly aware. And then this idea causes or produces a bodily movement--so that, together, that act of will and that bodily movement constitute an action. The action, of course, is my doing. But how does the act of will get into my mind? Is its getting into my mind not my doing? Do I have no control over it? If I cannot produce it when I want, then I cannot produce the bodily movement when I want. Why then would I think that a bodily movement which I could not produce was part of my action?

I must be able to control or produce the act of will.
But producing an act of will would be an action--not a
physical action, of course, but just like a physical
action, except for lack of bodily movement. It would
be a mental action. How are mental actions distinguished from non-actions? Are they, like physical
actions, caused by an act of will? If so, then that
act of will, also, is an action; and it will be caused
by another act of will, and so on.

What do I mean when I say than an act of will
causes or produces a certain bodily movement? The situation must be as Hume depicts it. First I experience
a certain act of will and then a certain bodily movement, and the first must regularly precede the second.
Would I then have reason to believe that a certain idea
produced a certain bodily movement? Certainly not; or
rather not in the right way. The only relevant experience I have is this: sometimes when I think of something, a bodily movement occurs. Sometimes I can think
so vividly of a cold winter's day that I can make myself shiver. I think of ice and snow and my skin contracts: I shiver. But thinking of ice and snow is not
having an act of will. I do not need to think of anything in order to perform an action such as raising my
arm. I cannot understand the proposal that an idea
could produce such movement of my arm.

Surely human actions are the actions of people. My
actions are my actions: they are the things I do. So
one would naturally think that if they had a cause, I
should be that cause. I should be the cause, that is
and not some act of will.[4] One would naturally think

---

[4]P.T. Geach, for example, thinks that statements
which "ascribe acts to agents" are "paradigm cases of
causal statements." He takes Hume to task for looking
for his (Humean) kind of "causal connexion" between an
act of will and a bodily movement when in his definition of will he has already ascribed an act (motion of
the body) to a person in the ordinary sense of (non-
Humean) causality: "The internal impression we feel
and are conscious of when we knowingly give rise to any
new motion of our body...." According to Geach, then,
when I "knowingly give rise to any new motion of my
body," I cause my body to move in the usual sense of
"cause." Geach presumably agrees with the idea that to
do something is to knowingly give rise to a motion of
the body. And to give rise to a motion of the body is
to cause it "in the ordinary sense of causality." When
acting, I cause the movement or movements of my body.
P.T. Geach, "Ascriptivism," Phil. Review, 69 (1960),
pp. 221-5.

that the person who did the thing which is an action and the cause of that thing would be one and the same. But how could I cause the happenings which are my actions? What is it for something to cause an occurrence? A rock falls down a cliff side. What caused the rock to fall? Water froze and cracked the pedestal of the rock causing it to topple and fall. I sneeze. Pollen falls on the lining of my nose, bringing about a chemical reaction which stimulates a nerve--which in turn makes me sneeze. Freezing water causes a rock to fall. Pollen falling on my nose lining causes me to sneeze.

What sorts of things can I cause? And how can I think of myself causing my own actions? I cause a lot of trouble wherever I go. I may cause a lot of commotion. But trouble and commotion are not actions. What am I to think of as actions? That is, what sort of things should I have before my mind as examples of actions? Actions are of many sorts. Making a deposit at the bank, turning on the hot-water faucet, hoeing weeds, laughing at a joke, making a right turn signal as I drive into an intersection, advising a student to take symbolic logic, telling someone the way to San Jose, wasting time at the race track. How could I possibly think of causing any such things? I must not forget that an action must involve at least one movement of my body. So surely it is not an action in its entirety that I am to think of myself causing but only that part of an action which is a movement of part of my body. I can cause a movement of part of my body--which is a definitive or important part of an action. It does not make sense to think that I cause my signalling a right turn, but surely I can cause my arm to go up--as I approach an intersection.

How am I now thinking? Most actions are complex and one of the simple parts of any complex action is a movement of part of my body. It is that simple part, a movement of part of my body, that I cause--and in so doing, I do the action in its entirety. Complex actions are of many different kinds and the simpler parts enter into the complex in all sorts of different ways. (1) I can, for example, turn on a light by flipping a toggle switch. And of course I flip the switch by moving my wrist and hand upward. That movement of my wrist and hand causes the switch to flip--which in turn allows electricity to flow through the filament of an incandescent bulb. The simple part, here, is the first in a sequence of causes. (2) I can signal a right turn while driving. I raise my left arm while driving into an intersection--and that is the action of signalling a right turn. The simple part, raising my arm, under

203

these circumstances becomes the action of signalling a right turn because of the part it plays in a social system.

The bodily movements, which are parts of complex actions, are the things which I cause. I cause my wrist to twist and my hand to move upward (and thus turn on a light); I cause my left arm to go up (and in so doing signal a right turn); but, of course, this is not right. When I raise my arm to signal a right turn what causes the movement of my arm? What kind of question is that? Perhaps it is a physiologist's question--what else could it be? A physiologist is lecturing to a class and says, "Suppose I raise my arm like this--so--to signal a right turn. Now what are the causes of that particular arm movement?" And now he goes on to give a detailed description of the bones, joints, tendons and muscles of the arm and says, "Nerve currents in the median nerve cause contractions of the deltoid and abducto humerus muscles which pull the tendons of those muscles." And he says other things of this kind. So perhaps in this way a physiologist talks of the causes of a certain arm movement. Of course he does not mention himself, the person who raised his arm, as one among the causes.

Consider again some things that a person may cause--things that I, for example, might cause. (1) I can cause certain things by my actions. I can make people uneasy by grimacing at them. How in some such way could I cause a certain movement of my arm? I might take a drug which causes my arm at unpredictable times to jerk upward. But this is a case where the drug would cause my arm to go upward, not a case where I cause my arm to go upward. Don't I cause the movement of my arm by taking the drug? No, that doesn't sound quite right. I think I should say, "I made my arm go up by taking the drug." What does that come to? I must mean that I contrived it that a drug should cause my arm to go up. Didn't I then cause my arm to go up--only indirectly and through the medium of the drug? No. I should not say that I caused my arm to go up by taking the drug or through the medium of the drug, or anything like that. Of course, I do not do anything like this when signalling a right turn, that is, I do not make my arm go up by taking a drug. There are other ways I can make my arm go up. I can stand near a wall and push hard against it and then when I move suddenly from the wall, my arm goes up. In this case, too, I think I should say, "I make my arm go up by pushing against the wall." I do not do anything like this either in order to signal a right turn. When signalling a turn there is nothing I do to make an arm movement. I cannot think of a case where I should say that I cause my arm to go up.

(2) Sometimes I can be the cause of things by my mere presence. "My presence at the committee meeting caused some people to be uneasy." By my presence I can cause embarrassment, nervousness, concern, a lot of raised eyebrows; but how could my presence at any place cause a movement of my arm? I can only think again of the way I make my arm go up by pushing against a wall and then moving away, but it is not my presence near the wall in this case that causes the upward movement of my arm. I am afraid that I am really trying to think of my presence at the base of my brain and then to think that I can cause a movement of my arm by creating nerve currents which make the muscles of my arm contract. But, of course, I cannot make heads or tails of the idea that I occupy a place at the base of my brain and then cause movements of parts of my body by my presence there.

Why must I do something or be some place in order to make my arm go up? I can, after all, simply raise my arm. When I signal a right turn I do not cause a movement of my arm. With no ado, I raise my arm in that way--the way in which one must raise his arm in order to make a signal for a right turn. This certainly seems a sensible reaction to take to the idea that I cause a bodily movement when I raise my arm. But I cannot take this reaction without ignoring entirely the philosophical question which set me on my way. I am trying to answer the question "What is an action?" And the answer is to start with the notion that "an action is an occurrence or set of occurrences which include a bodily movement." It would not do to complete the account with: "the bodily movement is something someone does--that is, it is itself an action." A bodily movement and an action cannot be identical. And even if they could be--which is impossible--the answer would be patently circular. It would amount to no more than "An action is an action."

I must not forget the question I am asking--and my understanding of it. I ask, "What is an action?" --where I understand "action as opposed to mere occurrences, that is, action as opposed to movements of parts of a body." But what--more concretely--is my understanding of the question? I think that mere occurrences--including bodily movements--are simpler than actions. Actions must be something more than bodily movements. When I look upon the world I can see only occurrences. Occurrences present themselves directly to my eyes. I do not directly see an action, but I can see something and take it as an action because of my upbringing and training in my culture and human way of life. Do I mean that? Surely not: that is too silly for words. Must I say that I can see movements of a humanoid form, or that I can see wheels and steel tubes, but that I cannot see my neighbor mowing his lawn? No. I must be able to see actions; but all the same, seeing actions is a more complex kind of seeing than seeing occurrences. If someone were unfamiliar with actions, he would see only occurrences--including bodily movements. Can I really imagine such a one? Here is a creature from another planet. He is blind to the "action-aspect" of the world. He can see the movements of my arms and legs but he cannot see me rubbing the painful swelling in my sprained ankle. He can see the movements of my mouth and cheeks, but he cannot see me smile. When I speak, he hears acoustical blasts--noises--changing in volume and pitch and rhythm. But he cannot hear me say something. He cannot know what I said. Can I imagine such a being? He cannot speak beause he is action blind and so has no grasp of saying something, telling someone something, relating, predicting, describing, or of any "speech act." Without that surely he has no language. But wait. Though he can't speak, he can think. He can think about the occurrences and movements taking place in the world: he can consider them in his mind. Perhaps he can picture them in his mind's eye. But no. Of course he cannot--for thinking, considering, picturing, are actions even though they do not involve bodily movements. One who is entirely unfamiliar with actions could not understand thinking, contemplating, meditating, considering, visualizing.

What can I mean then when I say that occurrences are simpler than actions? Well, occurrence words are simpler than action words. Occurrence language is simpler than action language. A child can see and have pointed out to him the masses, colors, shapes, and movements of things. So he can easily acquire a vocabulary of thing words and occurrence words. But action words require more. Before he can understand action words, he will have to learn about intentions, purposes, choices, deliberations, social groups and their organization, rules, laws and much more. This can have a plausible ring until I realize that I am saying that a child will have to wait to understand "eat," "get," "bring," and "give," "wait," "drink"-- while the world is first presented to him as an entirely non-human place of masses and motions, and he acquires the vocabulary to characterize that non-human world: "hard," "round," "smooth," "cubical," "shiny."

Well, then, I do not mean that occurrence words are

simpler in some genetic or historical sense. A child might well acquire an action vocabulary before an occurrence vocabulary--and still the action words might be more complex than the occurrence words. I mean "simpler" and "complex"--in meaning. When I explain (or state) the meaning of an action word or phrase I must use one or more occurrence words or phrases. The reverse will not be true. In order to explain or state the meaning of an occurrence word I do not need to use any action words. Thus, mention of some bodily movement or occurrence is part of an explanation of the meaning of an action word or phrase. When I explain or make explicit the idea of the action I must mention some bodily movement.

When I explain the action "raising my arm," then, I must mention some bodily movement. But what could this bodily movement be--a movement which is part of the action of raising my arm, but which by itself is less than the action of raising my arm? The movement is not that movement of my arm which I describe by saying, "My arm goes up." I stand with my side against a wall, and push outward against the wall with my arm. Then I step away from the wall. I find--to my amazement--that my arm goes up of its own accord. I do not raise my arm; it simply goes up. I am surprised by the movement. Of course, this "bodily movement" could not be part of the action of raising my arm. When I raise my arm I am not surprised or amazed by an upward movement of my arm. My arm does not move, then, of its own accord.

When I step from the wall and my arm goes up, I find that sometimes I cannot immediately stop the motion. Although I try to prevent my arm from going up, I do not have complete control over it. The bodily movement which is always part of the action certainly is not like that; that is, it is not a movement over which I have imperfect or incomplete control. Whenever I say, "My arm went up," it is not always the case that I am talking about something which surprises me or is out of my complete control. When I was very young and went to grade school, the teacher would many times turn to the class and say, "Will anyone volunteer to be the chalk monitor?" Of course every student was eager for the glory of being the chalk monitor. What a title to hold! How do I describe the almost frenzied response to her question? "Immediately twenty arms went up--and my arm went up along with all the rest." Of this occurrence I say--and say correctly--"My arm went up." However in this case I was not surprised or amazed by the behavior of my arm and my arm did not move of its own accord, out of my control. I did not try to interfere with the movement of my arm and find that I did not have complete control over it. Of course I could also tell this same story and say—and say correctly—"Twenty students quickly raised their arms, and I raised my arm along with all the rest." This is quite unlike the case where I make my arm go up by pushing against a wall. In that case, "My arm went up" contrasts with "I raised my arm." In the school-room case it is correct to say either "My arm went up" or "I raised my arm." Of course it is more apt, more exactly suggestive to say "My arm went up," and this, I suppose, is because "My arm went up" suggests that I raised my arm quickly and eagerly, so eagerly that my arm raising was like an involuntary movement, out of my control. In this case the words "My arm went up" seem to be used in a figurative way, whereas they are applied quite literally in the case where I made my arm go up by pushing against the wall. However, that is a dangerous thing to be saying. I certainly do not want to say or to suggest that the words "My arm went up" have some determinate literal meaning which they have and hold independently of the circumstances where they are spoken.

In any event the school-room case is of no use in my philosophical investigation. I am trying to analyze "I raised my arm" into "My arm went up" and something else. I am trying to think that the action, raising my arm, is partly composed of a bodily movement which is less than the action itself. In the school-room case, "My arm went up" cannot be the bodily movement which is less than the action because it is also describable in the words, "I raised my arm." "I raised by arm" surely describes my action. So in this case "My arm went up" describes the action also. "My arm went up" is not less than the action; it is the action.

The bodily movement I want must be less than the action, but it cannot be involuntary, out of control, or surprising. How can I characterize the bodily movement? I can project a set of coordinates on it and describe the shape and movement of color masses on those coordinates. "Dark bent shape through quadrant x at time t; through quadrant y at t_2...." But of what is this a description? It might be a description of a man, Herkimer, raising his arm. Or, perhaps the man, Herkimer, has just been pushing against a wall, and this is a description of his arm going up. Suppose I do not know which it is. Herkimer can stand against a wall and pretend to push and then he can step back and raise his arm. Also he can push hard against the wall—then stand back and his arm goes up. If I see the movement I cannot tell which it is. I cannot tell whether he has raised his arm or his arm has gone up.

I can simply describe this movement. But what have I
described? "Either Herkimer's raising his arm or Herkimer's arm going up"; and that could not be part of
the action of Herkimer's raising his arm. Or rather,
"Herkimer raised his arm or Herkimer's arm went up" is
not simpler in such a way that it would be part of what
it means to say "The man, Herkimer, raised his arm."
     Then the "bodily movement" is that which can be ex-
plained by anatomy, physiology, biochemistry and the
other relevant sciences. When I raise my arm, "that
movement is produced by these muscles contracting as
the result of electrochemical impulses produced by
chemical changes in the muscle cells...." And so on.
But that cannot be the "bodily movement" which is part
of the "meaning" of "action." In order to understand
"I raise my arm" I do not need to know anything about
the physiological or biochemical explanation of my arm
movement: I do not even need to know that it is subject to physiological or biochemical explanation.
     I have been examining the idea that an action is an
occurrence which I cause, and I cannot find anything in
an action which could be the required occurrence or
"bodily movement." Also I have been unable to make
sense of the idea that I cause an action or a bodily
component in an action. Surely then, I should reject
the definition. And if I reject the definition, what
then? Shall I search for another? I have no other
suggestions; I do not know in what direction to search
for another definition. I ought to be prepared for the
idea that the request for a definition is a mistake:
something is wrong with the question "What is an action?" But what is wrong? Perhaps it is the idea that
"action" is definable in the way that the question suggests.
     Actions are not reducible to any simpler things,
nor definable in terms of anything simpler than
actions. That seems the proper moral to draw. Then
will I not be able to say anything of a philosophical
nature about actions? I shall no longer expect to be
able to say anything in reply to the question, "What is
an action?" but I can still say something in answer to
questions about the natures of specific actions. I can
still address myself to questions like, "What is the
action of signalling a right turn?" or "What is the
action of hoeing weeds?" Signalling a right turn and
hoeing weeds are complex actions, and I can explain
what each is in terms of the simpler actions of which
it is composed. "Complex" and "simpler" mean the same
thing as before. I am thinking of complexity and
simplicity in "meaning." To explain the meaning of a

word or phrase for a complex action, I must refer to one or more simpler actions. A complex action is "composed" in some way of a simple action or simpler actions. Typing a page is a complex action which consists (in part) of the simpler action of striking a key. "Complex" and "simple" are relative terms. For any action of considerable complexity, there will be one or more simpler actions which compose it. And when one has enumerated those simpler actions, he has completed the "analysis" of that complex action so far as that part of the analysis is concerned, that is, that part which has to do with the composition of the action in terms of simpler parts. If there is any reason for it one can then turn to the analysis of one or more of the simpler actions. And for the simpler actions one can generally find other still more simpler components. Then one may turn to the analysis of those. And so on. But not "and so on ad infinitum." When the series of analyses is complete, it will end with one or more absolutely simple actions. Absolutely simple actions are such as raising my arm, moving my first finger inward, twisting my wrist, winking my eye. Consider the analysis of the action of an automobile driver signalling a right turn as he approaches an intersection. "Signalling a right turn consists of raising the arm." One cannot now go on to ask "What is the analysis of the action of raising the arm?" because raising the arm is an absolutely simple action. Firing a gun (in the usual way) consists in the absolutely simple action of moving the first finger in a squeezing motion.

Of course, when I give an analysis of certain complex actions I shall not always be able to specify one or a few simpler actions involved in them. Sometimes I shall have to specify the simpler action disjunctively. Consider the action of going to San Jose. It consists of one of these simpler actions: driving my car, taking a plane, taking a train, riding my bicycle, riding my motorcycle, or some other. It may be any one of these, and considering the nature of the action of going to San Jose will not tell me which one it is. For other complex actions I can do no more than mention a few of the many, many simpler actions of which it could be composed. Consider the action of disturbing someone. How could I begin to enumerate the ways in which I could disturb someone? I could make a loud noise, make a face, say something, introduce a hoodlum to him, and so on and so on. Perhaps, then, I should consider the structure and composition of actions by beginning always at the other end. I shall start with a simpler action and then list some series of complex actions which can be generated from it. I raise my left arm, I signal a right turn, I avert an accident, I save myself embarrassment. This is the method used by Alvin Goldman in his book, A Theory of Human Action.[5] But if I use only this method I cannot address myself to questions about the nature or analysis of actions such as, "What is the action of hitting a home run (in baseball)?" "What is the action of saluting an officer (in the armed forces)?" These appear to be clear and definite questions, and I think I know how to go about answering them. And even though I cannot always specify some simpler action, I can indicate the structure of the complex action by mentioning that it consists of "some" simpler action. "What is it to surprise a person?" "It is to do something which he finds unexpected." It still remains true that complex actions consist of simpler actions and those of simpler still, until we reach an absolutely simple action (or actions).

Of course there is more to giving an analysis of a complex action than merely enumerating the simpler actions which compose it. The equally important, and more difficult part, is characterizing the manner in which the simpler actions compose the more complex. Swinging the arms and twisting the body are simpler actions which compose "striking out"--but only if the swinger is playing baseball, taking his regular turn at bat, has already had two strikes called, swings at a legal pitch, and such. Alvin Goldman recognizes only four such modes of complication ("generation") of complex actions out of simple: (1) causal, (2) conventional, (3) simple, (4) augmentation. He claims that these four are exhaustive; and perhaps they are, but only because one of them, the "simple" mode is a catch-all. The list of complex actions which result from this mode of complication include such diverse acts of mine as fishing for bass, jumping farther than George, establishing my independence from my teachers, confessing that I had hostile feelings during our interview.

Undoubtedly the most interesting and important thing about many complex actions is their mode of complication from simpler actions. It is perhaps the main concern of such fields as philosophy of mind, philosophy of language, and philosophy of law. The modes of complication of many complex actions are extremely difficult to characterize correctly and completely. However, I am not now concerned with the manners of composition or complication of complex actions, but only with the idea that they are composed of simpler actions

---

[5]Englewood Cliffs, N.J., Prentice-Hall, 1970.

as parts and with the consequent idea that these simpler actions are composed of simpler until, in the
course of analysis, we arrive at absolutely simple
actions.

This way of looking at the analysis of complex
actions must lie behind John Austin's suggested
outline-anlaysis of speech acts or illocutionary
acts.[6] Such actions as promising, predicting, or
telling somebody something consist in making sounds.
If I make certain sounds (morphemes, words) while

---

[6]The historical facts concerning the manner in
which Austin thought about actions in general are of
little philosophical interest. The important point is
this: the program of analysis I am trying to characterize is so natural and elementary that it is hard to
imagine any philosopher not under its influence while
thinking about the "structure" of actions. Austin
never puts his analysis of speech acts into a systematic scheme which includes acts or actions other than
speech acts, yet he makes cryptic observations about
other actions which indicate that he is thinking of
speech acts and those other acts in the same way. On
p. 110-114 in How To Do Things With Words (Oxford,
1962), Austin compares his analysis of the "total
speech act" with that of other actions which include a
"minimum physical act" and other things which are
"consequences." The minimum physical act will be "the
making of some movement or movements with parts of our
body." The action of "killing the donkey" will include
not only the movement of "crooking our finger" but also
its consequences "a movement of the trigger, which produced..., which produced... which in turn produced the
death of the donkey." Austin compares such actions
with illocutionary acts. Our vocabulary for illocutionary acts marks off and distinguishes them from
their consequences in a way that has no parallel in the
vocabulary we use for other actions. Though illocutionary acts have consequences, they are not themselves
consequences of any simpler acts; they are produced by
"conventions." Austin mentions the possibility that
"perlocutions" are the consequences not of "illocu-
tions" but of "locutions." "Ought we not, in seeking
to detach 'all' consequences, to go right back beyond
the illocution to the locution--and indeed to the...
uttering of noises, which is a physical movement?
...Or is it? We have already noted that 'production of
noises' is itself really a consequence of the minimum
physical act of moving one's vocal organs."

These are cryptic and difficult passages, but I

212

observing the principles of grammar, I perform a
"phatic act." If I perform a "phatic act" while using
my knowledge of the meanings of words, I thereby perform a "rhetic act." If I perform a certain rhetic
act, in the right circumstances with the right intentions, and so on, I perform the action of telling
somebody something (or promising, or predicting, or
whatever). To bypass the technicalities: if I, who
know language, make the proper sounds, then I say
something, and if I say something in the right circumstances then I tell somebody something (or I
promise--or predict or whatever).

I suppose that one could then go on, if he wanted,
and ask "What is the analysis of making sounds?" or
"What is the analysis of making speech sounds?" and he
might then want to say that making sounds is composed
of the simpler actions of moving lips, tongue, cheeks.
Now these actions surely are absolutely simple actions,
and so there will be no philosophical questions about
their constitutions. A speech act such as telling
somebody something will consist then in saying something, and saying something will consist in making
sounds. I do not know whether the analysis of telling
is to stop with saying something or not. Or whether
the analysis of telling also includes the action of making sounds. Does the "idea" or "concept" of telling
something include only the idea of saying something, or
does it include also the idea of making speech sounds?
I do not know what to think about this. Perhaps it is
not an important point. The ideas of "saying something" or of "talking" or "speaking" certainly do include the idea of making sounds--the sounds of speech.

When I am under the influence of this picture of
complex actions composed of simpler parts, this seems a
perfectly obvious thing: to tell somebody something, I
say something--I speak--and to say something I make
sounds. Whenever I say something I make sounds--that
is what this picture inclines me to think. But what is
it for someone to make sounds when he speaks or when he
says something? He snaps his fingers when he speaks--
or he claps his hands or he beats on a drum while he is
speaking. Or he may have a strong lisp and make whist-
ling sounds when he speaks. Of course the picture of
analysis does not lead me to think of these things as

---

think they indicate pretty clearly that Austin was
thinking of complex actions involving simpler actions,
and simpler actions entering into complex through such
things as causation, consequences, and conventions.
The end of analysis is the "minimum physical action."

cases of a person's making sounds when he speaks. I want cases where a person does not make such sounds. What others are there? I may hear muffled rumbling sounds in the wall and find that they are made by somebody speaking in the next room. That is not the case I want either. Those sounds are not necessarily involved in speech; they are not essential to it. I cannot think of such cases--the cases which my picture leads me to believe are the ordinary routine ones.

Perhaps all of us always make sounds when we talk, but that is a fact which is so obvious and commonplace that we cannot **say** that we make sounds when we talk. Perhaps it is true, so obviously true that we make sounds when we talk that it sounds odd to mention it. But surely that is not right. If it were something obviously true I could take away the paradoxical sound of it by a proper preface. "Now I am going to say something so obviously true that it is not often spoken"-- and then I add "I have a nose in the middle of my face." Could I start the same way and then add "I make sounds whenever I speak?" Is that something obviously true? It sounds so strange that I wonder whether it is true at all.

There are sounds in speech; from a certain point of view speech is composed of sounds. Phonologists, phoneticians and others study the sounds of speech. But why, because there are sounds in speech to be studied, do I think that people make the sounds? Why do I think that speaking consists of the sub-action of making sounds?

Mynahs and parrots imitate human speech, and they certainly make sounds. The speech performance of a mynah is sometimes indistinguishable from that of a human. So if mynahs make sounds then surely humans, too, make sounds. Yes, but when do mynahs make sounds, and what sounds do they make? Well, they make shrieking and screeching sounds, loud whistles, and sometimes clicking noises. Humans can and sometimes do make the same sorts of sounds. But what of the mynah when he imitates human speech? Then we do not say that the mynah is making sounds, we say that he is talking. When we want to know about the ability of a mynah we ask, "Can he talk?" or, "What can he say?" We do not ask, "Can he make the sounds of someone talking?" or "What sounds can he make in the way of talking?" We do not say that mynahs make sounds when they talk any more than we say that humans make sounds when they talk. It appears that imitating a person speaking is no more making sounds than a person speaking is making sounds.

Many animals can make sounds. Some grunt, some chirp, some scream. Some animals can make many

214

different sounds. Also we have reason to believe that
certain animals are capable of learning at least the
rudiments of speech. Chimpanzees, in particular, seem
able to go quite a long way toward acquiring a language. Suppose that we take an animal which has the
ability of a chimpanzee to learn speech, but one which
naturally makes many different distinctive sounds, and
suppose that we teach him to use his natural sounds as
"words" of a language. Suppose that he can make a
grunt, a hiss, a hoot and a bark. Now I teach him to
make a grunt when I present a ball, a hoot when I
present a cube, and a hiss when I present a pyramid.
He quickly gets this right. Now I present the three
things together and teach him to point to one and make
the appropriate sound. He points to a cube, say, and
hoots. This is harder, but soon he masters it. Now
when there is but one object before him, I teach him to
bark instead of pointing. I'm sure this is very difficult, but suppose he shortly gets it--or at least seems
to get it. I show him a ball and he barks and grunts:
he makes the two sounds in that order. For a pyramid,
he will bark and hiss. Bark-grunt is much like "That
is a ball"; bark-hiss is much like "That is a pyramid."
     My animal makes sounds and he says something. He
speaks. Isn't that right? So at last here is a case
of saying something which essentially involves the making of sounds. But then I think that it is not that
simple. What should I really say about the performance
of my animal? It is not easy to evaluate such behavior. If I am not sure just what to make of his performance, I shall say, "He makes the right sounds in
the right order, but does he really have the idea?" On
the other hand, if I am quite convinced that he does
have the idea--and is well on his way to acquiring a
language--I shall probably say, "He's got it: he's
saying 'that's a cube'." Or, "He's saying 'that's a
ball'." At my animal's first success I shall think,
"He's making the right sounds." Later, after I have
become convinced that he has the idea I shall think,
"He's saying 'that's a ball'." Making sounds and saying something thus seem to be contrasted, and the more
convinced I am that he is really saying something, the
less appropriate it seems to be to say that he is making sounds.
     Suppose now that I must describe his behavior to a
visitor, a person who knows nothing about my experiments with the animal or of the animal's achievements.
He observes my animal and he says, "He's making a bark
and a hoot. I've never heard anything like that." Now
what shall I say? "I taught him to make certain of his
sounds in certain orders. He's well on his way to ac-

215

quiring a language. When he barks and hoots that means, "That's a cube'." Here now I describe him as making sounds and as saying something in the process. This shows that saying something consists in part of making sounds. Well, in this case perhaps it does, but it is only in this case that it does. Surely it is a peculiarity of this example. The animal is a natural sound maker: in his natural habitat, on suitable occasions, he barks, hoots, hisses, grunts. It is because he makes these many sounds that I selected him for my example. The ability to make these sounds evolved over the ages just as did the shape of his arms or the color of his coat, and so these sounds undoubtedly play an important part in his wild life. Perhaps one is a mating call, another a territorial call. Humans do not have such a repertoire of distinctive natural sounds. They do not have a mating hiss or a territorial bark. Of course they make sounds. When they are infants they gurgle, babble, and cry; and when they are adults they whistle, hum, clap their hands. These sounds do not enter in any immediate way into speech. I think then that the reason it is proper to say that my sound-making animal makes sounds when he says something is just that he is a sound-maker; he makes many natural sounds and he continues to make them. He makes his natural sounds on new occasions in new orders. I taught him to do that and that is his "speaking." My animal "makes his sounds" when he says something and that is my only reason for saying that he makes sounds when he speaks. If he learns to speak English, and comes eventually to speak English quite well, then certainly he will not be "making sounds" when he speaks.

Still at times I am inclined to think that the complex action of telling something consists in part in the simpler action of making sounds. In order to tell somebody something, a person must say something, and in order to say something he must make sounds. Saying something involves making sounds. I think I can see this: I think it is obviously so. I can contrive an example which I believe shows it to be so. Imagine a South Sea Island where a language is spoken quite unlike our own. The people live in small villages and there are many entertainers who travel from village to village doing various acts and putting on shows. One entertainer, a man named Kaydan, is an expert at making nonsense rhymes and songs. He makes all kinds of sounds, many quite like the sounds of the language, many quite unlike--all mixed together in a most wild performance. While travelling in the island I make a tape recording of him making his potpourri of sounds. I bring the tape recording home with me, and sometime

later I play it. Much to my amazement, I find that in
the string of sounds I hear are the sounds of the English sentence, "That is a daffodil." I positively know
that this man, Kaydan, knows no English; and so this is
a most amazing thing. But there it is; amid the
sounds of his performance, a perfect pronouncement of
the English sentence, "That is a daffodil."

To complete my example I must now imagine this most
unlikely series of events. Kaydan, the entertainer,
comes to America to live. His act is quite popular
here; so he remains in this country, and eventually he
learns perfect English. One day I hear that he has
bought a house down the road from me and I stop to see
him for a neighborly welcome. He takes me for a walk
in his garden. As we pass some unusual pink flowers, I
ask, "What is that flower?" He says, "That is a daf-
fodil--(It is a rare pink variety)." Suddenly I remember my old recording, and an idea comes to me. I start
my pocket tape recorder, and ask him again--as though I
had not heard him--"What is that flower?" He says,
"That is a daffodil." Now I return home. I find my
old tape of Kaydan making sounds and copy from it the
sentence "That is a daffodil." On the same tape I copy
what I have just brought home on my pocket recorder:
Kaydan telling me, "That is a daffodil." I play the
two performances, one after another and I cannot tell
them apart. In one Kaydan merely makes sounds, the
sounds of the English sentence, "That is a daffodil";
in the other he says something--he tells me something.
Now doesn't this example show that a person makes
sounds when he tells something or says something? In
one of these recordings Kaydan is making sounds; in the
other he is doing more, he is saying something and
telling something. I listen and I cannot tell the two
apart. Surely then he is doing the same in each: he
is making sounds. In one he is doing more than that,
but he is all the same making sounds.

When I listen to the two I cannot hear any difference between them. If I had someone play the two to me
without telling me which is which, I could not tell
which was Kaydan making speech sounds and which was his
telling me about the daffodils. From this I concluded
that Kaydan was doing the same thing in each case, that
is, he was making speech sounds. How could I have
reached such a conclusion? I must have reasoned that
when I cannot hear any difference between two things,
then what I hear in each case is the same. Sometimes
when I cannot hear any difference between two things,
there is still a difference between them to be heard.
Perhaps my hearing is bad or I have not been trained to
notice certain subtleties. I do not want any such

217

factors to enter my example. I assume that if I cannot hear any difference between the two recordings then there is no difference to be heard. No one with better hearing or an ear for subtle differences could hear anything I did not hear. Does it follow that what I hear in the two cases is the same? Certainly not. What I hear in the one case is Kaydan making sounds, in the other Kaydan talking to me. In addition to "what I hear" I can also describe the sounds I hear. "What do you hear?" "I hear a trumpet." "No, I meant what sounds did you hear?" "I think a middle C and A above middle C in a brilliant brassy tone." Can't I in a similar way attend to the sounds and describe them without regard to the "object," the thing or person or whatever? Yes. Of course. On each tape, then, I heard the sounds, t h a t i z a d a f o d i l. I thought I would describe what I heard in each case as Kaydan making sounds. I see that I would not. I certainly will not say what I was thinking I would. I shall not say this: "I can't hear any difference, but in each case I hear a person making sounds." Nor this: "In each case I hear a person making the sounds one must make if he wants to say 'That is a daffodil'."

I think now that "making sounds" is not part of the analysis of saying something or of speaking. I suspect my picture of the analysis of complex actions into simple leads me astray here--and in an important way. I suspect it casts an entirely false light on language--and on language acts or language actions. It suggests that speech consists of making sounds--and making sounds inevitably suggests such things as beating drums or ringing bells. This analysis suggests that language is a signal-system of sounds, and I think that that suggestion leads to a serious philosophical confusion. Sounds obviously enter into speaking, but not as involved in the simpler sub-act of "making sounds."

When I reflect on the failure of this proposed analysis of speech acts into the actions of making sounds, I suddenly find that I have reason to question the whole program of the analysis of complex actions into simpler.

(1) Do I understand where an analysis of complex into simple is to end? Do I understand what is meant by "an absolutely simple" action? Is smiling, for example, an absolutely simple action? Or does it consist of simpler actions such as turning up the corners of the mouth and raising the cheeks? When I smile, of course, I turn up the corners of my mouth. But is that the same as "In signalling I raise my arm"? Or is it more like "In lifting a hammer I contract the round pronator muscle"? When I lift a hammer I tighten that

muscle--among other muscles. I learned this in my course in physiology. Of course I cannot tighten that muscle on command. I cannot even pick it out as a clearly separate muscle in the lumpy bundle under my skin. So contracting that muscle is not an action, that is, it is not the sort of thing philosophers have been thinking of under the heading of "action." But perhaps it is--or ought to be--regarded as an "action." I can tighten my round pronator muscle by raising my arm just as I can make my heart beat faster by running around the block. Even if tightening the pronator muscle and making the heart beat faster are actions, they are certainly not actions simpler than raising the arm or running. Contracting that muscle, therefore, is not an action which is part of lifting a hammer. Raising my arm is an action which is part of signalling. Perhaps there is a mark of this difference. I can say, "When I raise a hammer my round pronator muscle contracts," but not "When I signal, my arm goes up." Yet I can say, "When one smiles, the corners of his mouth turn up" just as well as "When one smiles, he turns up the corners of his mouth." In this case I can use either the active verb (action language) or the passive verb (occurrence language). For the analysis of speech acts I suggested that the absolutely simple acts were moving the lips and moving the tongue. Is that right? "In saying something, one moves his lips and tongue." When would I ever say that? Imagine someone who is born deaf, dumb and blind--and that he has learned English and has learned to "communicate" by means of a tactual sign language. Now imagine that one day he says this: "I realize that I am quite unlike normal people. When I say something I use my fingers. What do normal people do?" Do I understand his question? I think not. Suppose that I ask, "Do you know anything about speech and speech sounds and phonetics?" and he answers, "People have mentioned these things to me but I do not understand them." Now, what am I to say? I must explain sounds and hearing. I must try to convey to him the idea that people speak. Can I do that? I really don't know. Perhaps I shall say, "In saying something, normal people move their lips and tongues." But also I might say, "In speaking, the lips and tongue move, and they make the sounds of speech." The lips and tongue make the sounds, not the speaker. I should not say, "In speaking, one moves his lips and tongue and makes sounds." That is, I should not say that unless I wanted to mislead the deaf, dumb and blind person into thinking that speech was more like Morse code than like his tactual language.

One of the reasons I have been led to think that

when a person speaks he makes sounds is this: I know there are sounds involved in speech, the sounds which phoneticians study, and I ask myself how those sounds get there. It is easy to answer "Persons make the sounds," but I have now seen that that is not right. There is not the action of making sounds involved in speech. Then how do the sounds get there? Perhaps the correct answer is this: the sounds in speech are not made by people, they are made by larnyx, lips and tongue.

(2) Not only do I not know how to terminate an analysis--having no clear idea of the "absolutely simple action"--in many cases I do not know how to begin an analysis of the required kind at all. There are many actions, which seem not to be absolutely simple actions, to which the whole idea of analysis into simpler actions seems not to apply. When I go walking with Jason he seems always to be looking for something; he seems almost apprehensive. Then he disappears every afternoon--he walks away and he seems looking for something as he goes. I ask him, "What are you doing for hours every afternoon?" He says, "I have been looking for an Indian pipe plant which grows around here at this time of year. I've never seen one." Looking for an Indian pipe is surely an action, and not an absolutely simple action. Well, in what simpler actions could it consist? Walking? Jason need not walk; he could ride a bicycle or go horseback. Thinking about Indian pipes? I suppose he must think about Indian pipes sometimes, but not always while he is looking. Not most of the time, in fact. He doesn't have to continuously remind himself of what he is doing, and refresh his memory of anything. Does he need to turn his head to and fro? Surely not.

I am at a loss, not knowing how to begin an analysis of looking for Indian pipes. And I can think of many, many actions where I should similarly be at a loss. Stalling for time. Entertaining someone. Improvising a tenor part while singing in a barbershop quartet. Modeling a suit for a designer. Sulking after I have lost a contest. Working up courage to talk to my supervisor. Looking for clues in a murder case. Shopping all afternoon for new shoes. Listening intently for a distant drum--which I never hear. Or, consider an action such as this. Suppose that I am an artist--painter--and I make a painting in which at last I succeed in something truly original. The action I have in mind is the action of establishing, through this painting, my originality, my independence of my teachers. What do I do to do this? I don't know what to say. Perhaps it's not what I do so much as the manner in which I do it: not the stuff, but the style.

   From the outset the scope of application of this program for analysis has not been entirely clear. It clearly is not intended to apply to omissions or acts of omission, such as forgetting to pay my insurance premium--but perhaps it does apply to the act which the omission is the omission of. So perhaps acts of omission present no special problem: I have only to give an analysis of an act and then add that it was not done. It is not intended to apply to "mental actions" or at least "purely mental actions" such as dreaming or visualizing. Also there is both an action and an attempt to perform that action: baking a cake and trying to bake a cake. It is not clear that the program for the analysis of complex into simple is meant to apply to attempts. And in some cases what I attempt to do does not come off: I fail. What I did was fail to get the nut off the badly rusted bolt, or I did not succeed in getting back to camp by nightfall. Is the program for analysis intended to apply to failures, slips, mistaken turns and such? But none of the actions I have enumerated fits into any of these excluded--or exceptional--categories: omissions, mental acts, attempts, failures. I begin to wonder whether the program for analysis applies only where it applies--to certain actions only; and so I wonder whether, in adopting the program, I have been feeding on a philosophical one-sided diet.

   (3) When I remind myself that the program for analysis grew out of thoughts about the question, "What is an action?" I have an even greater reason to be suspicious. I first discovered the hopelessness of reducing actions to "bodily movements" and causes. I let actions be irreducible; but obviously I was still concerned with finding their proper place in the physical world. The "absolutely simple action" replaces the "bodily movement." My conviction that a complex action must be grounded in an absolutely simple action may come from the same source as my original idea that an action must contain a bodily movement. This source, I think, is a Cartesian picture of things which I often have while doing philosophy. I think of myself in a world of physical things and happenings, of material bodies and their movements. In a way, I am insulated from this world. There are certain actions I can perform easily, but these are mental actions. I think. I dream. I wonder. None of these affect the physical world. They are not so much as the winking of an eye. How could I do anything which would change the movements of bodies in the physical world? If I am to perform a physical action it must begin with the movement

of some part of my body. I must gain a foothold for an
action in the world by moving some part of my body. I
can do that--move my legs and arms, head and lips,
foot, fingers, tongue, and other bodily "parts." I
have a great repertoire of such simple actions at my
command: I can wiggle my first finger, stick out my
tongue, rotate my foot at the ankle and nod my head. I
can do these things straight-off, directly. I do not
do them by doing things which bring them about, such as
pulling tendons, tightening muscles, sending nerve currents. So, whatever I do--whatever action I perform,
regardless of its complexity--I am led to think that in
the last analysis it comes down to one or more of these
absolutely simple actions. These simple actions provide the foothold for complex actions in the physical
world.

6. TRUTH AND FATE: FUTURE OCCURRENCES

Persons of the Dialogue: Scene: Room 314, Prince
   Sara   Lucian Hall
   Thayer   University of Oregon

Sara: Your friend, Harley Sander, will fall downstairs tomorrow at exactly 3:00 p.m. He will trip on the third step from the top and fall all the way to the bottom.

Thayer: Is that wishful thinking? I didn't realize you disliked Harley that much. Do you really want him to fall downstairs, or are you just letting some spleen out?

Sa.: That's a lot of questions at once. No, I really don't dislike Harley, and that wasn't wishful thinking, or fanciful spleen-venting either. I was just telling what will happen: Harley will fall downstairs tomorrow--at 3:00 p.m. exactly, and by tripping on the third step.

Th.: Are you serious? You don't mean that you have stretched a wire across his stairway or rigged it somehow so that he will fall?

Sa.: No. No. Nothing of the kind. I'm just saying that something unpleasant--maybe even hurtful--will happen to Harley tomorrow at 3 o'clock. He will fall downstairs, after tripping on the third step.

Th.: If you haven't rigged or arranged it, how can you possibly know that such a thing will happen?

Sa.: I don't know it. I don't know any such thing at all. I just said it. I said that Harley would fall downstairs tomorrow.

Th.: Why on earth did you say it?

Sa.: I thought you would never ask. I've just become a fatalist about such things--things, that is, that happen to people--and I wanted to show you the argument which convinced me of the correctness of the fatalistic view.

Th.: I should have guessed that you were up to some sort of philosophical shenanigans. How does your argument go?

Sa.: Let me unfold it for you step by step. It is neat and beautiful and very simple. You now have the first step. I said that Harley will fall downstairs tomorrow. Next, I want to show you that what I said implies that there is nothing anyone can do which will prevent it.

Th.: Well, suppose that I tell Harley that I have some reason to think that he might fall downstairs. Possibly he will take precautions. He might not use the stairs tomorrow at all. You don't mean to deny

223

that I can tell him, and that he might take it seriously, and might become cautious and do everything possible to avoid falling downstairs?

Sa.: Of course not. I only want to call your attention to a simple "logical fact"--if you like. What
I said implies that it cannot be prevented. I am trying to engage you in the simplest of logical exercises.
I want you to see that what I say implies various
things. Instead of "implies," logicians sometimes say
"entails." Also, logicians sometimes call this sort of
thing "immediate inference." What I say is, "Harley
will trip on the third step and fall downstairs tomorrow at 3 p.m.," and what I say implies all sorts of
things. It implies that Harley will not walk downstairs at 3 p.m. It implies that Harley will not run
upstairs at 3 p.m. And also it implies that nothing
can prevent Harley from falling downstairs at 3 p.m.

Th.: Yes, I understand now what you are asking me
to think. And it does not seem to me that this last
one, "Nothing can prevent Harley's fall," is like the
others. I certainly don't see this implication in the
same easy way that I do for the other cases. Can you
help me see that "Harley will fall downstairs" implies
that nothing can prevent his fall?

Sa.: Maybe I have been thinking about this so long
that I no longer have a sense for what your difficulty
could be. The implication seems just as "immediate" to
me as any of the others: maybe even more so. It's almost a case of "p implies p." "Harley will fall downstairs" implies that Harley will fall downstairs. It's
that simple.

Th.: But how do you get to "nothing can prevent
it"?

Sa.: If it were to be prevented, then Harley would
not fall downstairs. But I said, "Harley will fall
downstairs." What I said, then, rules out the possibility that Harley will not fall downstairs. It is
impossible that Harley will not fall downstairs. If
anyone prevents it, then Harley will not fall downstairs. But that is impossible. So it is impossible
for anyone to prevent it.

Th.: I find it terribly hard to follow that. But
let that pass for the moment. Supposing that you have
this implication, how are you going to get an argument
for fatalism out of it?

Sa.: Don't you see? Just as I said "Harley will
fall downstairs tomorrow," I could have said that anything will happen to anyone. I mean I could have mentioned anyone at all, and I could have said that anything was going to happen to him. I could have said,
"Carson will have a tire blow-out next Tuesday

morning," or "On October 23 Simon's hat will blow off his head and roll into the gutter." I could have said any of these things or any of an endless number of other things. And in each case what I say implies that nobody could prevent what I said would happen.

Th.: This is still a long way from fatalism.

Sa.: Yes, but be patient. All I need now is a little more logic. Of all the many, many things which I could say, a certain number of them together will make up part of the story of what will actually happen. If I could say just those certain things, then I could tell the complete story of everything that is going to happen to everybody. Of course, I can't do that; I do not know which of the many possible things to say. But no matter about that. Whichever they are, each one implies that nothing can be done to prevent the happening it is about. So of course, nothing can be done to prevent any of the future occurrences which are part of the complete story.

I ought to make one minor correction in this. I began by talking of happenings like falling downstairs and losing one's hat in the wind, and I said that nobody could prevent these things from happening. And now I want to generalize and say that nothing can be done to prevent any occurrence or happening whatsoever. The word "prevent" may become inappropriate when applied to things generally. I think we usually speak of "preventing" undesirable or unwanted occurrences. And, of course, many occurrences will not be undesirable or unwanted: many will be things we want to happen, many will be neutral--just plain happenings which we neither want nor do not want. It could be odd to say that no one can prevent some of these things. Suppose I say "Your prize apple tree will survive the sub-zero weather." It would be odd to say "No one can do anything to prevent the tree from surviving." But not so odd, maybe, to say "Nothing can prevent it from surviving." That might be just a way of saying "Don't worry, its survival is a certainty." At any rate, that's the only meaning I want when I say, "Nothing can prevent anything." Perhaps instead of "No one can prevent..." or "Nothing can prevent..." I should say, "No one can do anything which will make it not happen" or, "Nothing can make it not happen."

Th.: Yes. I see that you have a problem with language here--I suspect a more serious one than you think. But I should like to see whether I can understand the "logic" you invoke in order to get from the specific case to the generality. You go from "Nothing can make Harley not fall downstairs" to "Nothing can make anything not happen."

Sa.: Yes.

Th.: And you get the generality by saying that you could have said anything about any future occurrence in place of saying that Harley will fall downstairs?

Sa.: That's right.

Th.: And you think that if we could pick and choose correctly among the things that you could have said, then we could compose the complete chronicle of future happenings?

Sa.: Well, complete enough, anyway. It's true that there are many things I couldn't say because I don't know how to refer to certain future things. In centuries to come people will build buildings and bridges and monuments. I cannot say that such and such a bridge will collapse, because I don't know enough about the future to know whether people will build such and such a bridge or not. These are minor complications, though, and they do not affect the principles involved. If I can prove that most of the immediate future is fated, then I can easily imagine that someone in a future generation will take over and complete the details of my proof for his immediate future--and so on.

Th.: I can see that you are trying very hard to avoid anything like the construction of an "artificial language" in which you can refer to any future thing by "space-time coordinates," and encompass all future happenings by reducing all descriptions to "basic predicates," and that sort of thing.

Sa.: Yes. All of that is based on the idea that "sentences" are the carriers of implications. I don't want to talk about sentences implying that various future occurrences are fated. In fact, I don't know what that could mean at all. I want "what I say" to be the carrier of implication. I want to talk about "what I say," and "what other people say" and "what we might say."

Th.: This group of things, out of all the things which can be said, are the things which are true. Isn't that what you are saying?

Sa.: I tried to avoid putting it in that way, because I wanted to avoid any unnecessary problems about truth. One is always tempted at this point to try to classify all of the things which might be said into two groups: the affirmative ones, and those which are their exact contradictories. And then to invoke the law of excluded middle and say that exactly half of the sum of these two groups must be true. But I think this is a mistaken idea. It might work if we were dealing with mathematical expressions; but the "things said" which I am talking about cannot be treated in that way. And even if one could proceed in this way, he would then have the troublesome question, "What is it that makes half the 'things said' true?"

The main thing I discovered, I believe, when my argument for fatalism came to me, was that none of this has anything to do with the argument.

Th.: Yes. I can see that you have freed the usual argument for fatalism from some of its most troublesome features. You can bypass that difficult question about whether propositions are true at a time or true timelessly. And also the question about the meaning of that strange adjective "true."

Sa.: I was actually struck with wonder when this argument came to me. I was amazed at its simplicity and obvious validity. I felt very much as Russell felt when he threw his tobacco pouch into the air upon discovering the validity of the ontological argument for God. I feel that I have revealed the structure of the argument which many people have tried to state--but have failed to get put into the right form.

Th.: I realize that you are quite properly delighted by your discovery, and that you are also quite convinced of its correctness. I'm afraid, though, that I do not share your conviction of its correctness. I am slow about these things, and the older I become the slower I seem to become. I wonder whether you would mind going over one of its steps with me. The beginning of the argument caused me a great deal of trouble; and since I was not clear about that, I found it difficult to follow the rest of it to the inevitable conclusion.

Sa.: What step do you have in mind, and what do you find troublesome about the beginning?

Th.: It's the maneuver by which you get from the one thing you said about Harley to everything that you--and other people, even future people--might say. I appreciate the subtle way you began the argument in order to lay the groundwork for that step--but all the same, I do not quite understand it.

Sa.: You will have to tell me more specifically what troubles you.

Th.: In order to get your fatalistic conclusion, you need to be able to think about--or conceive--all of the many things which might be said about future occurrences. And each of these things must be such that it implies something about a future occurrence, namely, that it cannot be prevented. It's clear then that it must be the "thing said" in each case which carries the implication. What a person says must not imply the unpreventability of a future occurrence because the speaker knows something about the manner in which it will be brought to pass. The implication must not come

227

from the fact that the speaker is going to bring it about, or from the fact that he understands the hidden forces at work, or from anything of the kind. Is that a correct understanding of the requirements?

Sa.: Yes, that is exactly right, though you rather make it sound as though I had concocted the argument. I did not first think of the conclusion and then fix the premisses up so that I could get the conclusion out of them. The argument came to me all at once, and all of a sudden.

Th.: I don't mean to imply that you concocted anything. I'm only trying to see how it all fits together--from the standpoint of an outsider--and I need to understand how each piece makes its contribution to the conclusion. Your conclusion follows from the idea that there is this great multitude of things said which can be viewed in independence of anyone who says them.

Sa.: I don't like that reformulation quite as well, but I have no deep objection to it. The "things said"--as you call them--are things which might be said or could be said, though of course most of them never are.

Th.: At any rate, when someone says something, you imagine that there is "that something which he says" which can be thought of independently of the circumstances in which he says it, and other such considerations. And it is that "something which he says" which has certain implications--and these implications are carried solely by "what is said" and can be determined without considering the speaker or his circumstances.

Sa.: Yes. That seems quite obvious to me.

Th.: That's why I think you introduced very skillfully just what you needed in the argument from the beginning.

Sa.: What are you thinking of?

Th.: You just turned to me and said something--something quite unexpected and out of the blue. You said, "Harley Sander will fall downstairs" and you gave me an exact future time and some surprising details about the occurrence. And I quite naturally wanted to supply the missing background. I wondered how you were in a position to know such a thing. I wondered whether you had rigged his fall or knew of some scheme to bring it about. You told me that you just said it--and turned my attention to the implications of what you had said. Then you went on to the similar implications of other things which might have been said, but weren't.

Sa.: You sound as though you were suspicious.

Th.: Not suspicious, exactly. Though, yes, that's all right. Say I am suspicious. I wonder whether I could really follow this step you wanted me to take.

Sa.: It seems to me that you have already done so. You have certainly reproduced the line of thought quite accurately.

Th.: That's not the same as understanding it or following it. Here is the thing I wonder about: when you said "Harley will fall..." I was first nonplussed by it, and then I began to supply in my mind some of the things which might be expected to lead one to say such a thing. Then you ask me to take them away. And I wonder whether I can. I wonder whether I can think them all away.

Sa.: I don't see why not. Then, too, I don't see that it's important as long as you are able to consider "what I said" and see what it implies.

Th.: Surely I must be able to think them all away. It's only by thinking them all away that I shall be able to consider "what is said" in the same way that I am to consider it for the many things that might be said but never are. For those things, there will be no speaker--and certainly no one background--which is appropriate and pertinent to each. You are asking me to consider these things as though the speaker, his interests, the time, the place, the audience, and all such matters had nothing to do with it.

Sa.: Well, suppose that I am.

Th.: That's what I have misgivings about. Can I really? Can I think these things all away? Suppose you talk a great deal in your sleep, and suppose that I find you one day sound asleep on the couch, and you are muttering something. I come closer out of curiousity and I hear you very clearly say, "Harley will fall downstairs tomorrow at 3 o'clock. He will trip on the third step...."

Suddenly I remember your argument for fatalism, and I ask myself, "Does what she said imply that nothing can be done to prevent Harley's fall?" Or, "Does what she said imply that Harley will not run upstairs at 3 o'clock?" How do I answer my questions? I'm inclined to say, "That's silly. What kind of idea is that: the idea of something being implied by what a person says who is talking in her sleep?"

Sa.: Part of the difficulty here is that we cannot tell from what a sleeptalker says who the person "Harley" is in what he says. In fact we cannot tell whether Harley is a person. It might be a dog. Or perhaps "Harley" is the name of the sleeptalker's favorite chair. So, of course, we don't know who or what it is about.

Th.: We could easily remedy this by imagining that you say in your sleep, "Harley Sander will fall downstairs, that is, citizen Harley Sander of 412 11th Avenue, Eugene, Oregon...." And so on, filling in what you say so that any so-called vagaries of reference are made explicit. I do not see how that would make any difference. The question seems just as queer: "Does what she says imply that nothing can prevent his fall?"

When I ask a question about Harley I suppose I must be careful not to ask "Whom is she talking about?" because I must be concerned only with "what she says" and not with her talking. Anyway, she is not talking about anyone--not in any clear and straightforward way, because she is talking in her sleep, and in her sleep, I take it, she does not "talk about Harley" or talk about anyone or anything. But talking in sleep ought to give us a clear case of "what she says" in just the way you want it. If it does, though, it seems to check the next step in your argument, because there is no place for any question about the implications of what the sleep-talker says.

Sa.: Believe me, I feel the force of the question you are raising. I do not want to defend my argument against any objection, hell or high water. And I am beginning to see my beautiful argument slip away from me. Yet the more I think about it, the more I am inclined to believe that one can ask "What is implied?" after all. Perhaps there is an initial shock, but when it has worn off, I can think, "Someone said in her sleep 'Harley will fall....'" I can think, "Let me consider what it is that was said, namely 'Harley will fall.' Doesn't that imply the inevitability of a fall by Harley?"

Th.: Yes. I agree that this is slippery business. But now I wonder whether, after your initial shock, you do not allow yourself to think about "what she said" in an illegitimate way. I suspect that you take the words and say them over and over--while thinking in a philosophical way--and that the sleeptalking slips into the background and is forgotten. You are so engrossed in the words that you do not think where they came from. Now you just have "Harley will fall..." to think about. And I suspect that now you begin to think as we usually do with words that come out of context: we take the words as they might often, or might usually, be taken. That is, we supply the outline of a usual background or context. Sleeptalk is certainly not the usual way for something said to be said.

Sa.: It is not an easy matter. I cannot easily see whether you are right or not.

Th.: Maybe a more extreme example will help. Suppose you have a mynah named O'Casey who has unusual abilities. He can say many, many long English sentences. Also he makes many squeaks, whistles, and trills--and in addition he composes "songs" in the manner of the mockingbird, putting together long strings of trills and whistles and warbles, with an occasional squeak thrown in, improvising lengthy musical passages. One day you discover that O'Casey is doing the same sort of thing with his "English vocabulary." He mixes together strings of words, bits of sentences, and word sounds in original--and sometimes very funny--ways. Suppose now that one day he is engaging in this word-singing, and he says quite clearly, "Harley will fall downstairs tomorrow. He will trip on the third step." Just as you doubt whether you could have heard the bird correctly, he repeats the same passage. He says exactly the same thing again.

Now, let me ask, does what O'Casey says imply that Harley's fall cannot be prevented?--does what he says imply that Harley will not trip on the fifth step?

Sa.: Yes, I see, Now these questions sound completely out of place. Of course I want to defend myself. My first inclination is to say that this example is irrelevant, but I realize that if I were to give way to that inclination I should be saying the wrong thing. I want to say that it is irrelevant because O'Casey does say, "Harley will fall downstairs...." Of course, when I thought of all the things that might be said, I was thinking of things that might be said by people--not by mynahs, parrots, and other mimics. And I was not thinking of people talking while sound asleep.

Th.: Presumably the way you said "Harley will fall downstairs" was to be typical of the way these things would be said. It is hard for me to see how this differs in any significant way from the way O'Casey said "Harley will fall downstairs." You did not have any reason for saying what you said. You were not concerned with Harley or his future. You were not alerting me to an impending accident, or telling me something you thought I should know. You could just as well have spoken about anyone and any occurrence. After all, that was the whole point of your saying what you said--if I understand correctly. In place of what you said you could have said almost anything at all.

Sa.: Yes. That's right. Though, of course, when I said, "Harley will fall downstairs..." I knew what I had said. When O'Casey said the same thing he did not know what he had said.

Th.: There is certainly that difference. But is it of any significance? After all, we are not asking O'Casey to follow or evaluate the argument for fatalism. At most he is supplying us with a starting point, with something said. That's all you were doing when

231

you said "Harley will fall donwstairs." I'm inclined
to think that you were not really saying anything
either.

Sa.: But when I said it I was thinking of Harley
Sander and of his stairway.

Th.: But you agree, surely, that that does not matter. After all, we are trying to think of multitudes
of "things said" which will never be said at all. We
are trying to think of all these many things in complete independence of speakers, audience, purpose in
speaking, and all the rest. The only thing which matters is that the person who goes through the argument
thinks in the right way of Harley and what is said
about him. It doesn't matter where he gets the
"material" or "content" for his thinking. But he must
be careful in thinking about it, and if he does not
watch out, he may slip and think that someone actually
said something about Harley in the usual way, and then
he may try in his imagination to supply a little of the
missing context.

As long as he remains quite clear about what he has
on his hands, I think that he will feel that there is
no question about its implications. Or, rather, he
will feel that any question about its implications is
silly.

When I hear what you say and when I hear what
O'Casey says, I think of the same things. I think of
Harley Sander and his stair and I think of his tripping
on the third step and falling to the bottom. I think
that any question about the implications of what the
two of you say is equally inappropriate for either one.
It is as inappropriate for what you say as it is for
what O'Casey says.

Sa.: Well. I think, now, that you are right. My
discovery has turned out to be a wind-egg. I shall have
to make my fame in philosophy in some other way. But,
of course, I wonder why I thought what I did, and what
is the truth of the matter?

Th.: Those are dangerous questions. Instead of
taking on directly such big and serious questions, I
should rather just talk about the thing in a more
loosey-goosey way. Do you object?

Sa.: Not at all. What do you have in mind?

Th.: How were you thinking, I wonder, when you
discovered your argument? Or, more generally, how is
anyone thinking when--for a time--he finds your argument compelling? Isn't he thinking this? When a person says something, there is a component in it--in his
saying something, that is--which can easily be isolated. It is the "content," the "thing said," "what he
said," and it is this component which is the bearer of

the "logical attributes." This implies or is implied by other such things. It is inconsistent with another of its kind, or consistent with it. And, of course, it is the entity (or whatever) which is either true or false. I'm trying not to make this too stylized or graphic or definite. I don't want to caricature what we must be thinking.

When we have gone this far, though, it is tempting to think in a more pictorial way; and I believe we usually do, too. We imagine there to be bits or items of logical stuff, each being a sayable or thinkable thing, and each being either true or false. We represent them as letters or lines arranged on various levels. Arrows run from one to another indicating that the one at the head of the arrow implies the one at the point of the arrow. We think that we can then pick out and focus our attention onto one such thing and trace its logical connections with others--as though we were following the arrows leading from it to others and others to it. We may think of these bits of logical matter, and of course we may also **say** them. And so it becomes tempting to think of them as sentences--or at least as something one might write or pronounce or "utter" or read. If they are not sentences, then they are the logical shadows of sentences--or the logical accompaniments of sentences, or something like that.

Sa.: Yes. I can see that I am often tempted to think in this way and, of course, the farther one takes such thoughts the less plausible they become. But, before one takes off on flights of pictorial fancy, the first part of the story seems plausible enough. And until you raised your objections, I should have accepted it without question.

Th.: Should we ask, I wonder, where it goes wrong? At least, it doesn't fit the facts we have been concerned with; that is, we can't think of what people say about future occurrences in this way without seriously distorting things. Suppose that we try to see, in the case of your example, just where the story goes wrong.

Sa.: You mean, of course, the case in which I say "Harley will fall downstairs tomorrow. He will trip on the third step from the top...."

Th.: Yes, and you say this quite out of the blue, with nothing leading up to it--and without any thought about it at all. It pops into your head, and comes out of your mouth. You know nothing about Harley's habits, nothing about the possibility of his tripping on the stairs. The whole thing is completely outside your ken, your competence, your concern.

And now we want to consider what you say, and ask, "Does it imply... this or that?" Does what you say

233

imply that Harley will not go downstairs without a mishap? Does it imply that Harley's fall cannot be prevented? And so on. It certainly does seem that these questions are misplaced. It's not that the questions are hard to answer: the questions are strange and somehow improper.

Sa.: Now, the next question is: "Why is that so: why are these questions so strange?" And I suppose that someone who is pleased with the idea of isolable logical bits of information will say that it is because the phrase "what she said" does not suffice to isolate the logical bit. The trouble here, he will say, is this: when we turn to what she said and ask what it implies, we are thinking of what she, the speaker, implies and what the content implies at the same time; and because she does not imply anything we are puzzled by our question. But this is only because "what she says" does not refer to the content by itself but to the content as it is asserted in the whole speech setting.

Th.: Yes. I think that is the way a "logical-bit theorist" would explain the oddness of our questions about implication. But if he does not think that the phrase "what she said" will serve to isolate the logical bit of content, how do you suppose he does propose to isolate it? How will he explain what he understands by "the content"?

Sa.: If "what he said" is not the subject of the logical "attributes," I cannot imagine what is. "The thing he said" will certainly do no better at isolating the required bit of content.

There seems no more to this explanation than a refusal to admit that the story of logical-bits does not fit the facts. I think we must honestly admit that it does not fit the facts, and then ask why it does not.

Th.: What sort of answer do you have in mind for that question?

Sa.: It must be that one cannot say something in the way I tried to imagine.

Th.: But you did say something. Our discussion began with your saying something.

Sa.: Yes, of course. That's not the way to put it. There's no way of telling how to take what I said, and there is not room for a question about its implications unless it can be taken in some one of certain definite ways.

When I said "Harley will fall downstairs...," your first reaction was one of bewilderment, and you began to question me about how it should be taken.

Th.: Isn't that the natural thing for a person to do?

234

Sa.: And think of the many ways in which I might have said it. (1) I might have been rather playfully imagining what I saw in a crystal ball. (2) I might have been half seriously thinking that if I thought it and said it, I could make it happen by some voo-do of thought and speech. (I may have been very angry at Harley.) (3) I could have spoken as a result of post-hypnotic suggestion, being quite surprised at what I had said. (4) I might have been a "speaker-with-tongues," again quite surprised at the words which came out of my mouth. (5) I could have been in on a dirty trick which some of Harley's rowdy "friends" had set-up for him; and I told what was to be the outcome of this trick: Harley would trip over a wire and fall. And there are doubtless many more ways it could be taken.

Th.: You are giving a very good survey. Don't forget another. This will be (6): you might have been reporting a strange hunch or foreboding you had--wondering, from that and a few other experiences which had preceded it, whether you had some sort of psychical power. I believe they call it "precognition."

Sa.: Now of all these only (5) clearly allows for a question about implications. (3) and (4) are much like the case of sleeptalking. Maybe your (6) is like that too. (1) and (2) are only partly--and not seriously--statements about a future occurrence. (5) seems the only one which will clearly and definitely admit the question "What is implied?" I tried to make it out that what I said should be taken in that way, and yet I denied all the relevant background. I was not in on a plot or trick. I knew nothing. And even if I hadn't taken it all away, it is a strange thing to be saying, or a strange way of saying it. You would naturally have expected me to qualify or modulate what I had said somewhat. "It is likely that Harley will fall...." "If the scheme works, Harley will fall...." "There is a scheme underway to make Harley fall...." The whole thing is wrong from the start. One can't and doesn't pronounce on future occurrences of that kind in that way. It's not like saying, "There is a stain on the bottom side of that paper. Turn it over and you will see."

So, in trying to think "what I said" you naturally fell back on something like post-hypnotic suggestion or speaking with tongues. Or even like the muttering of a person in his sleep or like the chatter of an inventive mynah.

Th.: Yes. I know. You were urging me to take it as a serious, straightforward statement about a future occurrence; but you frustrated my every effort to take

235

it so.

Sa.: What I gave you was worse than a pretense, and it is no wonder, then, that it does not provide a place for a meaningful question about what it implies. One cannot pretend to make a serious pronouncement on something and then deny everything that would make it possible for him to make such a pronouncement. These denials can only suggest something like sleeptalk or babbling, but since these possibilities will be denied too, we are left with something worse than sleeptalk or babbling, something completely mysterious.

Th.: All the same doesn't it strike you as a plausible idea that in all these cases you mention there is a common element: they are all concerned with Harley's fall downstairs? And that common element is the "bit" we are looking for. If we can find it in all these different cases, then why can't we just consider it all by itself?

Sa.: That is a new big question. What would it be? "A possible future occurrence in the life of Harley Sander, namely, his falling downstairs." I don't know how one would formulate it. Whatever there is to the idea, though, most of it is not relevant to our inquiry. If one can satisfy himself that he has identified some bit or some content which is common to all of these, he must still show that that "bit" is the subject of the "logical predicates." He must show that it implies and is implied by others of its kind. And I cannot now imagine how anyone could show any such thing. Wouldn't he have to imagine someone saying or thinking it, all by itself; and isn't that just what I was trying to do in the beginning?

* * * * * * * * * * * *

Sa.: It suddenly occurs to me that we have been silly spending so much time on this one little point. Or rather, I should say that I have been silly to allow my argument to turn on this one little point. I think we have both forgotten one of the most elementary logic lessons. If one wants to construct an argument, he doesn't have to be in a position to assert or guarantee his premises or even have a hunch about the correctness of them. He can imagine, or suppose them—or as logicians generally say, he can assume them. So I can forget about saying that Harley will fall downstairs. I shall just suppose that he will, and then I shall argue from that.

Let's suppose, then, that Harley Sander will fall downstairs tomorrow. And let's suppose all sorts of

things that will happen, all sorts of future occurrences. Now I can treat any one of the supposals as a
premise and derive conclusions from it. "If Harley
will fall downstairs, then he will not walk down in a
normal fashion." "If Harley will trip on the third
step and fall, it follows that he will not trip on the
fourth step." So I can get the implication I want:
"If Harley will fall, then it follows that nothing can
prevent his fall." (Or better, "nothing can make him
not fall.")

Now I can get my argument back again without all
that flummery about **saying** that Harley will fall. Some
of the many things we can suppose will be correct; and
the correct supposals, when put end to end, will compose a pretty good catalog of what will come to pass.
Since it follows from each of these supposals that
nothing can stop or avert the occurrence in question,
it follows that nothing can alter or prevent what is to
be. So, what will be must be.

Th.: I don't see how this will overcome the difficulty. You are now thinking that a "supposal" will
be the bearer of "logical attributes," a "supposal"
will imply one thing and another. And I presume that
by a "supposal" you mean "what is supposed" or "the
thing that one supposes."

You will still need to think about a great multitude of "things supposed" which no one will ever suppose. And we will have all the same questions over
again. Imagine that O'Casey says, "I suppose that
Harley will fall downstairs." Does what he supposed
imply anything? We are in worse shape with supposing
than we were with saying. A mynah may say something,
but surely a mynah can't suppose something. Now, when
a mynah says something, we do not have anything at all
to consider: that is, we do not have anything that the
mynah has supposed.

Sa.: No. I have not made myself clear. I was
thinking of giving up that part of the argument. I am
now arguing for a more limited fatalism. Consider just
the things that I can suppose to happen. Then each of
my correct supposals about some occurrence will imply
that the occurrence cannot be prevented. That is good
enough. I can now show that a great, great many future
happenings are fated to happen. And I shall not presume to extend my argument to cover absolutely every
future occurrence.

The principle of the matter is what I am interested
in. After all, I can have other people suppose other
things. And when you put me together with many other
people, and give our supposal powers free rein, then we
can suppose a great multitude of things. Acting all

237

together, we can show that a great deal of the future is fated. And among these future occurrences will be many things of great importance such as sicknesses, accidents, marriages, births, and deaths.

Th.: I'm glad if we can find a way to put the business of saying or supposing behind us, because I should like to discuss another step in your argument.

Sa.: Which do you mean?

Th.: Grant that we can suppose that such and such will occur, and grant that from our "assumption" that such and such will occur we can derive various conclusions. How do you show that the conclusion you want can be derived? Suppose that Harley will fall downstairs. How does it follow from that "assumption" that nothing can prevent his fall?

Sa.: I hardly know how to spell this out any more than I already have. If Harley will fall, then he will fall, and if he will fall, then, of course, he will fall. And obviously if he will fall it can't be the case that anything will prevent him from falling. So nothing can prevent him from falling; if it did, he wouldn't fall, and we have assumed that he will fall.

Th.: Yes. That's what I wanted. That's the part of the argument I find it extremely difficult to follow. When I think about it, it almost makes me dizzy. The momentous meaning of it. And now if our supposal that Harley will fall is correct, then nothing and no one can prevent his fall. And if that particular supposal isn't correct, then many of our others will be; and the same sort of conclusion can be drawn from any of them.

Sa.: Yes, I'm sure you understand the argument well enough. But why the disturbance? I think you are genuinely disturbed.

Th.: No. I really don't understand it. I can't make it stand still so that I can bring it into clear focus. It flops in and out as though it were first too near and then too far. Sometimes it seems truistic. Sometimes it seems to cut from under me all the things my life is built on. Where can we begin on it? First I find it a little puzzling that you derive the intermediate conclusion "Harley will fall."

Sa.: That wasn't necessary. I was trying to spell it out in the greatest possible detail. "If Harley will fall, then he will fall."

Th.: That suggests from the outset that if the "assumption" is correct, then there is something inevitable about the fall. Also, perhaps, it suggests that you have put yourself in a position to say that Harley will fall.

Sa.: Of course, I don't intend either of those. I

was only trying to emphasize the content of our assumption. It is the assumption that Harley will indeed fall.

Th.: But that isn't our assumption. Our assumption is that Harley will fall, not that Harley will indeed fall. A person would say "Harley will indeed fall," surely, only when he is in a position to say very confidently that poor Harley will fall.

Sa.: Well, if that is troublesome, omit it. The step is not necessary. "If Harley will fall, then nothing can prevent it."

Th.: And of course the "if" marks the antecedent as an "assumption" or a "supposal." We are really only interested in the assumptions which are "correct," so that we can cancel the "if" for them. What I mean is this. We are thinking of a little "argument" which will go this way: "If Harley will fall, then nothing can prevent it. Harley will fall. Therefore, nothing can prevent it." We want to "detach" the conclusion "nothing can prevent it," and we can do so only by adding the premiss that Harley will fall. But, of course, we can add that premiss only when we take the assumption that Harley will fall as correct.

Sa.: Yes. Of course.

Th.: I wonder then what it is which makes our assumptions correct. What, for example, makes the assumption correct that Harley will fall? Is it this: when the day and the hour have passed, Harley will have fallen down the stairs?

Sa.: Yes, of course. For the most part, the only way we have of finding out which supposals are correct is to wait and see. If Harley falls downstairs at the proper time and in the proper way--as we had supposed-- then we know that our supposal was correct.

Th.: No. I don't mean "How do we come to know that our supposal was correct?" I mean "What is it which makes such a supposal correct?" Or "What does it mean to say that a supposal about a future happening is correct?"

Sa.: I do not understand very clearly what you are asking of me.

Th.: Well, actually, I don't either. But it does seem clear to me that there are two different matters here. One is: How do we find out that some supposal about the future is correct? The other is difficult to formulate. I don't quite know how to put it. What do you understand by a supposal being correct? If our supposal were not about the future, but about the present, it would be easy enough to understand the difference.

Sa.: How do you mean?

239

Th.: Let's just make some supposal of the kind you are talking about. How about this? "There is a trunk full of gold buried under my apple tree." The way I will find out whether the supposal is correct is to dig under the apple tree and find out whether a trunk is buried there. But to say that it is correct is to say that the treasure is there under my apple tree--whether anyone digs it up or not.

Sa.: How do I apply the analogy to something I say about the future? Suppose that I say, "A green apple will fall from your tree during the night." Finding out whether that is correct will involve your waiting under the tree--perhaps all night. But, of course, the apple may fall whether you are there under the tree, watching, or not.

Th.: No. I was thinking that just waiting--watching for the time to pass--for the future to become present--would be analogous to digging under the tree. Waiting for the future occurrence to take place would be finding out; but the supposal might be correct whether you found out or not. I see now that it is not a useful analogy. If I think of finding out as just waiting, and I want to say that the supposal might be correct whether you find out or not--this sounds as though I was saying that the supposal might be correct even if the future never came--or that it might be correct though time should come to a stop, or something like that.

Let me try again with my question. It is this: what is the whole force of saying "The supposal that Harley will fall is correct"? Now, will you accept this as the answer? "When the time has passed, Harley will have fallen."

Sa.: I don't see why not. I don't think I've ever had in mind anything more than that. The tenses create the difficulty you are struggling with, don't they? "Harley will fall," "Harley is falling," "Harley has fallen." All these are about the same occurrence. If the first is correct, then so are the other two. The occurrence which makes one correct makes the others correct also. I should not mind saying--if you like--that the correctness of the first, our assumption, amounts to no more than the correctness of the others.

Th.: This sounds truistic--and that, I take it, is exactly how you want it to sound. The correctness of the supposal that Harley will fall downstairs amounts to just this: when the time comes, Harley falls downstairs; or after the time has passed, Harley has fallen downstairs. The correctness of a supposal that X will happen consists, then, of no more than the fact that X happens.

240

But, you say, the supposal implies that nothing can prevent the occurrence of X. And if the supposal is correct, then nothing **can** prevent the occurrence of X. And so, of course, nothing and nobody can prevent the occurrence of anything at all. Because for each and every occurrence, there was a supposal that that occurrence would take place.

So, this is what it all comes to: when anything happens, the fact that it happens shows that it could not have been prevented or made not to happen. The fact that it happens means the relevant supposal is correct, and from the correctness of the supposal it follows that it could not have been prevented. So the fact that it happens is sufficient to show that it could not have been prevented.

Sa.: Well—yes—and no. I don't know what to think about that. There's my fatalistic conclusion, all right; but it has now come back to me in a surprising form. Something has gone wrong, and I cannot see exactly what it is. This puts it in a very different light. Perhaps I have just not lived long enough with my argument to accommodate myself to all of its consequences; and this one I certainly don't want.

I confess that I always imagined myself to be pronouncing occurrences unpreventable from one point in time, namely, the present. I always thought of myself as firmly ensconced in the present, and I was looking primarily toward the future. I was thinking primarily of future happenings when I thought of things which could not be prevented. Of course, I had thought of applying my argument to the past; but when I did I always thought of moving time backward so that the past was then future to me.

Th.: I don't see how one can profess to think of all past occurrences as things which cannot be prevented. I don't mean to make too much of the word "prevent" here. I don't see how one can think of past occurrences as things which he cannot make not to happen.

Sometimes we do talk of past occurrences in the way you suggest. Suppose that I put on my jacket and boots and I tell you that I am going out to close the barn door. "I want to keep the mare from getting out," I say. Now, you might say, "You can't do that. You can't keep the mare from getting out; she's already out." This is a joke; and you say this only because I have a mistaken idea about the occurrence in question. I think it has not yet happened, and you are, in effect, telling me that it has. "You can't do that" wouldn't be understandable unless I thought I could do it, and the only reason I think that I can is that I have a misconception about the matter. You don't mean

241

that you can imagine anyone who has a similar misconception about the occurrence of everything which has happened since the beginning of time--if time had a beginning--and to whom it makes sense therefore, to say "You can't prevent any of those things."

Sa.: No. Of course not. I've become terribly confused. It does follow from the correctness of an assumption that the occurrence could not have been prevented. And so it follows from the fact that it occurred that it could not have been prevented. You have got my argument right and you have made the correct tense adjustments. And the result is most paradoxical. Think of the conclusions to which it leads me. The fact that my roof leaks shows that the leak could not have been prevented. The fact that the forest fire started in the campground shows that it could not have been prevented. The fact that the water froze and cracked the engine block shows that it could not have been prevented. And so on and on.

I do not want to say such ridiculous things. But now I see that these things are precisely what the fatalist argument must lead one to say. The argument really boils down to this: the mere fact that something happens shows that it could not have been prevented. A fatalist must obliterate the distinction between things which could have been prevented and those which could not. I suppose that a hardy fatalist will say that there is no such distinction. He must say that a distinction which each of us makes with ease, with regularity and agreement, is no distinction at all. And that is too silly. If that is his only out, then I am no longer interested in his position.

No. I think that my argument is no good after all.

Th.: You change your mind about these important matters very quickly, and with ease.

Sa.: Well, I suppose that I've learned to take a professional attitude toward these things. I've just been appointed to an assistantship in philosophy, you know. I actually get paid for playing a part in dialogues like this--even though it is only enough for hamburgers and french fries. I wonder, though, what could have led me to make such blunders?

Th.: Maybe there is a mistake in thinking that a supposal about a future occurrence implies that nothing can prevent the occurrence.

Sa.: Do you see such a mistake?

Th.: No. But I suspect that if we went through the steps involved, while making the proper tense adjustments, we might turn it up.

Sa. Let us try.

Th.: Let's imagine that you make a supposal about

242

something which will happen tomorrow--something completely out of the range of your abilities to know or to predict, or even to have a reasonable hunch about. You suppose that the kitchen sink will stop up. What do you say? "Let's suppose that the sink will stop up tomorrow." Do I really understand this? I immediately think that perhaps you are going to give me a lecture on how to be prepared for household emergencies. "Let's suppose that the sink will stop up. What will you do? Call a plumber? Try to open it? Do you know how to go about it? Do you have the tools to open the trap? Do you suppose that a little lye or Draino would do the job?" So you might proceed, and then tell me that I should know more about these things than I do.

But no. I must put this supposal in an entirely different situation. You tell me that we are going to treat it as a premiss in some very simple logical exercises. And so you go on. Well, then, I shall try to engage in your logical exercises. "The sink will stop up" implies that water will not flow through it. Those implications are easy enough to see. Now how about this: "The sink will stop up" implies that nothing can prevent it?

Sa.: This last one is certainly different from the other two; but I do not see that the difference is significant. That is, I do not see that the difference affects the fact that there is an implication in each case.

Th.: How do we test--or get the feel of--the implication? One way is this. We deny the conclusion, and ask whether its denial is consistent with the premiss. If its denial is not consistent, then the premiss implies the conclusion.

Consider the premiss "The sink will stop up" and then consider "Water will flow through it," which is the denial of the conclusion, "Water will not flow through it." These two are surely inconsistent. One cannot accept both--without accepting an inconsistency. And that shows us--if we need any showing--that "The sink will stop up" implies that water will not flow through it.

Sa.: Yes. All that is easy enough.

Th.: Now take the same premiss "The sink will stop up" and consider it along side "It can be prevented." Are these inconsistent with each other?

Sa.: The question is, "Can I accept both-without being inconsistent?" And it seems perfectly clear that I can. It is quite possible that the sink will stop up and at the same time it can be prevented. I should say both of these things, for example, when I knew that the sink would stop up and I knew also that it could be

243

prevented--but I knew, too, that no one was going to do anything to prevent it. In order to get something along the right lines which is inconsistent with "The sink will stop up," I must consider something like this, then: "It can be prevented and it will be."

Th.: You don't need that much. You don't need "It can be prevented and it will be." It's only "It will be" that is inconsistent with "The sink will stop up." "The sink will stop up" is inconsistent with "It will be prevented."

Sa.: Yes. That's right.

Th.: So, "The sink will stop up" implies that it will not be prevented from doing so.

Sa.: This is a baffling thing we are thinking about. Now when I think again about this, it seems to me that "The sink will stop up" does, after all, imply that nothing can prevent it. Let me think it out. "The sink will stop up" is correct--that is, we are taking it as correct. So, if anyone did anything to prevent it, then it would not be correct. That is contrary to our assumption and shows that it is inconsistent with that assumption. So whatever anyone does, it cannot prevent the sink from stopping up. Even if someone tried to do something to prevent the sink from stopping up, he could not succeed. Regardless of how hard he tried, he could not prevent the sink from stopping up. So it would seem that nobody can prevent it.

Th.: That is really tempting. But let's go more slowly and see what you have done. We have "The sink will stop up" and we are taking that as correct. And you have agreed that what its correctness amounts to is that the occurrence takes place: the sink stops up, or the sink has stopped up. Anything that will prevent that occurrence is ruled out. So it is ruled out that anyone will prevent it. It certainly doesn't follow from this that if someone tried to prevent it, he would fail. If we spell out the implication along the lines which you followed, then this is what we get: "The sink will stop up" implies either that someone will do something to prevent it and fail, or no one will do anything to prevent it. We certainly do not get "Regardless of how hard someone may try, he is bound to fail." After all, we know that if anyone tried in the proper way he would likely succeed. And you have agreed that something like that is quite consistent with "The sink will stop up." That is, you agreed that "It could be prevented" is consistent with "The sink will stop up." Surely, "If anyone tried he could succeed in preventing it" is consistent with it also.

Sa.: How do you suppose I was ever led to think that "The sink will stop up" implies "Nothing can

244

prevent it"?

Th.: I can't now remember exactly how you laid out the argument for me. But from what I do remember of it, I think you reasoned something like this. If the sink will stop up, then nothing will prevent it. If it will stop up, it can't be the case that anybody will prevent it. So if it can't--absolutely can't--be the case that anybody will prevent it, then nobody can prevent it (or it cannot be prevented). This last step, of course, is the mistake. It really involves just the step from "Nobody will prevent it" to "It cannot be prevented."

Sa.: I don't see that so clearly.

Th.: It seems to me that what makes the slip easy is the language you use in marking-off the conclusion: "It cannot be the case that anybody will prevent it." If it can't be that anybody will prevent it, then it seems that nobody could prevent it. But "It can't be that anybody will prevent it" is just a way of emphasizing this: to say that somebody will prevent it is to say something inconsistent with the supposal. And as we have already seen: it may be the case that nobody will prevent it, and still be true that somebody could prevent it, if only he would.

Sa.: You know, now that I mull this over, I don't believe that I was guilty of that mistake. I think that I was taking--or trying to take--the supposals in such a way that they do imply that the occurrences in question cannot be prevented. So I think that I wrongly answered your question about the correctness of a supposal. My answer was wrong because it was not complete. After something has occurred we can learn from its occurrence that our supposal was correct; but there is more involved in its being correct than the fact that the occurrence took place.

Th.: But if there is more involved in the correctness of a supposal than that something should occur, how can the occurrence of that something suffice to show its correctness?

Sa.: Of course, it can't. I've become flustered. I'm trying to think too fast. That alternative will not do either. Neither alternative will do, and I cannot think of any other.

Th.: You mean that neither alternative will save your argument: you cannot give either answer and make your argument sound and at the same time plausible. The second answer will not do at all. But laying aside the requirements of your argument, do you suppose that the first answer is the correct answer? That is, do you think that what it means for a supposal to be correct is that the occurrence is taking place or has

245

taken place?

Sa.: I must confess that I have not been able to clearly understand this question.

Th.: Let's go back, then, to the specific question--in terms of your first example. You make the supposal that Harley will fall downstairs tomorrow at 3:00 p.m. Now is this what it amounts to to say that the supposal is correct? At exactly 3:00 p.m. tomorrow Harley is falling downstairs, or after 3:00 p.m. Harley has fallen down the stairs?

Sa.: The changes in tense make this most confusing. But it now seems to me that that answer is correct. After all, it can be nothing but a compression or summary of the way we talk about such things. Do we say that a supposal is correct because (and only because) the occurrence in question takes place? I am inclined to answer "Yes."

Th.: For an understanding of your argument, I think it very important that we get clear on this question, "What is involved in the correctness of a supposal?" If we were only interested in this matter as a logic exercise, then perhaps it would not be a very important question. We might readily agree that "Nothing will prevent Harley's fall" follows from the two premisses "If Harley will fall, then nothing will prevent it," and "Harley will fall." That is, we might agree that the argument is valid. Also, we might be satisfied with this: if "Harley will fall" is correct, then "Nothing will prevent it" is also correct. We might be satisfied with all of this without worrying much about what is involved in the correctness of "Harley will fall." We think we understand enough about validity to see that whatever it is--"correctness"--it can be transferred from the premiss to the conclusion. The validity of the argument guarantees that, and we do not need to worry ourselves about what correctness is.

When we are dealing with your argument for fatalism, though, we cannot be casual about this matter because your argument requires that a great many of your assumptions or supposals actually be correct. So we must ask, seriously, "What does it amount to for a supposal to be correct?"

Sa.: How can we say any more in answer to this question than we have already said? What more is there to be said?

Th.: Well, I should like to have before me some such supposals--where we are actually concerned with whether they are correct or not. And I should like to see, in terms of those supposals, what we are actually concerned with.

Sa.: Isn't that what we have done for the supposal that Harley will fall downstairs?

Th.: Not to my satisfaction. We have not considered whether we should say "That supposal was correct" or whether we should say "--is correct" or anything of the sort of such a supposal. And then I keep wondering about that odd requirement for "supposals" which your argument puts on us.

Sa.: What do you mean?

Th.: I mean that we must consider supposals which are about this occurrence and that--any old occurrence at any time--without regard to whether it is likely or plausible or whether we know anything about it at all. How can we imagine getting "supposals" of this kind? We say, "For purposes of creating little deductive arguments, let's suppose..." and we suppose anything at all--the wilder the better. And then we must ask seriously, "Is it correct?" "Was it correct?" "Will it be correct?" and such. How can I think of such supposals?

Sa.: I see. The trouble is that they are so disconnected from our lives and experience. Many of them are things about which we cannot even make guesses or have hunches or take any special interest at all. How are we to think about them? How about this? Imagine that we make up a game. We close our eyes and think in the most unregulated way possible of future occurrences--things we know nothing about--care nothing about--inconsequential and unpredictable and amusing things--anything whatever. And let us impose just one limit: we think of these things happening tomorrow. "Tomorrow Bertie will drop a fork," "An aspirin tablet will hop like a jumping-bean," "Something will drop into the kitchen sink, and plug the drain." We write these down, just for fun. Each of us makes a list. There is no further point to this; it occupies us for a little while, and then we go out to look for the winter wren singing in the forest.

These things we have written down are, surely, very much like the "supposals" we want to consider.

Th.: Perhaps they are. It is your idea, after all, and I suppose you should know. How are we to go about considering whether any one of them is correct or not, and what makes it so?

Sa.: Suppose that tomorrow evening I remember the lists we made. I find mine crumpled in my pocket; I take it out, look it over, and I am quite surprised. "Three of these things I wrote down are correct," I say. Isn't that what I should say? I mean I imagined in the game that those things would happen and they did happen. I wrote down that they would happen and they did happen. So what I wrote is correct.

Th.: When you make the discovery which you have made, then you say, "What I wrote was correct." Are you sure that that is what you should say?

Sa.: Well, no. That doesn't sound right, does it? But what should I say?

Th.: I'm afraid I can't help much. How about "turned out to be correct"?

Sa.: Yes. That sounds a little better. "One of the things I wrote yesterday turned out to be correct." No, that doesn't sound quite right either.

Th.: My ear is in agreement with yours. These are strange things to be saying. I wonder whether we haven't got a difficulty similar to that which we had with "saying." These things you wrote down, for all you put yourself into them, could have been produced by O'Casey--if we could teach him to write. But that isn't necessary. O'Casey could say these things, and we could write down what he said--so that we should not forget them. Now we look back and say, "One of the things O'Casey said was correct," or "One of the things O'Casey said turned out to be correct." Of course, we shouldn't say such things.

Sa.: But why not, I wonder?

Th.: I think the "things" have to come from some kind of thought or from some kind of speech with which we are familiar. Suppose that I have a considered hunch that something will happen tomorrow. Last winter a storm partly uprooted a tall fir tree which I can see through an opening in the woods from my kitchen window. It has been leaning ever since, and each new storm makes it lean farther. There is no doubt that one day it will topple over. One morning I sit at the window looking at the tree, and I am struck by the angle of its trunk. It has begun to rain and a wind is coming up. I say, "You know, I think this is the end for that tree. I'll bet it topples over before tomorrow." I think no more about this; but I look the next morning and find that the tree has fallen. Now what do I think? That is, what do I think when I remember what I said yesterday morning? "What I said about that tree's falling was correct?" "What I said turned out to be correct?"

Sa.: Yes. Now this language seems in order. And it seems to me that it would be all right to say either of these things.

Th.: Though they don't come to the same thing, surely.

Sa.: Yes. I see that there is a difference. "Was correct" implies that what you said was well founded. "Turned out to be correct" implies that there was guess work in what you said.

248

Th.: Well, we want those to which "correct" applies. That is, your argument requires that we compile "assumptions" about the future which are correct. And I think your suggestion must be right: only things which have some reasonable backing, things based on some evidence are "correct."

So if you want to compose a list of "statements" about future occurrences and then find among them many which are correct, the list cannot be produced by playing your game or by transcribing the sayings of a mynah. The things which are correct must come from people who know what they are talking about, and have some fair to middling—or better—reasons for saying what they say.

Sa.: Yes. I think you are right about this. And if I must supply "statements" such as these for my fatalistic argument, the scope of its application will be cut again—and very drastically.

Th.: We haven't yet got a very complete answer to our question, "What is involved in something being correct?"

Sa.: We have gone some way toward an answer. It now seems clear that only things which are based on some evidence can be correct. And even then, they need not be correct. They can be incorrect, of course. Also, they may "turn out to be correct."

Th.: How do you see this difference between saying something "was correct" and saying that it "turned out to be correct"?

Sa.: It seems to me that if the basis for what was said was not very substantial, or not properly applied or defective or something like that, then what was said "turned out to be correct."

Th.: And then, if the basis or reasons were sufficient we say it "was correct." This is very vague. I wonder whether we could see the sort of thing involved if we had a clear example before us?

Sa.: Can you invent a proper example?

Th.: I'll try. Suppose that we live near a large mountain slope. We are beginning to worry about the unusually heavy snowfall this winter on the mountainside. We wonder whether it may not create an avalanche—and possibly reach our house. So we go to inquire of a snow expert who teaches at the neighboring university. He says, "I've been watching that snow. I've plotted it on my contour map of the mountain side. I've determined its depth and weight. I'm confident that it will begin to slide by mid-week: I feel almost certain enough of myself to say it will begin to slide on Wednesday. I think you should move out of your place until the slide is over." We take his advice, and the snow does begin to slide on Wednesday and almost, but not quite, reaches our house. What do we say? "What he said was correct?"

Sa.: Yes, that seems quite right--or something stronger--"What he said was absolutely correct."

Th.: But suppose that later he revealed to us that his calculations were all wrong. He had been using the wrong map and his assistants had given him incorrect measurements of the snow. He now says, "If I had known, I should not have offered any prediction." What shall we say now? "Well, what you said about the avalanche--its time and all--was correct in any case." Is that what we should say?

Sa.: No. I think not. You're asking me to use my ear on "correct" and "turned out to be correct." "Turned out to be correct" certainly sounds better. Yes, I'm sure "turned out to be correct" is the right thing to say. "What you said about the avalanche--its time and all--turned out to be correct."

Th.: Let's try to examine all of the possibilities here. If his data and calculations were in order and he got the right result, then we shall say, "What he said **was** correct." If his data and calculations were all wrong, and he got the right result, we shall say, "What he said turned out to be correct."

Now suppose that his data and calculations were all wrong, and he also got the wrong results. What shall we say then of his prediction of the time of the avalanche? Let us suppose that he said, "There will be no snow slide this winter: there is nothing to worry about."

Sa.: Well, then what he said was not correct. That is, what he said about the non-occurrence of an avalanche on that mountain was certainly incorrect.

Th.: Then for something to be incorrect it is not necessary for it to be properly based on relevant evidence?

Sa.: No. But it seems quite clear that we should not say it was incorrect unless it could have been based on proper and relevant data. The snow expert's prediction could have been, and we thought it was, based on proper data and principles. He thought it was properly based for a while, of course. This is very different from a wild guess or pure fantasy--the sort of thing I tried to illustrate by my game.

Th.: Let me try to summarize what we have found. For something to be correct, it is not enough for what is said to be right. It must be arrived at by using the right data, making the right calculations, putting the relevant knowledge to use. For something said to be incorrect it is also not enough that the result be wrong. It must be arrived at by wrong data, miscalculations, a misuse of what is known, and so on.

Thus, for "correct" or "incorrect" to be applicable at all, the "statement" must be the sort that comes from some use of data and information. Or perhaps this is the right way to put it. It must be about an occurrence which is, to some extent at least, predictable; and it must grow out of a use of some of the proper data and knowledge.

Sa.: That is a fair summary.

Th.: Then "correct" or "incorrect" will apply to what one says about the future only where all these factors are present. Now your argument for fatalism required us to think of "assumptions" or "supposals" about future occurrences, and to think that some of them would be "incorrect"--but some of them would be "correct." And those correct supposals would imply that certain occurrences were unpreventable. We can now see that this is a mistake. Such things as your "assumptions" or "supposals" will be neither correct nor incorrect. We cannot ask, "What is implied by the correct supposals?" because there are no correct supposals--but, of course, there are no incorrect ones either. After all, for soundly based and carefully calculated predictions, it may be that the relevant occurrences cannot be prevented. And then perhaps you allow yourself to think that all statements about the future are like those.

Sa.: I see what you mean. If what one says about a future occurrence of that kind is correct, then the occurrence will definitely take place as predicted. It is as good as in the record books or in the bag. But even so, I wonder whether such occurrences really are preventable or unpreventable?

Suppose that the occurrence in question is the flooding of a stream, specifically this: the stream will overflow our dikes in the lowland at 3 p.m. tomorrow. We are trying our best to do what can be done in the face of an impending flood. The weather and stream expert has said, "The stream will overflow your dikes at 3 p.m." Someone might ask, "Does that imply that we can do nothing to prevent it?" And the answer might be "Yes. He has made an inventory of the available sandbags and equipment, and he has calculated that the dikes could not possibly be raised in time. His statement was based on a survey of all available manpower and resources."

In this example "what he says" implies the inevitability of the flood precisely because he has considered every means by which it could be prevented and has calculated that none of them will work. There is a great deal more in what he says than a mere calculation of the crest of the stream at a certain time. Suppose that he has said, "The stream will be one foot over your dikes tommorrow." Then we should certainly hurry and build our dikes several feet higher. And if we succeed, there will be no flood; but, of course, what he said was correct. The stream was one foot above the top of our former dikes. Will we say that that was unpreventable? At the time of his prediction we might say, "The stream will be a foot over the dikes tomorrow, and nothing can be done to prevent that rise in the stream."

Th.: But even then, he would not say "The stream will be a foot over the dikes tomorrow" unless he knew that there was no dam to be closed or that, if there were a dam, it could impound no more water. We can't imagine an expert on these matters making an irresponsible prediction. It is precisely his business to consider all of the possibilities for human control, and they are very clear and definite things, and very limited in number.

So, even when he says only "The stream will be a foot over the dikes," this implies that nothing can prevent it, because he has taken into account every possible preventive measure.

Sa.: Yes. I think that's right.

Th.: Where human action might enter the scene in an unpredictable manner, I suspect that things are quite different.

Sa.: What are you thinking of?

Th.: Suppose that a physics professor has prepared a long, gentle sloping inclined plane upon which to give his beginning students a demonstration of the laws of gravity. First he wants to show them how predictable things are. He tells them to start their stopwatches when he releases a ball at the top. And he says, "The ball will close a circuit at the bottom and turn on a light in exactly 30 seconds." Now suppose that after he releases the ball, some impish student raises the bottom of the inclined plane. Of course the ball will not now arrive at the signal point in the predicted time.

The professor has certainly based what he said on the proper data and laws, and he has carefully calculated his result. Yet what he said does not imply that nobody can prevent the ball's arrival at the end-point in 30 seconds.

Sa.: Yes, that's certainly right.

Th.: In our understanding of what he said, we do not hold him responsible for taking into account unpredictable human interference--or interference from any other unpredictable source. He certainly did not say, "The ball will arrive at the end in 30 seconds, hell or high water--so, nobody and nothing can prevent it."

Sa.: Yes. Statements such as these, though they are well based on solid data and properly calculated, do not imply unpreventability. I see what you mean. If the fatalistic argument derives from some model or picture of statements about the future, it cannot be such as these. It can only be statements about future occurrences which are outside the realm of interference by unpredictable forces, or which are based on a consideration of all the possible interfering forces. And such statements, I dare say, are not commonly made.

Maybe the things that astronomers say about future eclipses, occultations and such occurrences, will qualify. But does it make sense to think of such occurrences as preventable or unpreventable? Take a humble example of that kind of statement: "The moon will rise at 7:13 p.m." How could we think that nothing can be done to prevent it? Yet, I suppose that if I were explaining things to a child, I might say, "The moon will rise at 7:13 and no one can do anything to keep it from rising at exactly that time."

Statements such as these, it seems, do imply in this way that nothing can be done to keep a certain occurrence from taking place. And it may be that a sense of that implication was operating on me when I constructed my argument for fatalism. But surely there are other equally important things operating to sponsor the argument.

However that may be, we have come to see that only very special statements about the future can be correct, and only a small part of those imply that an occurrence cannot be prevented or made not to occur. These slim resources will not provide the fatalist with materials from which to construct his argument. We have come to see that the fatalist is mistaken about almost everything.

Th.: I don't think we ought to represent the things that we came to see in quite the way you do. I think of them as tentative summaries we have made at various stages in our discussion. If we were to think it all through again, we might go into greater detail, and invent more examples; and then we might well want to refine and qualify these summaries of what we have come to see.

Sa.: I'm convinced that our observations--as far as they go--are sound, and I don't think we should underrate their significance. I think we have turned up some principles that are of philosophical importance.

Th.: What are you thinking of?

Sa.: I think our discussion has obvious consequences for a "theory of truth." When it comes to
guesses, and hunches and predictions--to "statements"
about the future--I think that "true" must be much like
"correct," and "turned out to be true" much like
"turned out to be correct."

Th.: That seems plausible. In the examples we
have been using, we could probably substitute "true"
for "correct" and "turned out to be true" for "turned
out to be correct."

Sa.: Yes. And also we could substitute "not true"
for "incorrect."

Th.: Though I expect that "true" will apply in
some cases where "correct" will not.

Sa.: What are you thinking of now?

Th.: Something like a premonition. Suppose that I
have a premonition that I shall fall tomorrow and
injure my leg. I can't get it out of my mind, and I
tell you about it. And then I do fall and hurt my leg.
What do we say? "My premonition turned out to be correct" or do we say "My premonition turned out to be
true"?

No. Now I'll take it back. I thought that "turned
out to be true" might fit here. I see that it doesn't.
"Turned out to be right" would be the thing. And anyway this is about my premonition and not about "what I
said." "What I said yesterday about falling--well, it
turned out to be...." What? "Correct"? "True?"
"Right"? I don't know what to say. None of these seem
right.

Sa.: With regard to "statements" about future occurrences, I can't think of any example which will
bring out a difference. But anyway, I am interested
mostly in the fact that just as there is a difference
between "correct" and "turned out to be correct," so
there is a similar difference between "true" and "turned out to be true."

Th.: What has happened to "false"?

Sa.: "False" is surely a different matter entirely. There is a difference between being "not true" and
being "false." I'm not sure how to put it. In addition to being not true, things that are false are
deceitful, or deliberately misleading, or sham or hypo-
critical or something along those lines. There is
probably also a difference between "not correct" and
"incorrect." "Incorrect" is more nicely suited for
cases of miscalculation or theoretical error, "not
correct" for cases of innocent slips and blunders. The
difference, though, between "not correct" and "incorrect" is subtle, and is surely of no concern to us.
But the difference between "not true" and "false" is on

254

a different scale, and I think we should do well to avoid any equation of "false" with "not true."

Th.: What you say sounds plausible, but I have no confidence in my ability to see, or to comment out of the blue on the subtle differences between words. I mean, I do not like to consider such questions without putting a lot of examples before myself.

Sa.: You're right, of course. I think that my remarks about "true" and "false," for example, are on the right track, but I should not want to bet everything on them. I need to find examples, and I am quite prepared to change my mind in light of the examples. Part of what I am going on is the very obvious difference between "true" and "false" when they are applied to things other than "what people say."

Th.: What are you thinking of?

Sa.: Philosophers are concerned only with "true" and "false" as they apply to what people say--to "propositions" or "assertions." But the words "true" and "false" are used of many other things, and there is no a priori reason to think that the words will radically change their meanings as they are applied to one thing and another.

Th.: You're thinking of such things as these I suppose: we speak of a "true friend," and of a "false friend." We say that a lathe is "running true," and when it is not running true, we say that we must "true it up."

Sa.: Yes. And many, many more. We say that something flies "true as an arrow," but we do not say that a thing flies as "false as a crooked arrow." When a lathe is off-center, it is not "running false."

Th.: It certainly appears that "true" and "false" carry entirely different ideas.

Sa.: Also consider "true blue" which is a dye color that is especially fast. And we speak of a person or a group doing something which is "true to form." Biologists say that a sparrow hawk is not a "true hawk," and that a Douglas fir is not a "true fir." They mean that the sparrow hawk is not correctly classified with the hawks and the Douglas fir is not correctly classified with the firs. It seems to me that in all these many uses of the word "true" there runs the idea of something being trustworthy, reliable-- proper, as it is supposed to be or expected to be.

Th.: It seems hard to express one single idea running through all of those.

Sa.: Consider, though, the way in which "false" is different. We say that a store has a "false front," and a glass or bottle has a "false bottom." If we want to evade our pursuers, we lay a "false trail." A mask

255

is sometimes called a "false face." A person who sings in a voice far higher than his normal voice signs in falsetto (which is Italian for "false voice"). Dentures are sometimes called "false teeth."

Th.: This group seems a bit more unified.

Sa.: Yes. It's pretty clear to me that the basic idea is this: something is "false" when it is deceitful, when it is deliberately designed to confuse or mislead. And, by extension, something is called "false" when it could be deceitful or used to confuse or mislead.

Consider how the contrast between "true" and "false" comes out when we use them both of the same subject. A "true friend" is one who can be counted on. A person who is "not a true friend" is one who is not to be counted on. But a "false friend" is one who has betrayed--one who has deliberately betrayed his faith. "Not true" is "departing from the expected," but "false" is "departing from the expected--deliberately."

Th.: I suspect that you are on a useful track--or perhaps you are on many useful tracks--here. What about "untrue"?

Sa.: That's interesting: I confess I've not thought about "untrue" at all. We don't say of many things that they are "untrue," do we? A lover can be "untrue." A lover is "untrue" it seems when he is not true to his word--or his pledge. Both "not true" and "untrue" apply to what a person says. It seems to me that "not true" is "wrong," and "untrue" is "importantly wrong"; but I honestly have not thought about this, and I do not know what to say.

Th.: I should still feel much better if we had a lot of examples before us. What importance do you attach to this survey of "true" and "false" anyway?

Sa.: I agree. One should go slowly over this and proceed by constructing many examples. It seems to me surprising--and in a way shameful--that philosophers have not already made a careful and detailed survey of the uses of "true," "not-true," and "false"--because they have always been deeply interested in the "question of truth." Many philosophers have developed what they call a "theory of truth" and it is hard to see how they could do that without making a careful survey of the uses of such words as "true," "truthful," "truly," and others.

I started thinking about truth because I believe that our discussion of fate and the future puts us in a good position to shed some light on one of the questions philosophers have asked about truth. Philosophers have been exclusively interested in "true" as it applies to "what a person says" or to "assertions" or "statements" or something like that. And one of their questions has been, "To what does 'true' apply?" They have asked, "What is the bearer of truth?" or better, "What is it to which we attribute the predicates 'true', 'not-true', and 'false'?" And many philosophers have been strangely content with answers such as "propositions" or "statements" or some such. I think we can now see that any such answer is dead wrong.

Th.: How can you be so definite about that? Might not their answers be just as plainly right? In saying that their answers are right I mean only that you might have misunderstood them entirely, and they might be neither right nor wrong. They might be remarks of a terminological nature. The authors of such remarks might be saying only that they intend to call anything which is either true or false a "proposition" or "statement."

Sa.: But we have agreed that "false" is not the simple opposite of "true." That is, "true" and "false" are not like "true" and "not-true."

Th.: Well then, perhaps these philosophers intend to call by the name "propositions" anything which is true or not-true.

Sa.: That would be a very friendly and generous interpretation in a way. But in another way it would not--for then their question is not a very profound one--being only "What shall we call whatever is true or not-true?" Anyway, such philosophers make it clear that that is not their intended meaning. If that is what they meant, then they would have to agree that only a very limited number of things we might say about the future would qualify as "propositions": only those things which are predictable and which grow out of an effort to use the proper data and principles. I am sure that most philosophers would try to identify a "propositon about the future" not by looking at the way it was put forth--the position of the speaker, his knowledge, evidence and such--but by its "content." I think that they would say that anything was a proposition about the future if it was "about" some event or occurrence or action with a future date.

Th.: No doubt you are right in your understanding of this. Your interpretation does seem the likely one.

Sa.: Then these philosophers have simply made a mistake in saying or implying that anything about the future--wild supposals, pure guesses, anything at all about the future--is either true or not true.

It is obvious that some things are "true" or "not true" (let's not consider "false"), and some things are neither "true" nor "not true." That is, some things are simply not candidates at all. I think we have

257

turned up two important members of this group of non-candidates: (1) something that is playfully concocted about a future occurrence, such as the things we wrote down in my guessing game, and (2) something seriously said about a predictable occurrence, but which is based on a misuse of knowledge or data or comes from a miscalculation. We should not say, under any circumstances, that either of these "was true" or "was not true." But, when the subject is an occurrence which could have been predicted, and someone has offered a carefully calculated prediction of its occurrence, then I think we shall allow that it "was true"; or if the occurrence does not take place as anticipated, then it "was not true."

It looks as though we do not say that things are "true" and "not true" unless we believe that the speaker or writer of these things was at the time able to determine the relevant occurrences or non-occurrences. It looks as though what makes a thing a candidate for "true" or "not true" is our belief that the speaker was in a position to make the determination. If the speaker could not have made the determination at the time, then what he says is not a candidate, and is not now--or ever--either "true" or "not true."

Th.: If that is a peculiarity of things about the future, then a person ought to be able to say the most wild and irresponsible things about present or past occurrences, and they could be true or false.

Sa.: Yes. And isn't that the way it is? Suppose that one day we are talking about the funny names which some cities have: "Medicine Hat," "Bean Blossom," "Sweet Home." Then we turn to sheer fancy and think about names which cities might have. We do not know whether there are cities with such names or not: "Arthritis," "Woodpecker Glen," "Nuthatch Knoll." I become tickled by the name "Gnawbone" and I get carried away. I talk as though I were starting to tell a story. "Gnawbone is a town in Indiana, and yesterday a tornado tore up the trees on its main street...."

Well suppose that later you discover that there is a town named "Gnawbone" in Indiana; and you make inquiries about the weather and discover that the town was hit by a tornado on the exact day and the trees were torn up on its main street in just the way I described in my purely imaginary report. What now will you say to me? Isn't this all right? "You remember what you said about Gnawbone, Indiana and a tornado? Well, what you said was not pure fantasy: it was absolutely true. Everything you said was true--right down to the smallest detail: Isn't that right?

Th.: Well, it seems so. But I'm beginning to

wonder whether I can trust my ear with these strange
examples. Perhaps we ought to ask, too, whether
"turned out to be true" might not be used of present or
past occurrences? Couldn't I say, "What you said
turned out to be true?"

Sa.: Yes. I'm glad you brought that up. Here
"turned out to be true" seems to be the same as "I
found out it was true" or "It was found to be true." I
might say, "What you said about Gnawbone, Indiana
turned out to be true," and this seems to come to the
same thing as "What you said about Gnawbone, Indiana
was true: I found out just this morning that all of it
was true." And this is definitely not what "turned out
to be true" amounts to in our examples about the
future. To the snow-expert who used the wrong data and
made incorrect calculations, I shall not say, "I found
out just an hour ago that what you said was true," or
anything of that kind.

Th.: I wonder what you think of this suggestion.
Suppose I suggest that we have been concerned with the
conditions for **saying** that "statements" about the future are true or not true, correct or incorrect. That
is, we have not been concerned with whether something
is true or not true but only with whether we should say
it was true or not true.

Sa.: I'm not sure I understand what you mean.

Th.: I mean this: you might get your argument for
fatalism back again if you were willing to take a certain philosophical position. You might hold that **anything** said about the future--a supposal, a wild guess,
an idle imagining, or anything--is either true or it is
not true. It's just that we do not **say** that it is true
(or not true, either, of course). We only **say** that
carefully calculated statements about predictable
matters are true or not true. Someone who thought that
he could identify a proposition about the future by its
"content"--someone who did not think that he was making
purely terminological remarks--might defend himself in
this way. He might say that anything about the future
is either true or not true--it's just that often we
shall not **say** so.

Sa.: Oh yes. I think I understand what you are
suggesting. You mean that I should make a general
distinction between what makes something X and what
makes it understandable to say that something is X, and
then apply this to something being true and understandably saying that something is true. Those who make
this distinction generally say that the condition which
will make it understandable to say something is this:
the thing must be interesting, pointed, relevant, or
noteworthy. Unless what you say is one of these, it is

259

puzzling to say it. That is, it is puzzling to say something out of the blue, something which has no point, is not relevant to the circumstances--even though that something might be so. It is too dull, trivial, truistic, out of keeping, to be said without bewildering the hearer.

Th.: Yes. That is the usual view, and some philosophers have suggested that we should apply the distinction to the case of saying that something is true. I suppose that they think the condition for saying that something is true is a bit different, but they do not tell us what they think it is.

Sa.: First, let's consider the condition for saying something as it is usually understood, and see how it applies to one of our examples. Return to the example of the snow expert who made a prediction and then found that he had based it on erroneous data and incorrect theory. Even so, the snow slide that he predicted took place just as he said it would. We agreed that in this case we should say, "What he said turned out to be correct" (or "true"); and we should definitely not say, "What he said was correct" (or "true").

We can't interpret this as a case where what he said really was true although the condition was not right for us to say that it was true. If the condition for saying is to be the usual one, then the reason we cannot say that the snow expert's prediction was true is that it is not interesting or pointed or relevant. But that is ridiculous. It is relevant; it is exactly to the point; it is interesting. The status of what the expert said occupies the center of our attention. We say that what he said "turned out to be true" and we do not say that it "was true." If it really was true, we here have every reason to say so.

Th.: You are certainly right--assuming that the condition for saying something is the one which you have characterized. The philosophers who say--rather, imply--that the snow expert's prediction really is true must have in mind some other condition for saying something. It would have to be this: we can only say that something is true when it is a properly calculated statement about some predictable matter.

Sa.: What reason could anyone have for thinking that was a condition for saying something? Why should that be a condition for saying "It was true" and not for "It turned out to be true" or "It was right"? Surely that is a condition which anything has to satisfy in order even to be considered as a candidate for "true" (or "not true").

Th.: I think you are quite right. The suggestion

has no plausibility, and I brought it up only because I have read philosophers who hold such a view--or rather, they strongly imply that they hold such a view.

Th.: I believe that people who hold this view are not thinking of anything like our snow expert's prediction. I believe that they have before them only certain very simple examples. The cat is lying on the mat before me. Someone, speaking from the next room, asks, "Where is the cat?" Of course, I say, "The cat is on the mat." I do not say, "It's true: the cat is on the mat." Suppose instead that someone in the next room says, "Watson told me that the cat is on the mat. Is that right?" Now, I might well say, "It's true: the cat is on the mat."

With this example before him, our philosopher might observe: "We say that anything is true only when someone has said that thing--or is about to say it, or we think that someone might say it or think it--and so our saying that it is true is a way of conceding it, endorsing it, or confirming it, or something like that. The occasion for saying that it is true is that it has come to our attention and invites our agreement or disagreement. The philosopher seems to have in mind something like the usual condition for saying--as you have characterized it. He might then want to say that it can be true that the cat is on the mat, even when there is no condition for saying so: no one has mentioned the fact or is likely to be thinking about it. He might want to say this in defense of the metaphysical doctrine that every statement (or proposition) is either true or not true. Or he might say this in defense of a correspondence theory of truth. He might think that "true" means "corresponds to fact," and so he might want to say that the statement "The cat is on the mat" corresponds to fact--whether an occasion to say it has arisen or not.

Sa.: I can see that if someone started from such an example, he might think that he could find some such "theory of truth" reflected in it. But why would he then think that he could generalize from this example, and expect to find the very same elements in our remarks on the snow expert's prediction?

Th.: One can only guess about such matters. The philosopher may already subscribe to the doctrine that every proposition is either true or not true, and he might think that he can recognize a proposition in each case. Then, too, the philosopher may have been "feeding on a one-sided diet"--I believe that's what Wittgenstein has called it--I mean that the philosopher has been preoccupied with one example or one kind of example. I think that is the most common sin in philosophy, and the most excusable one: to overlook or ignore many cases or examples, particularly in a matter such as this, where there will be so very many different cases of so many different kinds. He may have been thinking of "is true," and may never have thought of "was true."

Sa.: Well, it doesn't seem such an excusable sin to me--especially if a person is in the business of trying to say something of utmost generality. And I imagine that someone who is trying to construct a "theory of truth," is in the business of seeking complete generality.

Not all philosophers have been quite so reckless in their generalizing about "truth." Some have sensed a peculiarity in "propositions about the future," and they have said that some propositions about the future are neither true nor not-true but have a "third-value." Thus they have been led to hold that only a "three-valued logic" is adequate for all propositions--since some propositions about the future do not have one of the usual two "values," true or not-true.

Th.: I thought the usual "two-values" were true and false.

Sa.: Well, they are; but I was trying to be amicable and generous on that point. I assume that by "false" these philosophers really mean "not-true."

Th.: How do they think of this "third-value"?

Sa.: Well, they call it "undecided" or "undetermined." At any rate, that's what the Polish logician, Lukasiewiez, calls it; and he is perhaps the best known representative of this view.

Th.: This makes it sound as though he (and the others) expected that these "undecided" propositions would, in time, be "decided."

Sa.: Yes, I believe that is the right way to understand them. They think that the third value applies to propositions about the future now, and that in time the propositions will acquire one of the other two values, true or not-true.

Th.: What do you think of this view?

Sa.: The philosophers who hold this "three-value" view show a proper sense that truth about the future is a different matter from truth about the past or the present. But they have certainly misconstrued and misrepresented the difference. One can't tell from what examples--if any--they derived their theory, but it would seem that they were thinking of cases like our snow-expert, the man who used the wrong data but whose prediction "turned out to be true" anyway. They must think that their third value, "undecided" or "undetermined," applies to predictions which are neither "true"

nor "not-true" but which may "turn out to be true."
And they think that when the predicted occurrences take
place, the propositions "become true." (Or, if they do
not take place, then the propositions "become
not-true.")

Now we have already seen that this is not right.
The fact that the snow slides on Wednesday, as the
snow-expert predicted, does not make his prediction
true. His prediction "turns out to be true," but this
does not show that it "was true." It certainly does
not show that it "is now true." These philosophers
make it hard to examine their view, because we do not
say of the expert's prediction that it "became true" or
"is now true." But if they had in mind something like
"turns out to be true," then they are mistaken, because when something "turns out to be true" it is not,
thereby, "true." (Neither is it "not-true" when it
"turns out to be not true.")

I suspect that the way they talk of three
"values"--"true," "false" and "undetermined"--grows out
of a misleading picture of the matter. They must think
of propositions as "things" which come into being and
then persist in time. And they must think that during
the time of their existence--their histories or
careers--they are subject to changes. And they must
think too that they change in the manner that Plato
imagined things to change: they lose one "property" or
"characteristic" and acquire another. Two "properties"
may be incompatible, and when one of the two comes in
it forces the other out. Thus "true," "not-true," and
"undetermined" are properties or characteristics of
propositions, and each is incompatible with both of the
others.

"True" and "not-true," they must think, are characteristics which propositions may have or acquire, much
as "generous" or "selfish" are characteristics (or better, "natures") which children may have or may acquire.
And just as there are children who are neither generous
nor selfish, there are propositions which are neither
true nor not true. And just as such "undetermined"
children may in time become generous or selfish, so
such "undetermined" propositions may in time become
true or not true.

I don't know how to bring this talk of "propositions" down to earth except in the way I did when I
tried to launch my argument for fatalism--that is, to
talk of "what someone says" instead. Surely "what he
says" or "what she says"--if it is the right sort of
thing which he or she says--will be a proposition.
Sometimes "what he says" will be true, sometimes not
true, sometimes it will turn out to be true (or not

true). Now something that endures in time, changes by losing and acquiring characteristics, natures, or traits, is a very misleading model in terms of which to think of "what he says." "What he says" may become more important with the passage of time, but that means that people learn to appreciate what he says. What he said may be more true today than it was when he said it, but that means that it applies to our times more pointedly than it did to the author's. We sometimes say, "What he said was once true but is not true now"; but that only means that times have changed, not that what he said has changed. The picture of "what one says" as a thing whose characteristics change is a source of great confusion. The nature of "what one says" does not change as a child's nature changes. It's character does not change as the color of an apple changes as it ripens.

Th.: In the beginning you said that you wanted to avoid any unnecessary problems about truth. But now you have certainly warmed up to the subject.

Sa.: In the beginning I wanted to keep any unnecessary complication about truth out of my argument for fatalism. Quite frankly, my desire to keep it out came partly from the fact that I did not think myself up to handling the matter of truth. But our discussion has given me confidence.

Th.: As for our discussion, I feel uneasy about some of the generalizations and summaries we have made. Perhaps we can justify them because we used them to set ourselves straight about your argument for fatalism. And, if they helped in doing that job, that is quite enough.

Sa.: All the same, I feel that that topic of truth with respect to the future is well worth careful discussion. It is a strangely neglected topic, and I think it might be philosophically important in all sorts of ways.

Th.: Then, I hope we may meet again soon and continue with this topic.

7. TRUTH AND FATE: FUTURE ACTIONS

When I am concerned with logic and logical theory, I can think about propositions and how propositions are true or false, and it can seem a helpful way of thinking. If it is not positively helpful, then certainly it is at least harmless. But when I turn to other matters, this way of thinking can get me into all sorts of troubles.

I get into trouble, for example, when I think about the future and what life might have in store for me. I know what the future will bring--not always, of course, but sometimes. The river will be at flood stage at 11 o'clock tomorrow. A total eclipse of the moon will begin at 12:04 a.m. The sun will set at 6:32 tomorrow, and then the temperature will fall rapidly. These, of course, are things that will happen. They result from the forces of nature and not from human agency. But also I know what people will do--not always, of course, but sometimes. Sometimes I know what someone is going to do because he tells me that he is going to do it or he tells me that he intends to do it. Of course, that alone is not enough to enable me to know positively what he will do. I cannot know that a person is going to do something just because he tells me that he is. I must know a great deal about the person who tells me and the way in which his life makes a place for what he says he is going to do. In short, I must know that he is the kind of person who will do this thing which he says he is going to do, and that nothing will deter him. In many cases, however, I know what someone is going to do even though he does not tell me: in such cases knowing what a person will do is more like knowing when the tide will turn or the sun will set. About some things some people are just as predictable as the tide or the sun.

Every year, at the end of spring term, our philosophy department has a picnic. These are dull affairs, but they are important to the members of our department because in recent years they have become fund-raising enterprises. And that is because several wealthy dowagers who have an "interest in philosophy" have become our regular guests and they enjoy doing things for us. They regularly supply us with money for guest speakers and travel and sometimes for research expenses. This year, a great gray dowager named Mrs. Woody has taken it upon herself to be our hostess, and she has prepared for the picnic a special kind of hot dog in which she takes great pride. If all goes well, we are going to ask her for a sizeable donation to

finance a department colloquium. Also, for the first
time, a new and outspoken young faculty member named
Boris will be in attendance. Boris is going to ac-
company me to the picnic, and the picnic is tomorrow.
Now I'm sure that Boris is going to make some trouble.
When Mrs. Woody serves her famous hot dogs, with great
fanfare, I know that Boris will refuse to accept one.
I know him; I know how he reacts to people like Mrs.
Woody; I know what he thinks about food, and in particular about hot dogs. There is just no doubt about it--
when she offers him the hot dog, he will refuse to
accept it. He will say, "No thanks. I'll just take
the salad," or something like that.

Boris cannot help himself. If I were to plead with
him, I know it would make no difference. It is not as
though Boris had never taken measure of himself. He,
too, knows that he shall do something that is impolite
and a bit cruel. He may think hard about it. "Surely
this one time I can make myself accept the greasy
rancid thing from the old fussbudget," he may think,
and for awhile he may half convince himself that he
will do the socially expected thing. But he knows--as
I know--that when the moment arrives he will get a
sickening in his stomach and he will say, "No thanks."
It is something he simply cannot control in himself.
he cannot keep himself from doing what he knows--and
regrets--that he will do.

Now this is the way "truth" gets into the picture
and creates a problem for my thinking about the future.
Some things I think about the future, some things I
say, are true. This one is true: "Boris will refuse
the hot dog." It is something I think about Boris and
about what he is going to do tomorrow, and it is true.
The fact that it is true implies that Boris has no control over himself in the matter. By concentrating on
the truth of that one thing which I think or say about
Boris, it seems I can lift it out of the situation in
which I think it or say it and consider what it comes
to all by itself. If it is the sort of thing which can
be true or false, then it is either true or false; and
this one is true. From the fact that it is true it
follows that Boris has no control over his action. It
follows that he will do what he is going to do whether
he wishes to or not. This is the first step in an argument that can lead me quickly into fatalism. Having
lifted "it" out--having concentrated attention on "it,"
I can next ask what "it" is. (One of the traditional
questions about truth, presumably, is "What is the
bearer of truth?") It is a "proposition" or "statement" to the effect that Boris will do something. It
is about Boris--Boris is its subject--and it predicates

of Boris a certain action, and one which is in the future, one which is to occur or to take place. It is true that Boris is to do that thing. The next question is "What does it amount to for it to be true?" And a good answer for a starter is this: if it is true that Boris is going to do the thing, then he is going to do the thing. So it is easy to see why he has no control over whether he will do the thing or not, because if there is any question about whether he will do the thing, then it is not true that he will do it. "It is true that he will do it" rules out the possibility that he might not do it. If it is true, then the matter is already settled. It is settled and determined in advance that Boris will do this thing (refuse the hot dog). Hence he has no control over what he is to do.

Now I am ready for the fatalistic conclusion. For, isn't each and every future action like this one in a most important respect--that is, in respect that it is true that it will be performed? I need only to generalize in order to get a truth about any person and every single thing that that person will do: about every single thing that a person is going to do one could say "He will do it" and that would be true. In other words, there is a true "proposition" or "statement" about everything that anyone will ever do. So, nothing that anyone ever does is within his control: no one has any control over any of his actions at all. Everything that everyone will do is settled in advance.

Richard Taylor gives a simple and eloquent exposition of the last step in this argument:

> Consider, then, that class of statements about some particular person--yourself, let us suppose--each of which happens to be true. Their totality constitutes your biography... the entire biography is there. It is not written and probably never will be; but it is nevertheless there, all of it. If... you have some way of discovering those statements in advance, then... you could hardly help becoming a fatalist. But foreknowledge of the truth would not create any truth, nor invest your philosophy with truth, nor add anything to the philosophical foundations of the fatalism that would then be so apparent to you. It would only serve to make it apparent.[1]

---

[1]Richard Taylor, **Metaphysics**, 2nd ed. (Englewood Cliffs, N.J., Prentice-Hall, 1974) pp. 68-9.

The further this argument goes, the more fantastic it becomes, and one naturally feels queasy about every step along the way to the fatalistic conclusion. One naturally wonders how it is possible to talk about propositions in such a wholesale way. One naturally wonders whether it is correct to say of a proposition about any future action that it is true. That is, is true now. One wonders whether it follows that a person has no control over a future action because a proposition is true to the effect that he is going to perform the action.

The argument begins with a clear example which gives us a "proposition" about someone's future action. Then we must see that that proposition is true and that its truth implies that the person has no control over his action. Then the argument generalizes: we can readily imagine similar true propositions about any future action. So it proceeds to the conclusion that no one has any control over any of his actions at all.

I must be clear in the beginning about that "proposition": it must be such that I can imagine one of the same kind for any future action. So I had best review carefully the means by which I produced that proposition by applying the notion of truth to some thought about Boris' behavior at the picnic. I must make sure that I have isolated something which I can lift from the context of the story; and so, without any similar story, I shall be able to imagine a similar thing for any future action whatever. Also I must see clearly how that proposition implies that the agent has no control in the matter of what he is going to do.

As it stands, the example with which I began does not clearly present me with a "proposition" about a future action. It presents me with a situation in which I know something about a future action of Boris'. I reflect on Boris, his presence at the picnic, the provocation he will confront, and what I know about his attitudes and his manner of reaction: I know that he will refuse the hot dog when it is served him. I do not want the proposition "I know he will refuse the hot dog." I want the proposition which gives "what I know," namely "Boris will refuse the hot dog." Suppose that a friend of Mrs. Woody's--a friend named Harriet-- comes to me with some anxiety. She says, "I understand that you are bringing Boris to the picnic tomorrow. Have you talked to him about Mrs. Woody and her childish attitudes?" "No. I haven't seen Boris in weeks." "What do you think he will do when Mrs. Woody forces her hot dog on him?" "Oh. Is that your concern? I don't need to talk to Boris to know what he will do." "Well, what will he do?" she asks. I say, "He will flatly refuse the hot dog." Here now, is what I say about Boris' future action, and that will give me the required proposition. I say, "Boris will refuse the hot dog" or something like that.

What about the truth, and the implication that Boris has no control over his action? Assume that what I say is true (for it is). Then does the truth of what I say imply that Boris has no control over his action? It seems clear that it does, but how can I show that it does? Perhaps I should look at a similar situation in which I explicitly say, "It's true that Boris will refuse the hot dog" and see whether that implies that Boris has no control in the matter of whether he will or will not refuse the hot dog. Suppose then that Mrs. Woody's friend, Harriet, says, "I understand that we may be in for a sticky time tomorrow: you think that Boris will refuse Mrs. Woody's hot dog." "I don't just think he will," I may say, "I positively know it." "How can you be so certain about anyone's doing such a thing?" "If you knew Boris, you would know that it's as good as done." "I still don't see...." "Well, it's true: you can count on it." (So the conversation might go. Perhaps I have strained a bit to make a place in the conversation for "it's true." The words "it's true" might come more easily if the question were about a person who told me of something that he himself was going to do. Say, George has told me that he is going to spill the beans about some secret deal. Then someone might ask, "I understand that George is going to spill the beans." And I might say, "That's true." But, then, is it clear that I am saying "That's true: George will spill the beans" as opposed to "That's true: George intends to spill the beans"?)

Doesn't "It's true: Boris will refuse the hot dog" imply that Boris has no control over his action? What is the problem with that? This: how can I tell that "Boris has no control" is implied by "It's true: Boris will refuse..." and not by the fact that I am in a position to say it's true that Boris will refuse? That is, how do I know that "He has no control" is implied by "Boris will refuse the hot dog" and is not implied by the conditions that make it appropriate for me to say that Boris will refuse the hot dog? What do I have in mind? What puts me in a position to say "It's true"? In this case, someone asks a relevant question. But no one needs to ask a question. I may anticipate a question: "You may have doubts about whether Boris will refuse the hot dog, but it's true; he will, there's no doubt about it." Although the conditions which will put me in a position to say, "It's true that Boris will refuse the hot dog" are much more limited

than those which will put me in a position to say,
"Boris will refuse the hot dog," they obviously have
nothing to do with the fact that what I say implies
that Boris has no control in the matter of what he is
going to do.

I am asking what follows from the fact that I say
(or am in a position to say) it as opposed to what follows from the substance of what I say. Suppose someone
asks me "Where was Lincoln born?" Then I might say,
"Lincoln was born in Kentucky." What is implied by
"Lincoln was born in Kentucky"? That Lincoln was not
born in Indiana or Illinois, for example. Is that the
way I am thinking? What follows from (or is implied
by) my **saying** it? Does it follow that I think someone
wants to know? Or does it follow that I have reason to
think someone wants to know?

What **is** implied by my saying something? Suppose
that I blurted out to Wheatstone, "Lincoln was born in
Kentucky." He might well ask, "Why on earth did you
say that?" and I might say, "I thought you wanted to
know Lincoln's birthplace. I thought you needed it for
last night's crossword puzzle. I noticed you were
still working on the puzzle." Suppose though, that
just after blurting out "Lincoln was born in Kentucky,"
I got up and walked from the room, leaving Wheatstone
to puzzle over my behavior. Would he think, "His
saying that about Lincoln could imply that he thought I
wanted to know Lincoln's birthplace"? I should think
not. What he might say is this: "The fact that he
said that could imply that he thought I wanted to
know." What is the significance of this difference?
Obviously "His saying that..." and "The fact that he
said that..." are different subjects. It seems to be a
feature of grammar that these two nomenalizations of
the verb "to say" yield different subjects. What might
we say about "his saying that"? "His saying that set a
new record for trivia." "His saying that dumfounded
his audience." "His saying that began a new line of
inquiry." Of course any of these can be reformulated
with a passive verb; then "saying" will become part of
a prepositional clause. "A new record for trivia was
set by his saying that." "His audience was dumfounded
by his saying that." And the same for others. "The
fact that he said..." cannot be substituted for "his
saying that" in any of these sentences.

What might we say about "The fact that he said
that..."? "The fact that he said that is enough to
show that he was lying." "The fact that he said that
will go down in history." "The fact that he said that
implies that he thought his audience was ignorant."
Where appropriate, these too can be rephrased in the

passive voice. "That he was lying is shown by the fact that he said that." "That he thought his audience ignorant is implied by the fact that he said that."

Should I indulge the impulse to say something summary? It is dangerous and will doubtless be wrong, but something like this seems to be involved here. "His saying that" refers to an action. "The fact that he said that" refers to a fact. One can anticipate, admire, condemn an action. One can find that an action brings or leads to peace, disorder, unhappiness. One can accept, emphasize, record, take note of, a fact. One can find a fact important, or insignificant, worth remembering. A fact is the sort of thing which goes with the "logical" verbs and predicates. But what good is all of this? "A fact is the sort of thing which can imply something." What have I accomplished beyond suggesting that something general stands behind the observation that "His saying that..." does not take the verb "implies," and "The fact that he said that..." does?

Now that I have cleared my mind a little, the question I should be concerned with is this: "What is implied by the fact that someone says something?" If I blurt out, "Lincoln was born in Kentucky" and then walk away, perhaps Wheatstone might think that I had addressed that remark to him, and he might conclude that I thought he wanted to know Lincoln's birthplace. He might think, "The fact that E. said what he said implies that he thought I wanted to know about Lincoln's birthplace." In such circumstances the fact that I say something might be taken to imply such things as these: I thought Wheatstone wanted to know, I thought Wheatstone might be interested, I thought Wheatstone had a misconception and thought it important that he be set right. But it is not just the fact that I said "Lincoln was born in Kentucky" which may imply something of this kind. It is the fact that I say it to somebody. If I just said, "Lincoln was born in Kentucky" while in somebody's presence, he might not know whether I had spoken to him or whether I was talking to myself. I might, after all, have been thinking aloud, and if so, he would not know what that fact implied. So what is implied by the fact that I say something depends very much on the circumstances: on whether I say it to myself or to somebody else, and on what preceded my speaking.

When someone asks me, "Where was Lincoln born?" and in reply I say, "Lincoln was born in Kentucky," then the fact that I say, "Lincoln was born in Kentucky" does not imply that I believe someone might be interested, or someone wanted that particular piece of information. The circumstances are not right here to

271

allow a place for thinking that anything of that kind is implied by the fact that I said "Lincoln was born in Kentucky." Regardless of the circumstances, though, whenever I say "Lincoln was born in Kentucky," doesn't the fact that I say it always imply that I know it or think that I know it? Certainly not, but sometimes it would. Suppose that I were a child, and my parents had successfully drummed into me the idea that I was never to guess or bluff. Now some adult asks (as adults sometimes do with the tone of a teacher giving an examination), "Where was Lincoln born?" I answer, "Lincoln was born in Indiana." Now some onlooker might observe, "The fact that he said that implies that he thought he knew." ("He wouldn't be guessing or bluffing.")

In the example of my conversation with Harriet, I have certainly made clear the relevant circumstances. Harriet is concerned about Boris' likely behavior. I know exactly what Boris will do, and Harriet is skeptical of my certainty. I say, "It's true that Boris will refuse the hot dog," and that implies that Boris has no control over his action. What I am trying to determine is this. Is it implied because of some feature of my speech situation? Specifically, is it implied by the fact that I said what I said to Harriet? The fact that one says something even when he is speaking to another person does not seem to imply the right sorts of things. "He thought someone wanted to know," "He thought someone might be interested," "He felt that he had something to contribute to the conversation." But the fact that I said to Harriet, "It's true: Boris will refuse the hot dog," certainly implies that I know that Boris will refuse the hot dog. And, whereas I am not interested in **that** implication, I am interested in what **that** may in turn imply. Does the fact that I know Boris will refuse the hot dog imply that Boris has no control over his action? No, that is not right: it doesn't sound right to say "the fact that I know" implies anything of this kind. It may be the fact that it can be known which implies that Boris has no control over his action.

What I want to determine is this. Is the fact that Boris has no control over his action implied in some way by my ability to know it? Or is it implied by what I say when I say, "It's true: Boris will refuse the hot dog"? When Mrs. Woody's friend asks me about Boris and about what to expect from him, suppose that I say, "I know that Boris will refuse the hot dog." That too would imply that Boris had no control over his action. (If someone asked me, "Does what you say imply that Boris has no control over his action?" then I should say, "Yes. It does.") But when I say, "It's true that

272

Boris will refuse the hot dog" does that imply that Boris has no control over his action because I know that he will refuse the hot dog? Surely it is the other way around. "I know..." implies that he has no control over his action because I can't know unless it's true that Boris will refuse the hot dog. If I know that he will, then of course he will. Surely what I say when I say, "It's true that Boris will refuse the hot dog" directly implies that he has no control in the matter of whether he will refuse or accept the hot dog.

But if I simply said, "Boris will refuse the hot dog" that, too, would imply that he had no control over his action. Truth, then, has nothing in particular to do with the implication. Why was I led to think that it does? Suppose now that I am the one who is interested in how Boris will behave tomorrow, and suppose that someone else, Frederick, says to me under these circumstances, "Boris will refuse the hot dog." Now, what Frederick says implies that Boris has no control over his action. Yet even though what Frederick says implies that Boris has no control over his action I çan still wonder whether Boris does have control over his action. Then I shall say, "If Frederick is right, Boris has no control over his action," or "If what Frederick says is true, Boris has no control over his action." Frederick says that Boris will refuse the hot dog, and what Frederick says implies that Boris has no control over whether he will refuse the hot dog or not. If I am interested in the implication of what Frederick says, then that is enough for me. But if what Frederick says is not true, then perhaps Boris does, after all, have some control in the matter of what he does about the hot dog. So, if I am interested in whether Boris does have any control over his action, I shall have to concern myself with the truth of what Frederick says. Its truth implies that Boris does not have any control over his action.

When I say, "Boris will refuse the hot dog," I am telling someone, quite sincerely, what I know about Boris' future behavior. And what I say implies that Boris has no control in the matter of what he is to do. But isn't it the truth of what I say which implies that Boris has no control over his action? That is a confused question. Only someone who has a doubt about what I say will raise the question. I have no such doubt: in my mind the question does not arise, and there is no reason why it should.

When I tried to think of a situation in which I should say, "It's true: Boris will refuse the hot dog," I thought of my being questioned by a skeptical friend of Mrs. Woody's. She wondered how I could be so

certain, and I said "It's true: you can count on it."
And what I said when I said "It's true..." implies that
Boris has no control over his action. But, after all,
she need not accept my guarantee when I say "It's
true...." She may still think that I am presumptuous
in talking about the future behavior of another person
as I have. She does not understand my reasons for
being so certain. She may think that no person could
be so predictable about such a little thing. I cannot
expect to quell her doubts merely by saying, "It's
true," regardless of how confidently I pronounce it.
If I address myself to her persistent doubt, what shall
I say? "It's true that it's true?" That would be
playful: it carries the flavor of a philosophical
joke, and is certainly not the proper thing for a serious discussion. No. I should probably say, "Well--it
is true" and likely I should go back again to talking
about my evidence, my understanding of Boris. Or I may
realize that I am already at the end and say, "Well, it
is true--whether you believe it or not."

   Where did I get the idea that it was the truth of
what a person might say which implies--if it does--that
someone has no control in the matter of what he is to
do? It can only be that in thinking as a philosopher--
with no example before me--that that seems the most
natural way to express my concern with whether someone
has control over his action or not. "If it is true
that he will do it, then he has no control in the
matter of whether he will do it or not." "He will do
it" I get from nowhere. I do not imagine any particular person who says "He will do it" or any particular
person about whom it is said, or any particular action
or situation, or any audience to whom it is addressed.
So, having no details, it somehow seems natural to use
the idiom of the skeptic. Perhaps--coming from no
one--I have no reason to trust it. And so I say to
myself, "If it is true that he will do it--then he has
no control over his action." This might be the explanation if I had one eye out to some person in some situation and some definite question--although I do not
concern myself with any details.

   Quite likely there is another explanation, though.
I do not have one eye out to some person or some particular action at all. I do not even imagine that
someone has said something: I do not have the words
"He will do it" or any other particular words in mind.
I want to speak with complete generality; so I say, "If
it is true that someone will do something, then he has
no control over whether he will do it or not." Of
course that is what I must say because no one will say,
"It is true that someone will do something"--that is,

no one will ever say that with anything like the relevant meaning. I want to talk about anyone doing anything in the future and what follows from that. I have no way to proceed except to say, "If it is true that someone will do something...." Naturally, I do not say, "If someone will do something, then he has no control over his action," because that puts me in the position of saying, with good reason (I know or think I know), "Someone will do something." And that is ridiculous--the idea that I have good reason for, am willing to bet that, someone will do something. The kind of schematic generalization I have in mind is not the sort of thing one can bet on or guarantee. It is not like "If that bird on the wire is a woodpecker, it will soon land upright on the trunk of a tree."

This seems to be the way I get the idea that truth is involved in the implication. And this also is the way the "proposition" comes in. The proposition and truth come in together. I go at the matter with a preconceived formula. I want complete generality, so I begin by thinking of such things as this: "A person says something to the effect that someone will do something." Or, I think, "A person says about another that he (that other) will do something." I have the idea that a myriad of specific things people might say are alike in being "propositions" about a person and to the effect that that person will do something. I want to say what any proposition of that form will imply. So, naturally, I say, "If any such proposition is true, its truth implies that the person in question has no real choice about the action in question." Or, "The truth of any such proposition implies...."

I begin with the idea that I could pull out of context and isolate "propositions" by thinking about truth. And that is a mistake.[2] If I consider an

---

[2]This may be the idea to which Wittgenstein is addressing himself in Philosophical Investigations, 136: "Now it looks as if the definition--a proposition is whatever can be true or false--determined what a proposition was, by saying: what fits the concept 'true', or what the concept 'true' fits, is a proposition. So it is as if we had a concept of true and false, which we could use to determine what is and what is not a proposition. What engages with the concept of truth (as with a cogwheel), is a proposition."

And perhaps I have been following Wittgenstein's advice: "But this is a bad picture. It is as if one were to say 'The King in chess is the piece that one can check.' But this can mean no more than that in our example of a situation where I say something of the relevant sort--I say "Boris will refuse the hot dog" or I say "It is true: he will"--then I do not get a "proposition" of a certain form out of this milieu by thinking about truth or thinking about the bearer of truth. Quite the contrary, I already have the idea of an isolated proposition as the bearer of truth. Giving almost no attention to the example, I can talk about the truth of a proposition to the effect that someone will do something, and, by taking only the most cursory glance at the example, I can pronounce that such a proposition will imply that the person has no control over his action.

Perhaps I am having trouble because I have surrounded myself with examples too soon--thinking that I might be able to extract "propositions" and "truth" from them, and then put my extractions together into the argument for fatalism. I have the schematism in my mind which provides the first two steps in the argument for fatalism. The generalization is already built into my way of thinking: "If any proposition to the effect that...is true, then that person has no control over his action." But I could not have begun with this generalization unless it seemed to be right. It must appear to fit some concrete details. Some example must lend support to it. Of course it does. And that is why I began with an example which seems to support it: the "proposition" is to be the substance of what I said when I said "Boris will refuse the hot dog," and that seems to be what implies that he has no control over his action. The argument, though, does not proceed from example to example--cautiously extracting the formal generality. The generality is built into my way of thinking about the example. "It is such and such a

------

game of chess we only check the king...the use of the words 'true' and 'false' may be among the constituent parts of this [language] game; and if so it 'belongs' to our concept 'proposition' but does not 'fit' it. As we might also say, check belongs to our concept of the king in chess...."

Whichever "picture" of "propositions" Wittgenstein is concerned with, my idea of propositions as bits-of-information is apparently more pernicious than his. And his chess analogy can even encourage me in it. Even though "truth" belongs to "propositions" in the way "check" belongs to the king, I can think of a proposition as something I can remove from the game and isolate and comment on just as I can do these things with the king.

proposition, which by its form implies that...."

Whenever I say of a person, "He will do...," do I say the same sort of thing in the required way? That is, can I find in the words "He will do..." a proposition about a future action of someone? Whenever I say, "He will do...," does what I say imply that he has no control over his action? Suppose I consider another example. It will have the same cast of characters and be set in the same place--the same people, and the same picnic; but now I know very little about Boris. He tells me though, that when Mrs. Woody passes him the hot dog, he is going to refuse it. He thinks this a funny, impish thing to do: he wants to see Mrs. Woody's reaction. He assures me that after the prank has had its effect, he will apologize to all and explain. I tell him that this is a stupid stunt; but I know just enough about him to know that he will do it. What do I say now to Harriet when she asks me what to expect from Boris? Suppose that I say, "Boris will refuse the hot dog. You might as well prepare for it." Now, when I say that he will refuse the hot dog, does what I say imply that he has no control over his action? It would seem not--because now I say that he is going to do something he has decided to do. But he decided to do it before he told me. What now, after his decision is made? I say now that he is going to do it. "Having said that he will do it, he will do it." Does that imply that, after the time of his decision, he has no control over his action? Doesn't that depend on the details? If he is going to think it over again and again, if his intention is not firmly fixed, if he is apt to chicken-out of his own commitment to the silly stunt, then of course he has control over what he will do in reaction to the hot dog. If I had known that he had not yet firmly made up his mind, I should not have said that he will do it. Instead, I should have said, "He will probably do it" or "I don't know whether he will do it or not."

If he will do it, though, if he will definitely do what he said he was going to do, then surely, after he has made his decision, he has no control over his action. Is that quite clear? (1) Having said that he will do it, regardless of how precipitantly, he may be the kind of person who simply could not allow himself to change his mind--to appear changeable. But (2) he might do just what he said he would do, light-heartedly--for a lark. He might not take it seriously enough to give it another thought one way or the other. I might say of case (1) that he had no control over his action; but I certainly shall not say that of case (2). If the circumstances were those of (2),

though, I should still say "He will do it. He intends
to, and he will certainly go through with the stunt.
He will not give it another thought." So, it seems
that my schematic-general way of thinking is not
supported by examples. The ideas I have of the
isolable proposition with all its implications do not
fit the facts.

Well, perhaps there are two different kinds of
propositions. Perhaps I can start from an example in
which "He will do it" does imply that he has no control
over his action, and more carefully generalize from
that to the kind of proposition I want. Return to my
original example. I say to Harriet: "Boris will refuse the hot dog all right." I might even draw the consequences myself. I might add, "You can bet on that.
He has no control over what he will do." Surely I am
drawing this consequence from what I said. I say "You
can bet on that" to make absolutely clear that I am not
talking off the top of my head, not just guessing. I
say "He has no control over what he will do" to make
clear what is involved in my saying "He will refuse the
hot dog." To someone paying close attention I need not
add these things. The nature of the question and my
tone should make plain that I am serious. And the details about Boris and his attitudes toward the picnic
should make plain what "He will..." comes to. When I
add, "He has no control over what he will do," I am making explicit something which is implied by "He will refuse the hot dog."

I say something about Boris and what he will do,
and what I say implies that he has no control over his
action. Here, then, is a sample of the kind of "proposition" I want. Why can't I now generalize from this?
"Any proposition of this kind implies that a person
has no control over his action--that is, the action
which is relevant." But what kind of proposition is
it? How do I get it extracted from the context? I
want the substance or the content of what I said. I
must leave aside my knowledge of Boris, his attitudes
toward hot dogs and Mrs. Woody-type people; I must
ignore the kind of person he is, the significance of
the event in question, and all of that; and I must concentrate on just what I said when I said, "He will
refuse the hot dog." Now what is it that I am supposed
to concentrate on? The words? Do the words carry the
substance of it? Can I represent the type of "proposition" as "what is carried by the words 'He will refuse
the hot dog'?" Can I take these words out of the situation, and have a certain understanding of them stick
with the words themselves, so that the words will represent a type of proposition? I say "Boris will..."

and that implies that he has no control over his action. And I want to say that what I say about Boris' future actions would imply that he had no control over his action, even if I were not in a position to say it. Of course, there is something right about that. I do not need an audience. No one has to ask me: I may be thinking aloud. Also I do not need to know it. I may be all wrong: Boris is not the kind of person I think he is. Whether I know it, or am in a position to know it, the fact remains: what I say implies that Boris has no control over his action. But I cannot say it unless I know or think that I know. No. That is too strong. I may just entertain the idea. The situation may be like that: Boris may be that kind of person. I can imagine that person and I can imagine the circumstances, and then imagine myself saying, "He will refuse the hot dog." And that is enough: then the substance of what I think, "He will refuse the hot dog," implies that he has no control over his action. And I do not know whether that is so, and I am not in any position to say such a thing. Or am I? That depends. If I were just to blurt it out to the first person who came by, that person would not know what to make of it. But then if I told him what I had been thinking, and told him that I was thinking aloud, then he would understand all right. So I have supplied, first to myself and then to someone else, the conditions in which I can say such a thing. Without those conditions, my hearers would not know what to make of my words "Boris will refuse the hot dog." And unless I imagined those conditions--unless I had been thinking of that possibility--I should not know what to make of my own words. In fact, I should not be able to think of them as my own words at all.

Suppose I were just to say, "Boris will refuse the hot dog." Suppose now, again, that I know very little about Boris. I am not thinking that he told me what he was going to do. I am not thinking that he is going to test Mrs. Woody's reaction, nor am I thinking that he is stiff and inflexible in such matters. I am not thinking that he detests hot dogs and people like Mrs. Woody. I am not thinking anything at all. Then what of my words? Where did they come from? Some power, some strange force must have moved my lips and formed these words. But what do the words come to? Is someone--through some strange influence--using my lips? But what can I make of the words? If someone is using my voice, what am I to make of what that someone says? There is no way to tell. Do these words imply that Boris has no control over his action? Certainly not. Not the words. What then? The substance of what is said. But that is what I cannot determine. Is the substance in the words; is it there, and I simply cannot make it out? There is no sense to that suggestion. Everything which might be there to give definite substance or content to my words, I have taken away. I took it all away when I took away everything except the words.

What has happened to my "type of proposition"? How am I to characterize it? What I say to Mrs. Woody's friend when I say "Boris will refuse the hot dog" gives me a sample of it. Any other samples will be like it in certain respects. But in what respects? They will be about future actions of people. They will imply that the people in question have no control over their future actions.

The next step in the argument requires that I detach the proposition even from what anyone says or thinks or might say or might think. Following Taylor's lead, I think: "About every future action of every person there is such a true proposition." I want only true propositions, but there will be others which are not true. I want to think only about the true propositions. From any such true proposition as this, it follows that the person in question has no control over the action which the proposition is about.

I must not only lift my sample proposition out of its surroundings, I must also supply another like it for each future action. But I am not able to get the sample proposition lifted from its surroundings. So I cannot even take the first step toward fatalism. I ought to be able to do better than that. When I attempt to lift out the proposition I must characterize it by type: it is about a person, and to the effect that he will do something--and above all it implies that he has no control over his actions. Surely I can see what it is about the "proposition"--about what I am saying when I say "Boris will refuse the hot dog"-- which implies that he has no control over his action. Yes, I am afraid that I can. When I say "He will refuse the hot dog" I am, in effect, saying that his action is the outcome of something very like a compulsion. If he ever comes to feel ashamed of what he did, he will say, "I couldn't help myself." Or he might say, jokingly but revealingly, "The devil made me do it." If that is part of the proposition--part of what I am saying--then I cannot get from a sample "proposition" of that type to the generalization: "For every future action of every person there is such a true proposition." That would be to say that every future action will be done compulsively--which is simply not true.

I have not done well in getting the argument for fatalism started; even so, I suspect that I have done too well. I suspect that my preconceived picture of "the proposition" has made me distort even the little I supposed that I could get. I have turned to a conversation, thinking that I could find there, and lift out, a proposition about a future action and one which implies that a person has no control over his action. I have assumed that "what I say" will give me that proposition. I have assumed that "the proposition" will be a tiny section of that conversation and that it can be represented by the words "Boris will refuse the hot dog" or more simply "He (Boris) will do it." I have talked as though, in saying just that, that "what I say" implies that Boris has no control over himself in the matter.

I have the idea that a proposition is a little section of a conversation—with a subject and a predicate. I have the idea that it is the "bearer of truth" and that it also carries whatever implication is present: in this case it implies that Boris has no control over his action. But where do I get these ideas? I think that I must distort my example in order to make it appear to fit a preconceived picture. I certainly do not get these things out of the example itself. I am talking about Boris with Mrs. Woody's friend Harriet. She wants to know what to expect of Boris at the picnic. I tell her that Boris will refuse the hot dog. I say, among other things, "Boris will refuse the hot dog." And now I step outside the example, assume the role of philosopher-logician and say, "That implies that Boris has no control over his action," or "What I say implies that Boris has no control over his action." What am I thinking of as "that"—which implies that Boris has no control over his action? Or what am I thinking of as "what I say"? I think now that nothing but my idea of the proposition guides me. "That" is "what I say" and "that" implies that Boris has no control over his action.

I tell Mrs. Woody's friend, Harriet, all about Boris and I emphasize how well I know him, and then I say, "Boris will refuse the hot dog." Harriet may say, "That implies that Boris has no control over his action," or she may say, "What you say implies that Boris has no control over his action." And she would be right. But what is she (she is no philosopher) thinking of as "that" or as "what you say"? Well, certainly not just "Boris will refuse the hot dog," taken out of the conversation and considered all by itself. But why not?

Suppose that Harriet and I have an agreement: I

281

shall tell her only of Boris' compulsive, and hence predictable, future actions. On other matters concerning Boris I shall remain silent. She asks me, "What can we expect of Boris tomorrow?" And I reply, "Boris will refuse the hot dog." She might think, "That implies that Boris has no control over his action." But, will she think that what I say implies that Boris has no control over his action? Certainly not. If she has almost forgotten about our agreement, she may remind herself, thinking, "The fact that he told me that implies that Boris has no control over his action." Here the implication is carried by the fact that I say something--given the agreement that I shall say such things only when the future action is compulsive. When I simply explain to Harriet what she should expect Boris to do tomorrow, I do not give this explanation against the background of any such agreement.

I am a professional golfer and I have broken my arm--near the shoulder. The break has been set, and the bone has healed, but I am unable to take a full swing with the clubs. My doctor says, "It will take time. You will not be able to take a full swing for several weeks." Does what he says imply that I have no control over whether I shall or shall not take a full swing in the next few weeks? It certainly implies that no matter how hard I try I shall not be able to take a full swing--not for several weeks, that is. Is it "what he says" that implies this? When I consider "what he says" I know that he knows all of the relevant details of my condition. Someone who knew very little about my condition could say, "You will not be able to take a full swing for two weeks," and what he said would imply that I had no control over whether I shall or shall not. But suppose that I had not broken a bone, and nothing at all was wrong--and now someone says to me, out of the blue, "You will not be able to take a full swing for two weeks." Well, I should simply not know what he was talking about. Does what he says imply that I have no control over the matter? I don't know what he was trying to say.

What am I struggling against here? Surely it is this: I have the idea that "what one says" is a proposition. That is, I have the idea that it can be represented by a short sentence taken out of a conversation or an example--and that it will stand by itself. What is one concerned with when he is concerned with what someone says? A person might have been listening to my conversation with Harriet. At one point in the conversation I turned my head and he could not hear what I said. He might say, "I could not hear what E.

282

said. What did he say?" The answer might be "E. said that Boris would refuse the hot dog." Can I now imagine that he might be concerned with whether that one thing which I said implies that Boris has no control over his action? I do not see how. Suppose that he had walked up to Harriet and me just a moment after I had spoken and impolitely said, "I did not hear what you said just then. What did you say?" If I felt at all inclined to answer I should of course say, "I said that Boris would refuse the hot dog." He might ask, "Who is Boris and what's that about a hot dog?" but I can hardly imagine him reflecting on the question, "Does what you said just then imply that Boris has no control over his action?"

If someone with a legitimate interest in the matter walked in on the conversation and asked about it, I should say that I was telling Harriet about Boris and his presence at the picnic. He might ask, "What did you say?" I can hardly answer his question with "I said that Boris will refuse Mrs. Woody's hot dog?" If he knew little of Boris or of tomorrow's social event I should tell him about them, and then tell him that Boris would certainly refuse the hot dog. And though it is unlikely, he might now ask, "Does that imply that Boris has no control over his action?" or even "Does what you said to Harriet imply that he has no control over his action?" Now, of course, "what I said" is not one sentence or one snatch of the conversation which he could not make out. His interest in "what I said" cannot be satisfied by giving him one sentence or a few words; and it is only his interest or something like it which will lead to the idea that "what I said" implies that Boris has no control over himself in the matter of whether he will accept or refuse the hot dog.

"What I said" when I talked to Harriet does imply that Boris has no control over his action, but I was quite mistaken in thinking of "what I said" as a proposition. I was simply mistaken when I wrote 'Boris will refuse the hot dog' implies that Boris has no control over his action."

BOOKS AND ARTICLES

Austin, J.L., Philosophical Papers, ed. J.O. Urmson & G.J. Warnock (Clarendon, Oxford University Press, 1961).

Ayer, A.J., Problems of Knowledge (Baltimore, Penguin Books, 1956).

Cassirer, E., "Le Langage et la Construction du Monde des Objets," Journal de la Psychologie Normale et Pathologique, XXX, (1932).

Chisholm, R., Theory of Knowledge (Englewood Cliffs, N.J., Prentice-Hall, 1966).

Ebersole, F., Meaning and Saying (Washington, D.C., University Press of America, 1979).

Ebersole, F., Things We Know (Eugene, Oregon, University of Oregon Books, 1967).

Geach, P.T., "Ascriptivism," Philosophical Review, 69 (1960), pp. 221-5.

Goldman, A., A Theory of Human Actions (Englewood Cliffs, N.J., Prentice-Hall, 1970).

Grice, H.P., "The Causal Theory of Perception," Proceedings of the Aristotelian Society, Supp. Vol. 35 (1961), pp. 121-68. Reprinted in G.J. Warnock, The Philosophy of Perception (London, Oxford University Press, 1967).

Grice, H.P., "Meaning," Philosophical Review (July, 1957).

Pitcher, G., The Philosphy of Wittgenstein (Englewood Cliffs, N.J., Prentice-Hall, 1964).

Putnam, H., "Is Semantics Possible?" in Language, Belief, and Metaphysics, ed. H.E. Kiefer & M.K. Munitz (N.Y., State University of New York Press, 1970).

Putnam, H., "The Meaning of 'Meaning'" in K. Gunderson, ed., Language, Mind and Knowledge, Minnesota Studies in the Philosophy of Science, VII (Minneapolis, University of Minnesota Press, 1975).

Quine, W.V., **Word and Object** (N.Y., John Wiley & Sons, Inc. 1960).

Rescher, N., "Action Descriptions" in **The Nature of Human Actions**, ed. M. Brand (Glenview, Ill., Scott, Foresman & Co., 1970).

Russell, B., **Analysis of Mind** (London, Geo. Allen & Unwin, 1921).

Sapir, E., **Selected Writings** (Berkeley, University of California Press, 1951).

Searle, J., **Speech Acts** (London and N.Y., Cambridge University Press, 1969).

Tayler, R., **Metaphysics**, 2nd ed. (Englewood Cliffs, N.J., Prentice-Hall, 1974).

Waismann, F., **The Principles of Linguistic Philosophy** (N.Y., St. Martin's Press, 1965).

Waismann, F., "Verifiability" in **Essays in Logic and Language**, ed. A. Fleur (N.Y., Philosophy Library, 1955).

Whorf, B., **Language, Thought and Reality**, ed. W.B. Carroll (Cambridge, Mass., M.I.T. Press, 1956).

Wittgenstein, L., **The Blue and Brown Books** (N.Y., Harper & Row, 1958).

Wittgenstein, L., **Pholosophical Investigations** (N.Y., Macmillan, 1953).

Ziff, P., **Semantic Analysis** (Ithaca, Cornell Unviersity Press, 1960).